Praise for
Soul in the Game

"A fascinating, often amusing, occasionally jarring journey – just like life itself. Vitaliy Katsenelson's *Soul in the Game* is one of those much-needed reminders that although we have no control over when we're born or when we'll die, we are the architects of how we live."
— **General Stanley McChrystal, Author, *Risk: A User's Guide***

"Vitaliy knows how to tell a story. This book reads like a conversation with Vitaliy: deep, insightful, inquisitive and civilized."
— **Nassim Nicholas Taleb, Author, *The Black Swan***

"*Soul in the Game* is a beautiful way to search for the lost value of happiness, strength and health."
— **Wim Hof, The Iceman, Author, *The Wim Hof Method***

"Wow! This is surprisingly good. Honestly I was suspicious (why should I listen to a money guy talk about life?) but I liked it a lot! Vitaliy brings an insightful, fresh perspective to the question of how to live life. He is caring and considerate, with a really engaging writing style."
— **Derek Sivers, Author, *How To Live***

"Vitaliy Katsenelson has been singled out by financial media for his brilliant investment strategies, but perhaps even more impressive are his philosophical writings. *Soul in the Game* is no ordinary self-help tome. I've never read anything quite like it: a collection of wonderful observations and insights about Vitaliy's native Russia (he emigrated to the US in the 1990s), parenting, living one day at a time, and – especially – creativity: in business, classical music, and art. Vitaliy's life is an integrated one, from which we can all draw some surprising and (like his investment approach) contrarian notions. This book is worth anyone's time."
— **Carl Bernstein, Author, *All the President's Men***

"Touching, honest and insightful – it's hard to put this down."
— **Morgan Housel, Author,** *The Psychology of Money*

"Vitally has captured much of the awe I hold for composer creators and he uses that insight to offer positive, constructive steps for us today who want to live life to the fullest."
— **Marin Alsop, Music Director Laureate, Baltimore Symphony Orchestra**

"The best investment you can make is an investment in yourself and in your relationships. Vitaliy's book is a big step forward in that direction. A must read!"
— **Gautam Baid, Founder, Stellar Wealth Partners, and Author,**
The Joys of Compounding

"*Soul in the Game* is a wonderful compilation of cogent observations and life strategies, derived from the author's unique personal journey. From classical music to the Classics themselves, Vitaliy Katsenelson both educates and inspires."
— **Jim Chanos, President, Kynikos Associates**

"A wise and irreverent narrative, replete with humor, life lessons and philosophical insights, which amply demonstrates that being a successful investor and a compelling writer are not mutually exclusive."
— **Leon G. Cooperman, Chairman and CEO, Omega Family Office**

"A treasure trove full of bite-sized actionable wisdom."
— **Rolf Dobelli, Author,** *The Art of Thinking Clearly*

"Vitaliy Katsenelson's engagingly readable life-a-log, *Soul in the Game*, parses so many spirits it will benefit most everyone. Wisdom, life-long learning, human capital, struggles, music composers, immigrant life, philosophy, family life, stoicism and so much more – presents for everyone in 76 enjoyable bite sized bursts. Have fun!"
— **Ken Fisher,** *New York Times* **Bestselling Author, Global columnist, and Founder & Executive Chairman, Fisher Investments**

"I thought it would take me a week to read the book, but when I started I could not stop and finished it in a day! After reading, I feel like I have spent one day of my life together with Vitaliy conversing with him through his warm words. His writing style is entertaining and at the same time it engages with the mind of the reader, making you think deeply about your own life. In every chapter, in every sentence and word, you can feel Vitaliy really put his SOUL into it."

— Héctor García, Bestselling Author, *IKIGAI*, and *A Geek in Japan*

"*Soul in the Game* is impossible to categorize. It is part memoir and part self-help book; it is part philosophy and partly about parenting; it is partly a book about writing, music history, and art appreciation. In the end, it is nothing less than a manual on how to live a good and meaningful life and achieve those most elusive and yet desirable of all states: balance and self-mastery. This book has changed me, and it will change you as well."

— Robert Greenberg, Composer, and Author, *How to Listen to Great Music*

"Part eclectic autobiography of a diverse life, part endorsement of critical thinking, part investing principles, and part how-to guide on how to be a complete human. *Soul in the Game* is always interesting, often funny, and at times profound."

— Greg Maffei, CEO, Liberty Media

"Vitaliy Katsenelson's craft is investing, his art is writing and his passion is to live a meaningful life. All are abundantly in evidence in *Soul in the Game*. Part memoir, part meditation, part self-help, with mini courses on Stoic philosophy and classical music, this book is personal, quirky, and marvelous. Invest some time with Vitaliy and you will be richer for it."

— Bill Miller, CIO, Chairman and Portfolio Manager, Miller Value Funds

"Vitaliy Katsenelson's book is a delight to read and contains a great deal of sound advice, including some nice tips on applying Stoicism in daily life."

— Donald Robertson, Author, *How to Think Like a Roman Emperor*

"Superb guidance on how to unravel what's really important in life. There's a gem of wisdom in each short, snappy chapter."

— Professor Jeremy J. Siegel, Professor of Finance, Wharton School, and Author, *Stocks for the Long Run*

"From Murmansk, Russia to Denver, USA. When Vitaliy Katsenelson immigrated to the United States from Communist Russia he had plenty of Skin in the Game. Now, a couple of decades later he has even more Soul in the Game. Katsenelson is a learning machine and is on the road to somewhere. He's going places. This book is his story. His life journey. You will be inspired. Congratulations Vitaliy on your latest (and best book). Like your mother, you might have been born in Russia, but you were made in America!"

— **Guy Spier, Author,** *The Education of a Value Investor*

"Vitaliy is a gem and *Soul in the Game* is a rare read worth relishing. I first met Vitaliy as a fan appreciating his value investing writing, became a colleague appreciating his valued investment ideas, and then became a friend appreciating and learning from how he finds virtue and values in family, fatherhood, and more. Taking threads from markets, music, art, philosophy, personal history, and universal humanity he weaves a tapestry worthy of kings and teaches us how to 'go long' the scarcest asset of all: making meaning."

— **Josh Wolfe, Founding Partner & Managing Director, Lux Capital**

Soul in the Game

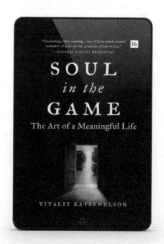

Soul in the Game:
The Art of a
Meaningful Life

Vitaliy Katsenelson

Harriman
House

HARRIMAN HOUSE LTD
3 Viceroy Court
Bedford Road
Petersfield
Hampshire
GU32 3LJ
GREAT BRITAIN
Tel: +44 (0)1730 233870

Email: enquiries@harriman-house.com
Website: harriman.house

First published in 2022.
Copyright © Vitaliy Katsenelson

The right of Vitaliy Katsenelson to be identified as the Author has been asserted in accordance with the Copyright, Design and Patents Act 1988.

Hardback ISBN: 978-0-85719-907-2
eBook ISBN: 978-0-85719-908-9

British Library Cataloguing in Publication Data
A CIP catalogue record for this book can be obtained from the British Library.

Whilst every effort has been made to ensure that information in this book is accurate, no liability can be accepted for any loss incurred in any way whatsoever by any person relying solely on the information contained herein.

No responsibility for loss occasioned to any person or corporate body acting or refraining to act as a result of reading material in this book can be accepted by the Publisher, by the Author, or by the employers of the Author.

To Jonah, Hannah, and Mia Sarah.
Because you don't read my emails.

Contents

Contents

Introduction – How to Read This Book

IF SOMEONE HAD suggested a decade ago that I would write a book that had nothing to do with value investing, I would have laughed. Even after writing two books on investing, I thought of myself as an investor who thinks through writing, not "a writer." I preferred to leave that stuff to professionals – the Dostoevskys and Hemingways – and stick to what I knew best: value investing.

However, over the years, I brought "life" stories about my childhood, my kids, and classical music as supporting actors (often as analogies) onto the main stage of my writing about investing. Kids change you; the realization of your mortality changes you – and writing changes you. It was just a matter of time before these life stories wanted to grow out of their supporting roles into lead roles.

Thousands of emails from my readers had a lot to do with that, too. Readers wrote that they came for the articles about value investing but stayed for the life stories (and my father's art; but more on that later). They encouraged me to turn my life (non-investment) essays into a book. They told me that reading these stories had made their lives a little better. Reading my essays nudged them to reflect on their own lives. Often, I even seemed to inspire them into action: to travel, to spend more time with their loved ones, or to just simply slow down and inhale life.

This book is about the most important investment you'll ever make: the investment in your life.

I hope a story or two in these "life" essays will touch you, add a ray or two of sunlight to your day, and motivate you to fill the gap in your life that needs filling.

This book is evergreen, and so I have structured it thematically, not chronologically (you will notice this in the variability of my kids' ages throughout the book). It started out just as a collection of stories I've written over the years. But as I was editing it, the writer in me took over. I ended up completely rewriting old essays and writing many new ones. Though it is not a traditional book with a story arc running through it, it morphed into more than just a collection of random stories. It is written to be read in sequence.

The book is loosely organized into six sections:

The **Student of Life** section has an autobiographical character. It takes you to Soviet Russia for my childhood, the fear that my aunt was an American spy, my family's emigration to the US, and our first (wonder) years in this great country.

Then it takes you on my most educational journey of all – being a parent. Those stories are full of joy and mistakes (kids don't come with an instruction manual), but also growth. Being a parent is the most transformative experience of all.

This section also features "Soul in the Game," an essay that provides a lens through which to view the rest of the book. It touches on everything one needs to find meaning in the creative part of their life. It is so important to me that I titled the book after it.

In **Inhaling the World** I share my experiences and impressions from visiting Santa Fe, San Francisco, Switzerland, France, and Italy with my family. I discuss topics ranging from how visiting a modern art museum can enhance your trip to an IKEA store, to Jeffersonian lunches, to the caloric content of uncooked fish. If this section inspires you to see a bit more of the world, I have succeeded.

One Day at a Time is the self-help part of this book. Well, kind of. I am not dispensing self-help advice; I am just taking you with me on my journey of learning about how to stick to a diet, sleep better, work out, meditate (a little), and firm up new habits through trial and (a lot of) error. I'll share personal finance advice that was given to me by a friend when I got married – advice that eliminated any bickering about finances from my marriage!

I was almost done editing this book when I stumbled onto Stoic philosophy. I was so taken by it that I put editing on hold and embarked on a five-month learning and then writing journey about Stoicism. This spilled into **Stoicism – The Philosophy For Life**. It's a mini-book within this book, with two sections of its own. One section focuses on Stoicism as an operating system for life, and the other outlines a value system that could lead you to a happier and more meaningful life.

Soul in Creativity houses my essays on... you guessed it, creativity.

Creativity is a thread that runs throughout the whole book. I have found that creativity is a secret sauce that makes life more meaningful; it's what draws me out of bed every morning.

I share with you what I've learned about the art and process of writing, not to mention how the music of AC/DC can turn you into a better writer. And you'll learn how I structured my life to have time to run an investment firm, do investment research, spend time with my family, and still write the equivalent of a book a year.

The essay "Pain, Opera and Investing" explores an excruciatingly painful professional period in my life. Most importantly, it offers tools (based on Stoic philosophy) for coping with pain. This essay sat in my virtual drawer for years; I couldn't bring myself to publish it, until now.

After I finished writing the essay "Creative Roller Coaster," I realized that I *had to* take all my life essays and publish them as a book to share with others. There was an instigator who was singlehandedly responsible for my starting to work on this book: Pyotr Ilyich Tchaikovsky. I explore Tchaikovsky's struggles as a composer, which I can *so* relate to as a writer; though I get the feeling that this struggle is universal in all creative endeavors, not just composing and writing.

Tchaikovsky brings us to the last section, **Melody of Life**. In this series of essays, I delve into the lives of classical music titans –Tchaikovsky, Schubert, Liszt, Brahms, Chopin, Berlioz, and Bruckner.

Though these essays about classical music and composers may seem out of place in this book, they continue to tug on this thread of creativity. Today we listen to the music of these superstars, and it still moves us (to me it is the best drug of all). We call them geniuses. But their talent and success, which seems evident to us, was anything but evident to many of them. Just like the rest of us, they were full of insecurities and went through a lot of personal and creative struggles, accompanied by a lot of pain. There is a lot we can learn from them.

By way of summary and conclusion, in **The Art of a Meaningful Life** I collect the breadcrumbs I left throughout the book and connect the concept of soul in the game, Stoic philosophy, creativity, and lessons from classical music composers by means of an art and craft framework. Oh, and I break the fourth wall.

Finally, if you are questioning why a relatively young adult with plenty of life experiences still ahead of him writes an autobiographical book, read "Intermission – Stop Eating Sugar" (the book's conclusion): It will answer this question.

My advice to you: Read this book as if each essay is an email that just appeared in your inbox. You are invited to ponder for a while before you move on.

For reasons that will become apparent as you read the next essay, I also had to include a few of my father's paintings in this book. You can find them in the middle painting section. And you can always see more of his artwork at katsenelson.com.

I approach this book the same way Zeno, the founder of Stoicism, approached his students. Zeno did not claim to be a physician – he saw himself as a patient describing the progress of his treatment to fellow patients in the hospital beds beside him.[1] Grab a bed next to mine and let's have a conversation about life, creativity, Stoic philosophy, classical music, and other fun topics.

---

1 D. Robertson, *How to Think Like a Roman Emperor* (St. Martin's Publishing Group), pp. 32–33.

Student of Life

*Stories and lessons from
my life as a child, a parent,
and everything in between.*

Born in Russia, Made in America

Warning: If you skipped the book's Introduction and went directly to this chapter (something I'd normally do), you just ventured into a jungle without a map. Friendly advice: Read the introduction first.

Red October

I SPENT MY YOUTH in Murmansk, a city in the northwest part of Russia, located right above the Arctic Circle.

Murmansk owes its existence to its port. Thanks to the warming of the Gulf Stream, the port doesn't freeze during the long winters, providing unique access to Russia from the north. During the Cold War, Murmansk's coordinates must have been on the speed dial of the US military, as it is the headquarters of the Russian Northern Navy Fleet. Fans of Tom Clancy's *The Hunt for Red October* may remember Murmansk as the home base for the submarine Red October.

The winters are cold and dark; Murmansk makes Seattle look like a sunshine city. For six weeks every winter we lived without daylight. On those days during the winter when the sun would grace us with its presence, I still wouldn't see it. In the morning I'd be walking to school in complete darkness. The sun would come out for 30 minutes around noon while I was in class. I'd walk home in complete darkness.

The city was so desperate for sun in the winter that it even created a day celebrating the sun, called Hello Sun. All this sounds awful, I know. Especially for my kids, who have spent their whole lives in Denver – with its 300 days of sunshine a year. But I was born into that life. I embraced it and never really thought twice about it.

Though I never felt it, I can see now how my parents' life was very difficult. Murmansk is located so far north that the ground is permafrost – there is no vegetation to speak of. Most food had to be brought from other parts of the country. Murmansk had an abundance of fish (after all, it was a fishing port) and bread; that's about it.

When I was a teenager, a few years before we left for the US, Russian bureaucrats figured out that if you grind fish, you can feed it to chickens. Suddenly we had an abundance of chickens. Unfortunately, the chickens that were fed fish tasted like fish. When I moved to the US, I could not eat chicken for ten years.

There was no fruit in stores during winter. In September, my parents would pickle cabbage in giant jars that we kept on our windowsills so it wouldn't spoil. Pickled cabbage was one of our few sources of vitamins in winter. We'd also drink what was called "fish fat" (fish oil), an extract from cod liver that was our source of vitamins A and D.

Today when people look at me, at 5'10" (on a good hair day), standing next to my 19-year-old son Jonah, who is 6'3", they ask me why he's so tall. I explain that I grew up in a place that had no sun or vegetation, and thus my diet, in addition to lacking vital vitamin D, lacked all other vitamins, too. Then I add that if I had grown up in Denver I would have been 6'5" and blond.

My mother always worried about what we were going to eat. Store shelves went through different phases of emptiness. Every month we were given vouchers that allowed us to buy a few pounds of meat, per family member – if the store had meat. Even when they had meat it was for a short time and we had to stand in long lines to get it. My parents never complained. It was our life and the life of everyone around us. I did not know any other way.

But my parents had known a different, gentler life. My father grew up in Moscow. Being Jewish in the 1950s was difficult in Russia. There was hidden (not in-your-face) anti-Semitism. My father aced math in high school, and even tutored other kids in the subject. Yet when he applied to university, he somehow "failed" the math test. I don't know whether, if he had applied to other universities, they would have accepted him, but the rebel in him decided to go study in a godforsaken place at a school that would accept him without even an entrance exam – Murmansk Marine Academy. They accepted anyone who was able to fog a mirror.

Late in the 1950s my father met my mother while visiting his relatives in Saratov, a beautiful 400-year-old Russian city on the Volga River. My mom was my father's distant relative (not blood-related). They fell in love, and she moved to Murmansk. My mom must have loved my dad very much to move from the comfort of an intellectual life in Saratov (she played piano and violin and went to the symphony on a regular basis with her parents) to the hellhole that Murmansk was at the time. It was better in the 1960s than it had been in the 1950s, but it was still a fisherman's town, where the only music you'd hear was the drunken sailors belting out bawdy seaman's chants as they stumbled through the streets.

My parents could have left Murmansk for Moscow or Saratov. But all their friends were in Murmansk and my father had a great job there that he loved. He was a gifted and much-loved professor. My father had taught most of the high brass who occupied positions of power throughout Murmansk, and thus if we needed something my father knew someone who knew someone. That was Soviet Russia: Every single company or organization was owned by the government, and to get anything you had to know someone. That included simple things like my brother wanting to transfer to a different school, or my parents wanting a larger apartment for their growing family to live in. As I write this, I realize how weird this sounds. Welcome to socialism.

This "power" my father had was born completely out of love and respect. My father liked walking home from the Academy, which was two miles (this is where I got my love of walking). This 30-minute walk always turned into a two-hour walk-and-talk journey, as my father would meet people he knew and stop and have a ten-minute conversation with each. I think he enjoyed being loved and respected by others. He is a warm, honest, well-rounded, non-judgmental human being, and a great listener. People love that. I remember the admiration with which people looked at my father.

If we moved from Murmansk, he would have had to give that all up. My mom could never ask him to do that. I only understand now, almost 40 years later, how much my mom loved my dad – she shielded him completely from the difficulties of the outside world. She just let him be him – he taught and painted. Worrying about what we were going to eat was my mother's burden. Though this was a difficult life, we never starved. In fact, I didn't know anyone who went hungry.

My mom gave up a career for our family. She had a graduate degree in physics from the university in Saratov, but in Murmansk took just a part-time job working at an institute that studied the Northern Lights. Her work and her own interests were always secondary to the family. She put my father, my brothers, and me at the center of her life. In her late 40s, she found a sliver of daylight in her day and joined a choir. That is the only thing I remember my mother doing for herself.

Life takes a terrible turn

My mother and my father were born a year apart. Both of their birthdays are in May. I remember May 1983 vividly. A few days before my father's 50th birthday, I was playing outside, holding a bottle that had a broken bottom. My friend hit the bottle, which flew right into my face, breaking the skin right under my right eye (I still have a scar). I ran home with blood running down my face. I remember Mom's calm face when she saw her youngest child with a cut right next to his eye and covered in blood. I remember her calling the ambulance and calming me down. Miraculously, I did not lose my eye – the bottle had stopped just nanometers from the eyeball. I spent my father's 50th birthday in the hospital.

A year later my family was not so lucky. On May 6, 1984 – a day after her birthday – Mom was hospitalized with an enormous headache. She was diagnosed with brain cancer. Knowing my mom, she had probably had the headache for weeks but hid it, not wanting to ruin her or my father's birthday celebrations.

A day after Mom was hospitalized my father took me to see her. That was the last time I saw the mother I had known.

Even at that time, as she was suffering enormously, I don't remember seeing any fear or self-pity in my mother. She could not bring herself to think about herself and, on that last day with her, I remember her quizzing my father about my brother Leo and giving instructions about what my brother Alex needed to do in school.

My father fought for her using everything he had. All his energy went toward saving her. He found and brought a neurosurgeon from Saint Petersburg, who promised the moon – full recovery.

When people of science see a loved one facing death, they'll cling to anything, even the empty promises of pseudoscience. I vaguely remember my father reading and reporting that water sent through a contraption that contained electricity and salt helped some people with cancer (or something along those lines). My father constructed that contraption and made that water for my mother.

Neither the surgery nor the contraption helped.

Murmansk's population leaves Murmansk in the summer months and goes south (not much different from New Yorkers moving to Florida in the winter, except that half of Murmansk emptied in the *summer*). We needed as much warm weather and sunlight as we could get to warm our bones and store up heat for the coming winter. (That is how my mother jokingly explained it to me.) In those two or three summer months my family usually traveled to Moscow and Saratov to visit both sets of my grandparents, or visit other parts of the country.

Summer 1984 was different.

My brother Alex was 17 (he is six years older than me) and was sent to a resort in Tajikistan. My oldest brother, Leo, was 21 and a cadet at the Murmansk Marine Academy, so he stayed in Murmansk. My father stayed, of course, with my mom in Murmansk. In late May, my father gave me 15 rubles and a sack of sandwiches and put me on the train to Saint Petersburg.

It was a two-day journey. My father's friend met me at the Saint Petersburg station and drove me to a pioneer camp in Pushkino, a small town south of Saint Petersburg. Fifteen rubles was a lot of money for a 10-year-old kid (though I'd turn 11 in a few weeks). As weird as it may sound, the very first thing I bought with this money, at one of the train stops, was the darkly satirical anti-war novel *The Good Soldier Švejk*. There was definitely something seriously wrong with me. I should have bought a toy instead.

I never thought I'd be one of those people who say, "When I was your age I..." and describe how hard their life was. But the thought of putting one of my kids on a train without a cell phone and location-tracking software on their iPhone, sharing a train car with complete strangers for two days, is unfathomable to me. The irony is that they could do this, and they'd be absolutely fine. I would not be fine.

A month later, my father's friend picked me up from the camp and put me on the train to Moscow. In Moscow I was greeted by my brother Alex. I spent the rest of the summer with grandparents in Moscow and Saratov.

When we arrived in Murmansk in late August, I did not recognize my mom. In fact, the mother I knew was gone. My mother was a beautiful, vibrant, smiling woman with brown hair. Now there was a woman in our house with a short buzz cut and grey hair, who looked nothing like my mom. I did not understand how all her hair could turn gray in two months – only years later did I learn that she had colored her hair brown.

The surgery did not go well. The cancer kept growing. Mom did not recognize anyone but my dad. She called him Papa. She spent most of her time in bed and could barely speak. She spent a few more weeks in our apartment but had to be hospitalized as she got worse.

Looking back at my 11-year-old self, I am shocked by how clueless I was. My mother was dying, and I was going about my life as though nothing had happened. In fact, I remember enjoying my newfound freedom – my mother was not there to mother me, and my father was busy taking care of her.

That guilt for leading a normal life while my mother was in the hospital hooked up to an IV still haunts me to this day. But psychologists would opine that this was a self-preservation mechanism that allowed an 11-year-old to cope with his mother's dying. It was too devastating for me to process, so I blocked it.

In early October, Mom's sister Natasha came from Saratov to stay with us.

The evening my Mom passed away I remember as vividly as if it was yesterday. I was home with Aunt Natasha. The hospital called and asked to speak with my aunt. She took the call in another room. Then she came out, hugged me, and told me that her sister, my mom, had passed away.

I still don't know why, but we went to the hospital. We were sitting in the lobby and my aunt was talking to administrators. I was sitting by myself. Someone asked me a question, and for the first and the only time in my life I found that I could not verbalize the words in my head. I remember just giving the questioner a puzzled look.

Thirty-something years later I realized that I never said goodbye to my Mom. Not really. My Mom, the woman I knew, died a day after her 50th birthday when she was hospitalized. I did not say goodbye to her; I did not know she was dying. A woman with a buzz cut and grey hair that did not even look like my mother is the woman that died.

My father

Stoic philosophers have a practice called negative visualization. You imagine you are going to lose something or somebody. There are two reasons to do this. First, it may make a loss less painful; and second, you'll appreciate that thing or person. This is great advice for anyone.

The Roman Stoic philosopher Seneca wrote, "We should love all of our dear ones ... but always with the thought that we have no promise that we may keep them forever – nay, no promise even that we may keep them for long."

For months after my mom's death I was terrified about losing my father. I had nightmares about it. That fear of losing my dad was seared in my brain. Without knowing it, unintentionally and unwantedly, I was doing negative visualization.

I hate finding a silver lining in my mom's death, but there was one. Losing my mother brought me closer to my father – not just in the months that followed her death but for decades, right up to the present. I lived with him until I got married in my late 20s. In my 30s and 40s I made sure to see him at least a few times a week. We'd go for morning walks. I stopped in for breakfast several times a week. A few times a year we'd go on trips, at first just the two of us (including to South Africa and Europe) and later with my kids. Our relationship is much deeper than just father and son; we are friends.

Imagining losing my father (negative visualization), right after I lost my mother, made me appreciate my father so much. My dad and I also got closer after Mom's death because he had to come out of the academic bubble that Mom had allowed him to live in. Instead of sharing parenting responsibility with her, he was solely responsible for me now. I was his sole responsibility now. My brothers, who were both cadets at the Marine Academy, required a lot less care than me.

My father rose to the occasion of being a single parent. I was a lighthearted kid, but I was also lazy and lacked the ambition to study. My teachers decided I was not a good student, and I didn't want to prove them wrong. My father had difficult material to work with, and he did the best he could. He also believed in me and always showed it, and eventually that belief paid off. (I am not congratulating myself here for lifetime achievements, but I have exceeded the very low bar I set for myself when I was a kid.)

When I face a difficult situation or when I evaluate my behavior, I ask myself, "What would my father do?" My father is and always will be my role model. He is a role model not just for his intelligence, kindness, calmness, patience, and constant curiosity to learn, but for his bravery as well.

Our apartment in Russia was on the fifth floor. A family with eight children lived directly below us. My father jokingly called them the "Garlics." All their kids, like garlic cloves, looked the same; we could never tell them apart.

One day when I was 13, I came home from school for lunch. On my way back to school, as I was coming down the stairs, I smelled smoke coming from the Garlics' door. I rang the bell; I knocked; no one answered. I ran back upstairs and got a hammer, went back down, and started hitting the door, trying to open it. My father came down a minute after me, realized the situation, and quietly and decisively moved me aside. He told me to go to our apartment and call the fire department. He rammed the door open and walked into an apartment engulfed in fire. He went into every room and finally brought out two kids (five and seven years old). They were scared to come out from hiding under a blanket in their bedroom. If he had waited for the fire department, the kids could have burned to death or suffocated from the smoke.

At a school ceremony staged by the fire department, I was given a watch with the inscription, "For saving kids in a fire." I had done absolutely nothing other than be at the right place at the right time and call the fire department. My father, on the other hand, had risked his life.

That was 30-plus years ago. You won't see my father's medal anywhere in his house. (I don't think I've seen it in 30 years.) He never told this story to any of his friends. He is a person who is so comfortable with himself that he doesn't seek external approval and is thus naturally modest.

A few years later after Mom's death, my father married my stepmother, Feyga, whose son Igor is as close to me as my brothers are.

Not military material

Murmansk revolves around its port, and its academic institutions are geared toward producing a workforce for the fishing and merchant marine industries. It was always assumed that I'd attend either the Marine College or the Marine Academy. Both were semi-military schools where the students (cadets) had to reside in dormitories, wear navy uniforms, follow strict military-like rules, and take orders from navy officers (and ask no questions).

Russia had a draft army. It was not concerned about recruitment and thus treated its soldiers very poorly (an understatement). The pay was only high enough for soldiers to afford the postage to write home asking for money. Russian youth looked at serving in the Russian army as akin to a two-year prison sentence (at least when I was there; I have been told that has changed). Army avoidance in the late 1980s was not about fear of death, as the war in Afghanistan was over, but stemmed from the dread of losing years of one's youth and the dismay of humiliation, as the older soldiers commonly abused the younger ones. A very sane friend of mine entered a psychiatric institution and faked mental disease just to avoid serving in the army.

My father and both of my older brothers graduated from the Murmansk Marine Academy. My father taught at the academy for 27 years. Neither my brothers nor I had any dreams about being seamen. Quite to the contrary, Leo could have been a philosopher (now he is an engineer). Alex wanted to be anything but an electrical engineer (he is now a successful real estate broker in Denver and has gone back to his art roots and become a terrific artist too). Our choices were limited: Either attend one of these two semi-military schools or join the Red Army.

By the time I finished eighth grade (the equivalent of tenth grade in the US), the law had changed: Cadets from the Marine Academy lost their draft exemption, but college cadets were spared. I enrolled in the Marine College and dreaded every moment I spent there. I lived in an army-like barracks, and wore a navy uniform. I hated taking orders from commanding officers and had no interest in the subjects I studied, but the alternative was even worse. This is what you do when you have few choices; you take the least poisonous alternative.

My aunt in Siberia

My father has two younger sisters. One lived all her life in Moscow, while the other moved with her family from Moscow to Siberia in 1979. For a long time, I wondered why my aunt and my cousins in Siberia never visited or called us. It seemed so uncharacteristic of our family, who were always very close. In the summer of 1988, my father finally told me that my aunt had not really moved to Siberia; she had emigrated to the United States of America. My immediate reaction was resentment. The first words out of my mouth were "traitor" and "spy."

It sounds a bit silly now, but you have to understand that I was a child of the Cold War. A couple of times a month my class walked to the movie theatre (this was before VCRs had reached Murmansk) and watched propaganda documentaries about decaying capitalistic America, infested with the homeless, where black people were lynched, the poor were exploited by the rich, and people were poisoned by hamburgers (later, of course, I learned that the part about hamburgers was not a complete lie).

Russian movies showed Americans as evildoers, usually spies whose single goal in life was to destroy Mother Russia – the whole country was brainwashed. When I was nine years old, I attended a pioneer camp and went on a field trip. A foreign tourist, mesmerized by my smile and internal beauty (okay, that is just a wild guess), gave me bubble gum. My camp teacher, in horror, took it away, yelling that I was lucky to be alive, as it was probably poisoned.

My father was not at all surprised to hear the words "traitor" and "spy" come out of my mouth. He calmly explained that despite being well educated, his sister's family had lived in poverty because they had faced the invisible anti-Semitic wall that is so often encountered by Jewish people in Russia.

He also explained that he hid the truth about my aunt's whereabouts from us because the consequences of the truth leaking out to local authorities would have been dire. My mother and he could have lost their jobs, and my brothers and I would never be permitted to leave the borders of the country, which for (future) seamen would have been devastating. In fact, his sister who stayed behind was demoted due to my aunt's departure for the United States; she was deemed guilty of betrayal by association.

Second-class citizen

Though my parents always tried to shield us from anti-Semitism, I was often made aware that there was something wrong with my being Jewish. Even as a little child, I often encountered a second-class-citizen attitude toward me.

"Nationality" was a mandatory line in Soviet passports and was a required disclosure on every application. When I was seven, my parents, hoping that I had a hidden music talent (I didn't), signed me up for singing lessons. While filling out a standard application, the teacher asked me the usual questions: parents' names, address, phone – and nationality. I vividly remember being filled with shame and staring at the ground as I said, "Jewish."

Russia was not South Africa under apartheid; there was no formal discrimination against Jews or segregation. Though Stalin was going to send all Jews to the Far East, his timely death interrupted that endeavor. I'd be lying if I said that we constantly felt anti-Semitism in Russia; we did not. It sporadically touched parts of our lives and some people were impacted more than others. Other than the anti-Semitism my father encountered in the 1950s, when he applied to universities in Moscow, we were impacted even less by discrimination than most Jews were. Murmansk was a city of immigrants, a melting pot that somewhat came to life in the 1960s and 1970s.

But I always thought of being Jewish as a nationality. Until my late teens, I never related being Jewish with a religious identity. My parents and grandparents were not religious. The premise behind all organized religions was "debunked" by teachers in Soviet Russia from the first grade forward. I don't think the "God doesn't exist; it's all a mass delusion" lecture was in the curriculum, but the message was consistently the same from all our teachers. My father says my teachers were just a product of their environment, and he is probably right.

Come to think of it, I did not know a single religious person of any religion. My parents had a lot of Jewish friends who for the most part were either teachers, scientists or doctors, and none of them were religious.

Coming to America

After the *glasnost* ("transparency," "openness") reform of 1985, the decades of brainwashing were slowly supplanted by the truth. In the late 1980s few people could afford VCRs, but little VCR movie theaters were popping up in basements of apartment buildings everywhere, consisting of several TV sets hooked up to a VCR. Unlike state-owned theaters, they were not censored and had the freedom to choose their repertoire.

Picture and sound quality were terrible, as VHS tapes were copied dozens of times before they made it into a VCR. Movies were dubbed by one monotone voice that translated all characters. But none of that mattered; we were hungry for variety, and American cinema was it. After watching hundreds of these flicks, it became painfully obvious that America and capitalism were not so rotten after all. And despite what my camp teacher told me, Americans did not really have any intention of poisoning little kids.

But we were shocked to discover that Americans ate dogs. Okay, this needs an explanation.

As the relationship between Russia and the Western world started to thaw, Americans and Europeans started to send food to help Russians. I remember one day we got a box full of canned and packaged food. All this food looked new and exciting to us. It was so different from the food we were used to that it might as well have come from Mars.

There was a can that said, "Hot Dogs." My English was good enough to know the words *hot* and *dogs*. What you need to understand is that the term *hot dog* doesn't (or at least didn't) exist in Russian. There were sausages and there were links (thin sausages). We were shocked that Americans would kill dogs and then eat them hot.

In 1990, my "Siberian" aunt invited us to join her in the US. Just a few years earlier the possibility would have sounded absurd to us but, despite America's cruel eating habits, we decided to emigrate.

My father saw no future for us in Russia. So, on December 4, 1991, we found ourselves in New York City. We stayed there overnight and a day later we were in Denver. A new and in many ways harder (at least at first) life started, but we never regretted leaving Russia.

Our coming-to-America experience lacks the color and drama you might expect. Pan Am had oversold its coach class, so we got a free upgrade and flew first class from Moscow to New York. In 1991, the road for new immigrants from Russia had already been paved by the hundreds of thousands that came before us a few years earlier. At the airport we were greeted by my aunt and half a dozen friendly strangers (people from her synagogue), who brought us to a fully furnished apartment that my aunt and these strangers had prepared. The selflessness of these supposedly self-obsessed capitalists was shocking to all of us. With the help of my aunt, these strangers, and Jewish Family Service (a terrific organization that helped a lot of Russian immigrants), we were able to get on our feet relatively quickly.

Another shock to us was that Denver looked nothing like New York or Los Angeles. It didn't have many skyscrapers; nor did it have palm trees. My image of America had been wrongly colored by Hollywood movies, which were usually set on the coasts, not in flyover country. We were also shocked at how underdressed Americans were (at least in Denver). Russians, just like Europeans, paid attention to how they dressed. Americans (unless they lived in NYC), not so much.

I had studied British English in school, though *studied* is an overstatement. This was raw memorization, with zero practical speaking experience. I soon discovered that my Queen's English was worthless. It was good enough to buy a pack of cigarettes, but beyond that I could barely understand anything. Americans spoke in full, run-together sentences, not in discrete words.

The lack of language did not stop me from looking for a job. My aunt taught me to say, "I'd like to fill out a job application." Armed with this important sentence, a winning smile, and a lack of fear, I knocked on the door of every business in a two-mile radius. (I later discovered that a few of them were strip clubs.) After a few months of knocking, I got a job at a health club folding towels and cleaning locker rooms.

TV was a great educational tool. In fact, the show *Married with Children* is responsible for a good portion of my day-to-day vocabulary, and for a while Al Bundy was my role model (not for too long, though).

My new American life was exciting – new friends, new country; everything was new.

My father and stepmother initially had a very different experience. The first few years must have been excruciating for them – they had a family to feed. My father could not teach, so he turned to painting. My stepmother was a doctor in Russia; she got a job doing housekeeping at a hotel. As you can imagine, it was a difficult and painful transition for her. My father, wonderful human being that he is, would come to the hotel late in the day, let her rest, and do the beds for her. To this day, when we stay at a hotel, my father makes sure we leave a big tip.

After a few years in the US, my father started to make a living selling his art, and my stepmother quit working and became his "business manager." She spoke English for both of them.

Becoming an investor

When we first arrived, I was not a resident of Colorado and could not afford to pay out-of-state college tuition fees; so I found myself going to high school to learn English. This was quite a shock, considering that I had left Russia three months before my college graduation. I was the oldest kid in high school, but I didn't mind.

After I graduated, my American life followed the normal trajectory of that of an average, fresh-out-of-high-school kid. While enjoying the benefits of being single and living with my father and stepmother, I worked full-time and went to university.

After dating a half-dozen majors (and just two girlfriends) in my first few years of university, I was very fortunate to discover what I wanted to do (more accurately, what I love to do) – investing. That discovery, like most things in life, was serendipitous.

I got a job with a small investment firm in Golden, Colorado: PVG Asset Management. It was run by two wonderful human beings, Joe Pecoraro and Bill Rahmig. In the early 1990s PCs were fickle and PVG needed someone to constantly fix them. I never got formal training, but I tinkered with my own computer and became good at fixing software issues.

I knew little about fixing hardware. One day Joe asked me to replace a video card on the company's server. This was in the middle of the day. I'd have to ask everyone to stop working so I could shut down the server. I don't remember if it was out of laziness on my part or I really did not want to ask everyone to stop what they were doing. I made the brave (and very stupid) decision to install the video card on the running, fully powered server. I did not get electrocuted. I did, however, fry the server, including the hard drives and the data stored on them.

What came next was a shock to me. I expected to be fired or at least yelled at. Nothing of the sort. Joe made some jokes. Bill saw how upset I was and tried to make me feel better. They understood that it was an innocent (though idiotic) mistake. Both Bill and Joe focused on solving the problem I had created. A new server was bought. An IT firm was called in. Data was restored from backup. A day later the firm was back in business. That was it. This incident, which cost a company half a year of my annual salary, was never brought up again. Thinking about it today, I realize that Joe and Bill set a standard for how I should behave as the CEO of IMA, when I find myself in similar situations: With respect, grace, calmness, and a little bit of humor.

Joe fell in love with my father's art (and he is still the largest collector of my father's paintings). Almost three decades later, we are still friends. In December 2017, out of nowhere, I received an incredibly kind email from Bill, congratulating me on "what I had turned into." Sadly, Bill passed away a month later from a freak case of pneumonia.

Back to the '90s. Hallway conversations with Joe and Bill sparked my love affair with investing. I stopped dating other majors and committed to a monogamous relationship with investing. A few years later, when I was done with school, I knew I wanted to be an analyst. Sadly, PVG did not need any. I started looking for another job.

I needed every advantage I could get. So, in addition to applying for jobs posted in newspapers, I pulled out the yellow pages and faxed my résumé to every single investment firm in Colorado (this was before email).

As luck would have it, IMA – a money management firm tucked away in a leafy Denver suburb – received my fax even before the company posted a job for an analyst in the newspaper. I still remember that afternoon. I had just come home from school. My stepmother told me that "a very pleasant gentleman" had called me about a job opening. I called him back. His name was Mike Conn, founder and then-CEO of IMA. As I talked to Mike, I learned that IMA's office was only three blocks away. I offered to be there in 10 minutes. Mike agreed.

What took place was not a traditional job interview but more a casual conversation. I instantly liked Mike. He had grown up on a farm near a town of 300 people in Iowa. He was the first in his family to go to college. But he did not just go to college; he graduated from Harvard. He turned out to be full of interesting stories about history, books, movies, and his own adventures, which included race-car driving and being a vent man (a crew member responsible for fueling a race car during a pit stop) in the Indy 500 race. I have yet to meet a person who is better at talking to anyone about anything and not wanting anything from that other person, except a good conversation.

It helped that Mike knew Joe and Bill. He called them. They must not have mentioned the server incident. A week later I was hired.

Years later, Mike told me that I was the only person he interviewed. I am forever grateful to Mike for taking a chance on me in 1997. I had little investment experience. I had a heavy Russian accent (I had been "off the boat" for only six years), but Mike saw in me a burning love for investing and a desire to learn. Mike is my mentor, friend, and chess sparring partner (though he's been telling me that I have a Russian genetic advantage over him).

I've been with IMA ever since. IMA is the longest relationship I've ever had; it even predates my marriage. I started as an analyst, then gradually progressed to managing portfolios, and in 2014 I became CEO.

A writer is born

A few years after I joined IMA, I started teaching a graduate investment class at the University of Colorado in Denver. Though I enjoyed teaching, I "retired" after seven years, for two reasons. First, I absolutely hated giving out grades, especially bad grades. I suffer from "I want people to like me" syndrome. When I gave out a bad grade, I felt worse than the student receiving it. And second, I simply got bored. Teaching the same class over and over again loses its challenge after a few years.

Also, in 2004, I started writing for TheStreet.com. At the time, TheStreet was an interesting experiment. Unlike typical financial websites, where all content is written by career journalists, the bulk of TheStreet's stuff was created by professional money managers opining on the markets, the economy, and stocks. TheStreet provided an audience and a safety net – editors.

I was new to writing but discovered that I really liked it. I wrote almost daily. Unlike teaching in a classroom, writing never bored me. Still doesn't – I don't let it bore me. If a subject stops pushing the boundaries of my knowledge or curiosity, I move on to the next one.

Though writing is something you can get better at with time, when I look objectively at that period I see that my own opinion of my writing was improving much faster than the writing itself. Less than a year after I began writing, I had the audacity to submit an article to the *Financial Times,* one of the most respected publications in the Western Hemisphere. To my surprise they published it; and shockingly, they went on publishing my articles regularly.

One of the pieces I wrote for the *Financial Times* had a kernel of an idea that I thought would be interesting to explore more deeply. In late 2005 I approached John Wiley & Sons with a proposal to turn that idea into a book. Eighteen months later, *Active Value Investing* was born. I am so glad that I had that youthful arrogance then – I was punching far above my weight but didn't have the self-awareness to know it. There is no way I'd be able to do that today.

Writing my first book cracked a small opening in the doors of other publishers, and I waltzed right through them. My articles started to appear in big publications – *Christian Science Monitor, Barron's, Fortune* – and then I became a columnist for *Institutional Investor* magazine and won several prestigious (in very small circles) writing awards.

Somewhere in between writing for TheStreet.com and the *Financial Times,*

I started emailing my articles to a few dozen friends and relatives. Let me be completely honest: I was spamming them. They had not asked me to send them articles, but they were too kind to say so. Some, probably out of pity, even encouraged me.

Writing is an externalization of your internal conversation, and even as I type this I can hear myself talk. It is a conversation with someone, and for that someone I visualize my email readers, my friends and relatives. The fact that my initial email readers sometimes replied and commented on my articles made this visualization much easier. Even when I was writing a column for *Institutional Investor*, I was mentally writing to my email subscribers, not magazine readers. This way I was not writing to strangers but to friends and family, and thus I was less guarded, more honest, and could just be my casual, sarcastic self.

A few years after I started writing I found myself entering into the "There must be more to life than this" chapter of my life (to quote the immortal Freddie Mercury). It dawned on me there was more to life than just investing. But this was a glacial process, which started with my father's art. I love my father, and he is a phenomenal artist, so I started to include his paintings in my emails.

Then, a year or two later, I started to include classical music. One day I was working on an article and listening to music. I don't remember what piece it was, but I do remember that it moved me. I dashed off a few paragraphs about it, added a few links to YouTube, and appended it to my investment article email. Some people were indifferent to it and said nothing, but as I continued to do this, many people started to thank me for including classical music, as it rekindled their love for it.

The reaction to my father's art was very interesting. A year or two after I started including his paintings with my articles, there came a day when I forgot to insert a painting in the email. To my surprise I got polite but still quite strident emails that said things along the lines of "Vitaliy, your articles are fine, but please don't send them without your father's paintings." In other words, my emails had turned into something akin to *Playboy* magazine – my readers were actually perusing them for the pictures, not the articles. (I learned from this experience. I do not want to get similar emails from readers of this book, so I included my father's art in this book.)

My personal life morphed into my writing in a gradual way, too. Since I was still "just writing to friends and family," I started to share stories about my kids, our trips together, my self-improvement journey, and nostalgic recollections of growing up in Russia. Over time, writing about life became as important (and at times more important) to me as writing about investing.

As I have mentioned in the Introduction, many readers told me that though they came for investment articles they stayed for my life articles, my father's paintings, and classical music. These responses kept me coming back to write about life. Readers wrote that my life (non-investment) articles made a difference in their lives. A few told me to stick to investing and shut up about my personal adventures. I tell them, in that case they can just pick and choose articles on ContrarianEdge.com.

I know that I've been the biggest beneficiary in this relationship. Writing about classical music has inspired me to learn more about it. As I write about my family and my life, I appreciate them more. When I write about deeper subjects, the trip to the subconscious always leaves me recharged and newly curious. This writing journey has changed me. It has turned me from a one-dimensional value investor into a student of life; it has made me a better person. (I'll explore in greater detail what being a student of life means to me as we go along in the book.)

Made in America

I got married in my late 20s, and my wife Rachel and I have three wonderful kids – Jonah, Hannah, and Mia Sarah. You'll get to meet them soon.

At times I wonder how my life would have turned out if we hadn't emigrated to the United States. Was I disadvantaged coming to this country when I was 18, hardly speaking a word of English? I have thought a lot about that. I think I had a disadvantage for maybe the first few years, especially when I applied for that first job at Taco Bell and couldn't understand a thing the hiring manager asked me (I did not get that job).

Once I learned English and acclimated to the culture, I had an unfair competitive advantage: I had a drive to succeed. A lot of immigrants have it, because they see the contrast between where they came from and what America has to offer. I am not sure if my kids will have this drive, and that is okay.

But I also had another competitive advantage – incredible parents. My most important job today is to be for my kids as good a parent as my parents were to me.

It took me a while to get used to Americans smiling all the time and not telling you what they really think. Russians are very direct. They do not do small talk, and they tell you what they think to your face. It took me years (and being fired a few times) to realize that a person smiling at me may not necessarily mean they are happy with me or my job performance.

I began to wonder whether I preferred Russian directness or American politeness. Then my brother Alex and I visited Russia for a week in 2008, and I felt like a fish out of water. People looked at my constantly smiling face with suspicion, obviously questioning my mental state. I, in turn, got tired of their directness very quickly.

I guess I was born in Russia but made for America.

Soul in the Game

"Do not act as if you had ten thousand years to throw away.
Death stands at your elbow. Be good for something while
you live and it is in your power."
– Marcus Aurelius

THE CONCEPT OF having soul in the game is very near and dear to my heart. When someone has soul in the game, you instantly recognize it. I know, you want to know which soul and what game I am talking about. We'll do this, but first let me tell you about Jiro.

There is a wonderful documentary, *Jiro Dreams of Sushi*. It depicts 85-year-old Jiro Ono, proprietor of Sukiyabashi Jiro sushi restaurant in Tokyo. By outside appearance you'd think it was about the most unexciting restaurant you'd ever visit – a hole in the wall in a subway station with a seating capacity of ten at the sushi bar. That's it! Not a restaurant you'd think would be worth making a documentary about.

Then you learn that this hole in the wall is the first sushi restaurant in the world to receive three Michelin stars. There are millions of restaurants in the world, and as of this writing only 135 had three Michelin stars. This tiny place is where Barack Obama and former Japanese Prime Minister Shinzo Abe went for sushi on the American president's official visit to Japan.

What is so special about Sukiyabashi Jiro? It simply has incredible-tasting sushi. Every piece of sushi is crafted with the same care that Rembrandt took as he laid brush strokes on his masterpieces. Jiro is an artist in constant, unending pursuit of trying to make the best sushi in the world, and he has achieved it. He dedicated every waking moment of his life to making the best sushi – and some not-waking ones, too. That's why the documentary is called *Jiro Dreams of Sushi* – Jiro thinks about sushi so much that ideas of what sushi to make come to him in his dreams.

You can see this constant pursuit of perfection in little details: Jiro said that he recently realized that if the octopus is massaged for 45 minutes instead of 30, then this extra 15 minutes brings out an important flavor. Or, when a couple comes to the restaurant, Jiro makes the pieces of sushi for the woman slightly smaller. He explains that women have smaller mouths, and he wants the couple to finish each piece of sushi at the same time. He wants them to enjoy each piece together. Everything he does has this sort of incredible focus on every tiny detail.

Jiro is an example of total dedication to one's craft – he undoubtedly has soul in the game.

So, what is "soul in the game"?

Let's start with soul – that's the immaterial part of us, our essence, the dearest part of ourselves. The game is whatever creative endeavor we are deeply involved in, be it running a company, creating art, writing, investing, or making sushi – any creative pursuit that you believe is worthy of your effort and time. When you have soul in the game, this pursuit has all of you, every ounce of your attention and strength and love.

I learned about soul in the game from one of my favorite thinkers, Nassim Nicholas Taleb. In his book *Skin in the Game*, Taleb touched just briefly on this concept, but it really stuck with me.

Before we go deeper into soul in the game, let's discuss its cousin, skin in the game – a concept Nassim expounded on.

Skin in the game can be summed up in one sentence: You want to associate with people who will share not only upsides with you but also downsides. When someone is getting paid to sell you a product but captures no downside in the transaction (this describes the bulk of Wall Street transactions), that person doesn't have skin in the game, and his advice may not be in your best interest.

You and I would not want to eat at Jiro's restaurant if Jiro and his apprentices never ate the sushi they made. Eating their own sushi connects their self-interests to ours: Not being sickened by uncooked fish.

I've designed my investing firm IMA so that we have skin in the game.

Our business grows and shrinks with our clients' success, but we don't see that as real skin in the game; it's a nail clipping from my pinkie in the game, at best. No, I have skin in the game because all my family's liquid net worth – all my life savings – are invested in the same stocks my clients own. I and the people dearest to me (my family) share the upside, and most importantly the downside, of my decisions for IMA clients.

Soul in the game is the elevation of skin in the game to a much higher level. Now, the proprietor is connected to the product or service more than just through sharing upsides and downsides with his customers; his creation is indistinguishable from his identity. His self-worth is completely interlaced with his creation. Just as with Jiro and his sushi.

Taleb relates the concept of soul in the game through a discussion of artisans. When you love what you do, your work stops being *work* and becomes a craft; and no matter what it is, you do it with pride, love, and care.

Jiro's documentary touches on that concept as well. After ten years of apprenticeship, Jiro finally allows his apprentice to make an egg custard (*tamagoyaki*). That becomes the apprentice's sole focus for months. He goes through 200 batches before Jiro is satisfied with his egg custard and calls him *shokunin* – an artisan.

Here is what being an artisan, having soul in the game, means to me (with Taleb's help).

Artisans have sacred taboos. They won't break them for financial benefit.

My father was an artisan all his life – not just as an artist but as a teacher, scientist, and inventor. When we lived in Russia, my father earned his living as a professor, teaching at the most prestigious university in Murmansk. Bribes in Soviet Russia were as common as tipping at Denny's. My father was constantly offered bribes for a passing grade, and he always declined without a moment's hesitation. This explains our modest life in Russia.

Once, however, my father came close to sacrificing his sacred taboo. My mother was gravely ill. She needed medicine that could not be bought in the pharmacy (again, remember, this was Soviet Russia). A parent of a student "had connections" and volunteered to come up with the medicine if her son got a passing grade. But even then, my father tutored her son for weeks until he passed the exam, rather than just hand out a good grade where it was not deserved.

When we moved to the United States, my father was 58 years old – too old to learn a new language well enough to teach in it. Painting, his hobby, turned into his profession. Unlike most Russian intellectual immigrants, who ended up driving taxicabs or cleaning hotel rooms, my father blossomed in the US as an artist. He loved being an artist. But he always had taboos. For him, it was art first and profession second. He never allowed money to influence what he painted. If a patron ordered a painting, he'd only paint it if it was interesting to him. He never allowed what sold to determine what he created. The art was his north star, not the money.

For an artisan, the love of his craft (which often borders on art) is his primary motivation; financial considerations are always secondary.

Warren Buffett says that he tap dances to work. He goes to work not because he cannot wait to earn another billion – he is giving the bulk of his money away, anyway – but because he loves investing. He is an artisan; investing is his art and craft. (I discuss this topic in greater detail in "Art or Craft.") He has often mentioned that, for him, building Berkshire Hathaway has been akin to Michelangelo's painting the ceiling of the Sistine Chapel.

Jiro's restaurant has only ten seats. The cost of the meal is a prix fixe of $300. There is no menu – Jiro gives you 24 pieces of sushi in the sequence he chooses, to achieve the best dining experience. It is impossible to make a reservation at Sukiyabashi Jiro. In fact, Michelin recently removed its three-star rating because of the inability of the public to make reservations. This had no material impact on Jiro's business – demand clearly outstrips supply. If money was a primary driver for Jiro, he could have expanded the restaurant to a hundred seats, opened a chain of them, or doubled his prices. He has not. Money is a secondary consideration – not a goal but a byproduct of what he does. His primary pursuit is to make great sushi, and financial success has ensued.

I can relate to this sentiment: investing is an incredible intellectual riddle that I have the privilege of attempting to solve every day. It is a never-ending journey of self-improvement. Though I don't have Buffett's wealth – nor do I aspire to have it – I feel exactly the same way about tap dancing to work (though at times I ride a bike or drive a car to get there).

At first unintentionally and later intentionally, I sculpted the perfect job. Thinking about investing and portfolios doesn't just start when I come to work and stop when I go home. I have not yet achieved Jiro's level of dedication – I am yet to dream of stocks. But they do follow me around. It's a bit unhealthy, and there's always a tug of war between work life and family life, but I still wouldn't change a thing.

If I won a billion dollars in the lottery, my daily life wouldn't change a bit – I'd just have to work harder to make sure my kids didn't get spoiled. I cannot see myself doing anything else with my life. At some point, as IMA continues to grow, if I feel our size is impacting the quality of our investment decisions or the service we provide to our clients, I'll put the brakes on growth. We'll simply stop accepting new clients. I am fine with "ten seats."

Artisans are students of life, for life. I think of my father when I write this. In his late 60s, when he was already an established artist who had won many national exhibitions and had work exhibited in museums, he discovered a local artist whose paintings he admired. When he learned that this artist taught masterclasses, my father signed up without hesitation. He did not have to think about his pride or what he had accomplished; he saw someone he could learn from. So he did.

This student of life concept is very dear to me. It was a competing title for this book. I will repeat this point several times throughout the book, because it is worth repeating: Maintaining the attitude of being a perpetual learner, being openminded to new knowledge, is paramount in preventing your ego and your success from fossilizing and stifling your learning and self-improvement. Which brings us to our next point.

Artisans constantly strive for improvement. Jiro has been making sushi for over 70 years and is still learning. He says, "Even at my age, in my work… I haven't reached perfection… There's always a yearning to achieve more. I'll continue to climb, trying to reach the top, but no one knows where the top is." Making the best possible sushi is his sole goal; he is obsessed by it. Jiro's oldest son shares his father's values. He has said, "Always look ahead and above yourself. Always try to improve on yourself. Always strive to elevate your craft."

Artisans have a very narrow, single focus. Jiro said, "I do the same thing over and over, improving bit by bit." Stoic philosopher Epictetus said, "You become what you give your attention to." Single focus combined with a drive for constant improvement, while being a student of life, adds up to an incredibly powerful force.

Claude Monet's painting of Rouen Cathedral sums up the nature of artisans as lifetime students, striving for improvement, and with a single focus. In 1892, Monet, father of the Impressionist school of art, rented an apartment across from Rouen Cathedral. (I touch on this story in greater depth in "The Art of a Meaningful Life.") For the next six months he painted a single subject – the cathedral. Monet studied light. He wrote: "A landscape does not exist in its own right since its appearance changes at every moment, but the surrounding atmosphere brings it to life – the light and air, which vary continually."

Monet had a single focus. He was completely consumed by the cathedral and the light that fell on it. He wrote to his wife, "I work like a mad man; I cannot stop thinking of anything else but the cathedral." He completed 30 paintings of the cathedral over the next three years. (He finished many of them in the studio afterwards.)

Monet was 52 years old, a very accomplished artist, and he had been painting for over 40 years. He was not too old to study light – he was a student of life for life. He wanted to improve.

Finally, **to have soul in the game, your pursuit has to be a net positive for society as a whole.** This one is less tangible, but it doesn't make it less important. The definition of *shokunin* goes beyond being a craftsman and having technical skills. It also implies an attitude and a social consciousness, an obligation to do one's best for the general welfare of society. This aligns well with one of my core values: Leave the world a better place than you found it. What is the point of life otherwise?

By the way, this is not just an altruistic endeavor, it's also a selfish one – all that you add to the world reciprocates back to you and improves your own life.

This is how I strive to lead my life. Just as important, it's how I want my kids to lead their lives, too.

Hold sacred taboos.*
Love what you do.
Be a student of life, for life.
Focus, and strive for continuous improvement.
See art in it.
Own it.
Have pride in it.
Be a net positive for society.

If you do all this, you may or may not have the fattest bank account, but you are guaranteed a fulfilling and meaningful life. It's that simple: Have soul in the game!

I'll leave you with Jiro's advice for the rest of us: "Once you decide on your occupation... you must immerse yourself in your work. You have to fall in love with your work. Never complain about your job. You must dedicate your life to mastering your skill. That's the secret of success... and is the key to being regarded honorably."

Share this chapter with a friend:
https://soulinthegame.net/zxj/

---

* For artisans, money is a second derivative of what they do; the quality, the craft, comes first. Over the years, with the advent of computers and consultants, an elegant but flawed theoretical framework, Modern Portfolio Theory, scientized and institutionalized investing. Large pension funds and foundations employ an army of consultants that slice and dice manager performance data (this is where computers become very handy). Inflows and outflows in a manager's fund are completely driven by his short-term performance and how he compares against his peers and benchmarks. This is not an abstract process to a money manager, because his bonuses and employment itself are tied to the success of the assets he manages. He – it's usually he – has a wife, kids, and bills to pay. These incentives are powerful and turn institutional investing into the Wall Street version of the Hunger Games, where winning and staying in the game is often more important than doing what is right for the client.

The concept of long term doesn't exist in this game: If you're fired in the short term, who cares about the long term? Managers start emulating benchmarks – if you stray far from the benchmark, "You are not doing what you were hired to do." What your peers own becomes more important in your buying and selling decision-making than what will generate attractive long-term risk-adjusted returns (risk in this case being not volatility but permanent loss of capital).

But when a client turns their life savings over to you and you know your decisions will have direct consequences for their life, playing the Hunger Games should never even enter into the equation.

There's an old saying: Companies get the shareholders they deserve. It's true of investment firms as well. We wear our values on our sleeves, and we get the investors we deserve. IMA is lucky to have attracted clients who share our values. Our growth as a firm may have been slower than some on Wall Street, but growth for the sake of growth has never been our priority.

If you listen to conversations happening at IMA, you'll often hear, "It needs to have soul in the game." It's at the core of everything we do. Neither the company nor I will ever have an extra ounce of reputation that we'd want to spare. After all, a reputation takes years to build but can be lost in minutes. If we do things with soul in the game, we'll make mistakes at times, but we'll never have to worry about our reputation.

Roman Emperor and Stoic philosopher Marcus Aurelius said, 'Do every act of your life as if it were your last.'

Speechless (Future) Father

PARENTING IS THE most difficult and yet the most rewarding job I have ever had and ever will have.

I was not prepared to be a parent.

Jonah was born 13 months after Rachel and I got married. Rachel was 22 and I was 28. I remember the day Rachel told me that she was pregnant. I was reading in an armchair. I closed my eyes and did not say a word for an hour. I was speechless, and not because I was overwhelmed with happiness. I was in shock. We were living paycheck to paycheck, paying off student loans. My computer of a mind was running spreadsheet simulations of how we could afford this child – diapers, daycare, education.

I am overwhelmed with guilt writing this today. I cannot even imagine the emotions Rachel went through during that hour. I called my father and shared with him my "happy" news and my concerns about it. He was calm; I could sense him smiling on the other end of the line. He said, "There are six billion people in the world. There are billions of parents out there. They've figured it out; so will you." I only vaguely remember what I did after that conversation, but I did firmly embrace the inevitable – Rachel and I would be parents.

Jonah was born in 2001, Hannah in 2005, and Mia Sarah tipped the scales toward a female majority in our household in 2014. You are about to meet them.

In the essays you are about to read, I am writing about the happy days, the highlights of parenting. Those are the moments that inspired me to write. But there were plenty of difficult ones.

Jonah did not sleep on his own until he was ten – Rachel and I had ten years of sleep deprivation. It took me ten years to figure out a solution – I bought an iPod. I put it on a shelf for him to see and told him it was his if he slept on his own for 20 days straight. That did the trick. As you'll see later, out of all my kids, Jonah is the only one who responds well to bribes. Thank you, Apple!

I wish I could say that I had a firm belief that Jonah would be standing firmly on his own two feet when he grew up. I did not. Until he was 16, I silently worried about Jonah's future. His grades were horrible. Everything, including his grades, was everyone's fault but his. He had zero drive to learn. I did not know what to do.

Then, during the summer before his senior year in high school, he went on a trip to Israel with a group of kids from Colorado. He came back a totally changed person. It was almost as if a maturity switch had been turned on. He started to take school seriously, and his GPA tripled from 1.3 to 3.9 from his junior to his senior year. He started to keep promises he made. Today, Jonah is 19, and I have no worry in the world about him.

Hannah... there is supposed to be no such a thing as a perfect child. But I cannot think of a single worry or headache that Hannah gave us. I kept losing her in the mountains when we went skiing (she was four), but that was my fault, not hers.

Mia Sarah, when she was seven, decided she didn't like mayonnaise. But her not liking it is not just confined to her plate. She decided that no one in our home could have it. I'll be eating a salad in the evening. She'll come downstairs to check my plate for mayonnaise. She checks the location of the mayonnaise bottle in the fridge to see if it's been moved. If she sees any member of our family eating mayonnaise, she starts crying. I did some light research on the subject: Mia Sarah is not alone in hating mayonnaise; there is even a word for it – *mayophobia*. President Obama is a member of the exclusive "I hate mayo" club, though he probably allows other members of his household to eat it. Not our Mia Sarah.

Just like any other normal family, we rush to be on time for school in the morning, and everyone is stressed. Breakfast is eaten on the go. Lunch is packed last-minute. We are constantly late. Kids argue in the car about what music to listen to. Yogurt is spilled in the car. The normal stuff. Keep this in mind as you read my stories about parenting: They are not written by a professional parent, but by a regular father who entered into parenthood speechless (for an hour).

Here She Is

O N JANUARY 11, 2014 my wife, Rachel, and I were blessed to bring into the world another American citizen who has the right to become the American president – a baby girl, Mia Sarah Katsenelson.

Rachel had wanted to have another child for a while. Our son Jonah is 12 and daughter Hannah is eight, so it was a long while. But I felt two was plenty, and we had a perfect set – a boy and a girl. But this year I turned 40, and my selfishness took over. I realized that Jonah will probably ski with me for another five years and then go to college, and Hannah for maybe another nine. Then it hit me: I need to plan ahead. I need a long-term ski buddy.

So, to my dear wife's considerable shock, I requested a baby. When I mentioned that maybe we should have another child, her immediate response was, "Are you writing another book?"

See, we had a deal – if I write another book then we'll have another child. For several years, I did not want to have another child, nor did I want to write a book, so it was a non-issue. (Mia Sarah's birth gave a greenlight for this book, which is how you come to be reading it now.)

The new baby changes the dynamics with the kids. Our concern was about Hannah – she was not going to be the youngest anymore. But she seems to be coping okay with it for now – we have been bribing her with ice cream, and we went skiing a few times. She is getting as much attention as she got in the past, at least from her brother and me (while Mom focuses on her baby sister).

We did not cheat and find out the sex of the baby ahead of time. It is our third child, so we wanted to add suspense to the waiting. When we asked our kids if they wanted a boy or a girl, Jonah said he wanted a boy and Hannah wanted a girl. Hannah's logic was very straightforward: "I already have a brother, so I want a sister." That's almost like "I already have a dog, now I want a cat." Jonah's thinking was similar. We knew one of them would not get their wish.

Not knowing the gender made the pregnancy experience so much more exciting and fun. Almost everyone in our large family was convinced it was a boy. My mother-in-law and my stepmother were adamant; they argued with incredible conviction that the shape of my wife's stomach indicated it was a boy. They made almost a scientific case of it, backing it up with countless examples of how stomachs in the past looked. (I have it all on tape to embarrass them in the future!) I had zero insight, but their conviction made no sense and woke up the contrarian in me, so I went on record (iPhone) saying it was going to be a girl.

It also made a conversation with a rabbi friend – who would perform the circumcision if it was a boy – a bit interesting. "Rabbi, there is a 50% chance that I may need your services in January."

Also, my wife had two sets of baby clothes – blue and pink. This is something I still don't understand. I don't think babies are picky about colors. But what do I know?

It hit me yesterday that another dynamic in our household has changed as well: Males are now the minority.

This Is What
Happiness Feels Like

*"Children are the living messages we
send to a time we will not see."*
— John F. Kennedy

YOU REALLY DON'T know what true emotions are until you become a parent. As I am writing this at 5 a.m., I have headphones on and I'm listening to Beethoven's "Moonlight Sonata." It's dark outside, and my wife and three kids are safely asleep.

This is what happiness feels like.

I know that in two hours they'll wake up. We'll have breakfast and I'll drive them to school. Jonah (my 16-year-old) will be bargaining with me about what music we'll listen to – classical will not be his first choice. Hannah will be on Jonah's side. Mia Sarah (my almost-four-year-old) will offer her preference, which is always the same: "Wheels on the Bus Go Round and Round." We'll compromise. Jonah has a learner's permit, and he'll be driving us through a beautiful park. I'll hug and kiss them, drop Jonah off at high school, Hannah at middle school, and Mia Sarah at preschool.

I am overwhelmed with emotions just writing this. This is all finite. One day they'll all be grown up. The house will be empty and days like today will be distant happy memories. I never want days like this to end. I really don't want my kids to grow up, and a bat mitzvah is another reminder that they are! Someday I will no longer be hugging and kissing them in the morning and driving them to school.

The stock market, economics, politics somehow seem so trivial next to this.

My daughter Hannah had her bat mitzvah a few days ago. It was one of the most important days of her life. For a Jewish girl it ranks somewhere close to getting married or having a firstborn.

In my speech at Hannah's bat mitzvah I wanted to express my love for her and tell her something meaningful about becoming bat mitzvah. Expressing my love for her was easy; the latter part was difficult, as you'll see.

Here is the speech:

Dear Hannah,

When I think of you, the word that instantly comes to mind is *sunshine*. Since you were very little, you always smiled. I'd wake you up in the morning, and no matter how early it was, you'd open your eyes and smile at me. Always.

You started skiing when you had barely turned four. You had no fear. No hesitation. You only had one speed – forward. Of course, skiing came with its own set of challenges for me. I kept losing you at Keystone or Vail.

If your Mom knew how many times I lost you, she'd have learned to ski and started skiing with us.

I just choose to look not at how many times I lost you but at how many times I found you.

When I lost you the first five times, I panicked. You were so little and these ski resorts are so large. I had a full head of hair when we started skiing, but after the first season, not so much.

When you went missing you wouldn't panic or cry. You'd ask someone for a phone and call me. Laughing, without a worry in the world, you'd say, "Dad, I am here."

You have always been happy within yourself. Wherever you go you bring sunshine with your smile.

This internal happiness is very rare.

Stay this way.

I was thinking about what Jewish advice to give you today. I was a bit conflicted. I grew up in Soviet Russia, where there was no religion. I am not just talking about Judaism. From the time I was seven years old, I was taught in school that "religion is the opioid of the masses."

Until I was 18 I thought that being Jewish was a nationality. And in Russia it was not a good one.

My parents and grandparents were not religious, and thus my upbringing was not religious. I realized that I have a unique perspective on religion. I've been looking at the Jewish religion as an outsider looking in. So here it comes.

What does it mean when a child, a girl, becomes bat mitzvah? Since I grew up in a very Jewish but also a not very religious family, I had to look the subject up. I went straight to the source of all modern wisdom: Wikipedia.

Bat Mitzvah according to Jewish law is when the girl becomes responsible for her own actions ... bears her own responsibility for Jewish ritual law, tradition and ethics.

Let me tell you what this means to you in theory. I want to stress the word *theory*.

Now you are eligible to be called to the Torah.

Since Mom takes you only to orthodox synagogues where only men are called to the Torah, this is unlikely to happen.

Of course, if you really want to be called to the Torah, just say a word and I'll drive you to a Reform synagogue. Even if it is on Shabbos.

You have a right to be legally married, at least according to Jewish law.

I think what the sages really meant is that you now have the right to be married to books and to learning.

Also, knowing your Mom, for whom PG-13 really means PG-21, you'll make one Jewish boy really, really happy after he finishes dental school; and you'll become anyone your gentle heart desires to become, as long as people call you Hannah Katsenelson, MD or Hannah Katsenelson, CFA.

As a Katsenelson you carry the torch of your ancestors. They all had an insatiable thirst for knowledge and learning that doesn't stop with college graduation.

My father, your Grandpa Naum, already had a PhD when he went to university to study English at 76 years old. His mother (my grandmother) Emily (we gave you your middle name after her) studied English and took singing lessons well into her 70s. My father's father, my grandfather Volodya, translated scientific papers from other languages well into his 80s. And this is just my father's side of the family...

You learn for as long as your heart beats.

Until today, according to Jewish law, Mom and I were responsible for your actions.

Again, according to almighty Wikipedia, "Traditionally, the father of the bat mitzvah gives thanks to God that he is no longer punished for the child's sins."

Maybe other fathers have to do that; I don't. The only sin I can think of that you committed is being a better skier than your father. A 12-year-old girl being a better skier than a 44-year-old man in his prime – this is just wrong.

Now you have a duty to follow the 613 laws of Torah.

This is really the topic I want you to think about.

I want you to think of being Jewish as three things: tradition, religion, and philosophy. Where one starts and another begins is often hard to tell.

Here is what I suggest you do. Take religion like many Americans have learned to take President Donald Trump – *seriously but not literally*. There is an incredible amount of wisdom in the Jewish philosophy.

However, when you have 613 rules (mitzvahs), it is very easy to get lost in the trees and not see the forest. The rest of the world is struggling to keep ten commandments; Jews have got 603 more to follow.

As an outsider looking in, I can see how following all these rules can be overwhelming and can often turn into a meaningless journey driven by fear.

Just as you skied without fear, don't do anything in life out of fear.

I love that Jewish religion and philosophy encourage you to question everything.

That is why there are three synagogues for every two Jews. We all need a synagogue we don't go to.

Question everything. Look for meaning. If you accept all 613 commandments, do it by choice, not because you feel you have to.

Finally, in your life you're responsible not just for yourself and your future family but for your brother and sister. And since Jonah and Mia Sarah are in the audience, this message is to them as well. Your siblings should always be the most important people in your life. Always.

Hannah, my sunshine, I know that when you grow up (which according to Jewish law starts today), you are going to become what you already are – an incredible, kind, thoughtful human being who is going to keep lighting up everything around you with your presence.

Mom and I are very proud of you.

Mazel Tov!

Why Do I Torture My Kids... with Classical Music?

A T FIRST IT was a subconscious decision of mine to torture my kids with classical music.

Somewhat by inertia, I was following in the footsteps of my parents. That's what they did, and that's what I'm supposed to do. However, I realized recently that I am re-gifting. Instilling a love of classical music is one of the best gifts my parents gave me.

Just as in any typical Jewish family, my older brothers suffered through several years of music school. Neither one liked taking piano lessons, but they took them. My parents finally saw the writing on the wall and pulled them out of music school when my oldest brother pulled some keys off a piano keyboard.

I was spared from taking piano lessons, but for a different reason: my mother passed away when I was 11 years old. My father was suddenly alone with three kids. He signed me up for piano lessons, but when I showed little interest, he didn't have the energy to nudge me further. I quit after only a small handful of lessons.

Ten years later, when I was 21, I took piano lessons again, this time completely of my own free will. But I didn't want to start with the basics – that was too boring. I went right for the (classical music) jugular: Rachmaninoff's *Piano Concerto No. 3*, my favorite piano concerto. Which also happens to be one of the most technical piano concertos ever composed. Needless to say, I failed miserably.

Both of my older kids have taken piano lessons, but neither one showed much interest (my youngest is only four and has so far been spared). My wife and I tried different teachers, but in the end we realized piano was not in the cards for our oldest kids. It is my job as a parent to nudge my kids to try new things, and maybe push them a little (enough to overcome their natural laziness – it's a lot more fun playing outside than practicing the piano). But at the same time, as a parent I need to know when to cut my losses and move on.

Though my parents nudged us to play piano, they never forced us to listen to classical music. They taught by example. They listened to classical music when we were around. They always spoke positively about it. They admired people who listened to it. They took us to concerts. I didn't care much about the music, but patiently waited for intermission – those were the rare occasions when they'd buy me dessert (a huge treat in Soviet Russia).

This exposure made it easier for me to fall in love with classical music later in life.

Classical music is complex. I'm generalizing, but classical music is often more complex than pop music. There are a lot of themes (stories) going on in the music; they are like underground currents that you don't encounter unless you swim in the river awhile. Though we can instantly fall in love with some pieces, many require us to work – we need to listen to them more than once to hear them, to *understand*.

By exposing me to classical music, my parents created a musical foundation for me. My mother loved Rachmaninoff's *Piano Concerto No. 2* – she played that record many, many times. I liked small parts of it when I was very young, but when I heard Rachmaninoff's 2nd concerto when I was 18, the whole piece suddenly clicked with me – I *understood* it.

My parents opened an incredible world to me that has definitely made my life better and richer. Classical music, just like any art, has an ability to unearth emotions we did not know we had and that our dictionaries often cannot describe. It makes us feel. Yes, just feel. That is an incredible gift. Today I could not imagine life without it; it would be plain, pointless, and simply boring.

Now I know why I torture my kids. My job as a parent is to pass this gift to them, though they may not unwrap it until decades later.

Reading
and Listening

I DON'T THINK I'VE ever seen anyone so obsessed with reading as my 12-year-old daughter Hannah. I remember when it started. She read a book or two. To encourage her to read I volunteered to pay her $10 per book read. For the next few months she read nonstop. I was slightly concerned that she was gulping books for money and not for the pleasure of reading. However, a few months and $120 later she came to me and said she didn't need to get paid to read. She felt guilty because I was buying the books as well as paying her. I was glad she had made that decision. I have never seen anyone – really, anyone – so engrossed in reading. All she thinks about is what book she'll read next.

My wife and I don't set any limits on how much money Hannah can spend on books. When Hannah wants a book, she looks first in a digital library. If it isn't available there, she buys it on Kindle or we go to Barnes & Noble. Our trips to Barnes & Noble are my favorite part of her reading addiction. I am so glad that Barnes & Noble stores are still around, as we go there almost once a week now. Our only rule is that Hannah can buy just one book at a time – that's what keeps us going book shopping.

Sometimes on Fridays, when I pick up both of my girls from school, I take Hannah and her almost-five-year-old sister, Mia Sarah, to Barnes & Noble. It used to be a bookstore with a Starbucks in it. Post-Amazon and the digital apocalypse, it turned into a Starbucks that sells books and toys. I hadn't noticed how many toys they carry until I visited it with Mia Sarah. On our first visit she wanted me to buy her toys. She and I made a deal: We only go to Barnes &

Noble to buy books (and Starbucks cake pops). Now, even before we walk into the store, she says, "Dad, yes, I know we only buy books here."

While Hannah is conquering her teen books section, Mia Sarah and I search for her book in the kids section. My hope is that being close to books and having a positive experience associated with them, will encourage Mia Sarah to become a reader just like her older sister. Also, we're creating our little tradition – going to bookstores.

At her preschool graduation ceremony, Hannah was asked what she wanted to become when she grew up. She thought for a second, smiled, and said, "I want to be a writer, like my daddy."

I had never thought of myself as a writer, but rather as an investor who writes. Hannah didn't know the difference. When my kids see me work, I'm either reading or staring at my laptop.

Reading has had an interesting side effect on Hannah: Over the last few months she has started writing stories. Her writing is very colorful and highly descriptive; her stories are dramatic, and the characters in them are very dark (Freud would have had a field day with her characters).

This happened to me when I started writing: I started reading for two people, for the reader and for the writer in me. As a reader you are focused just on the content, but as a writer you start paying attention to how this content is packaged and delivered. You start paying attention to sentence structure and to the author's voice.

My two older kids have expressed little interest in investing, which makes me slightly sad – it would have been awesome to research stocks together. Hannah and I had a conversation about that recently. Her mother wants her to become what every Jewish mother wants her offspring to become – a doctor. I told Hannah, "Don't try to please us in your career choice; the only person you want to please is yourself. We'll support whatever choice you make. We just want you to be happy, and if you are happy we'll be happy with you."

This brings me to a question I get asked often: How do I get my kids to listen to classical music? I have found that there are a lot of similarities between instilling a love for books and a love for classical music. For both, it's a very delicate process that involves a lot of gentle nudging.

I am anything but an authority on parenting. I attended the same university of trial and error as every other parent. But I've been thinking about this topic a lot as classical music has gradually taken a larger and larger role in my life. It is an incredible world, and I want my kids to be part of it.

I found that my kids, especially when they were young, would go to great lengths to spend time with me; and just like all kids, they love sweets. When I take kids to classical music concerts, we make part of the trip about food, be it Dairy Queen, burgers and fries, or cookies during intermission.

I still remember my father taking me to see Alexander Borodin's *Prince Igor* when I was 11 years old. I sat through the opera without too much fidgeting. And I still remember two things: a short fragment from the aria of Prince Igor – "Oh, give me, give me freedom so I can repay for my shame" – and, even more memorable, the dessert cake my father bought me during intermission. I waited patiently for intermission, because I was promised a cake. This was more than 30 years ago. My paying Hannah to read was another such gentle nudge.

Falling in love with classical music is a process. The music is not always easy to *understand*; it requires *work* – those are the words my father used to describe classical music. Listening to something you don't yet appreciate *(understand)* is not necessarily fun; it may be hard *(work)*.

However, my parents listened to classical music at home, in addition to taking me and my brothers to concerts. They exposed us to the music, and that is all you can do as a parent. When I heard this music later in life, it had already been deposited somewhere deep in the memory bank of my childhood. My kids and I listen to classical music at home and in the car going to and from school. At times we watch YouTube music videos together.

Mia Sarah was exposed to classical music through watching cartoons like *Little Einsteins*. A few days ago she came to me and said, "Dad, what is this music – da da da daaa?" She was singing the opening bars of Beethoven's *Symphony No. 5*. I fired it up on YouTube, she sat patiently on my knees, and we even conducted together. She lasted about seven minutes, which was plenty.

As a parent, trying to instill in your kids a love of reading or listening to classical music requires a lot of diplomacy (bribing with *your* time, sweets, and sometimes, yes, money), setting an example by listening to classical music or reading, and simply being there with them (my favorite part) by taking them to bookstores or classical music concerts.

Share this chapter with a friend:
https://soulinthegame.net/bjf/

There Is No *I* in *Hannah* (But There Are Two in *Vitaliy*)

I AM SHOCKED BY the maturity of my 14-year-old daughter, Hannah (and the immaturity of her father).

Last summer Hannah started playing volleyball. She really fell in love with the game. She went to volleyball camp and joined a volleyball league in September.

At first, Hannah played on a team for 14-year-olds. She was one of the best players. Her coach told her that he wanted to make her a team captain. Then the program director noticed Hannah's play and told me that Hannah had "good hands" and suggested that we transfer her to a more advanced team of 15-year-olds (Hannah had just turned 14). I instantly started calling her "good-hands Hannah."

My wife and I hesitated a little, because we weren't sure if it would be better for Hannah to be the best player on a weak team or a weaker player on a better team. (Malcom Gladwell would suggest the former.) But Hannah told us that she really wanted to get better and it would help her to be on a stronger team. She joined the more advanced team. This was a month ago.

Yesterday, Hannah and I got up at six in the morning to drive to a tournament that was an hour away in Colorado Springs. Hannah's team played four other teams. Each game has two or three sets. Hannah stood on the sidelines for all the games and did not touch the ball even once.

I was really upset, for two reasons. First, I was thinking, what was the point of using our Sunday to drive 65 miles and spend eight hours in a very noisy arena (you don't know what loud means until you hear 200 teenage girls scream non-stop), just to see Hannah's teammates play and Hannah sit on the sidelines. If I am honest with myself, this reason was more about me. We could have been skiing instead, or doing something else fun.

The second reason was the one that was really breaking my heart. I saw Hannah on the sidelines while the other girls played, and I felt that she must feel like a second-class citizen. But Hannah smiled throughout and cheered and high-fived her teammates when they scored. I looked at her and thought, she must feel miserable inside. Her pain must be my pain times a hundred.

Hannah's team won every single game. The team moved on to a higher division. At the end, every player got a victory pin. They took a group picture. Hannah was incredibly excited and happy. Her father... not so much.

When we got in the car to drive back, I asked her if she wanted me to talk to the program director about going back to the old team. Hannah said this:

Dad, absolutely not. Being part of the team is not just about playing in the tournaments. It is participating in the practices. This was a very important tournament where we had the chance to move up to the next division. If I were my coach, I wouldn't have played me, either. I am new to the team. She doesn't know me well yet. Also, I am not as good as other girls on the team. They've played for years; I started less than six months ago. I learned so much watching the games from the sidelines. I could see the mistakes of the other girls and learn from them. I learned a lot today. I know where I need to improve. I need to work harder. Dad, I also got a victory pin!

I said, "Maybe we should go skiing during tournaments when they don't play you. What's the point of us being there?"

Hannah retorted, "You don't understand! If I don't show up, then who is going to give them emotional support? When I'm on the sidelines, I'm cheering them on. I'm helping them. My team won! This is very important. I am part of the team."

I was speechless. We drove for two minutes in silence. I had thought the smile I saw on Hannah's face during the tournament was sitting on top of giant pain. I could not have been more wrong. She was happy for her team. She felt like she was part of something bigger than her.

My brother Alex called me and asked if Hannah got to play. (I had called him a few times during the tournament, complaining about Hannah not playing.) I told him what she told me. I said, "She is so much smarter and more mature than her father. My 14-year-old daughter showed me what it means to be part of a team." I have no idea if Hannah will be playing volleyball a year from now (I hope she will), but I know she is prepared for the life ahead of her. She'll be a great asset to any company or organization she decides to start or join.

And one more thing. Ten years ago I would have looked at spending a full day at these tournaments as a chore. Driving an hour each way. Did I mention 200 teenage girls screaming? There are so many other things I could be doing. But a while back, I realized that there is a finality to everything in life and especially to kids being... well, kids. This changed my perspective on life. Instead of looking at driving my daughter to tournaments as an obligation and feeling victimized for being forced to do it, I *choose* to do it. And I really, honestly look forward to doing it. As we drive, Hannah and I listen to music and podcasts, and we talk. We go to lunch. We spend time together.

Girls' Gambit

IT ALL STARTED after Hannah watched *The Queen's Gambit* for a homework assignment. She told me I had to watch it. I did. I loved it. But then Hannah said, "Dad, let's play chess."

Okay, I have to do a pause and rewind. I grew up in Russia, where chess was a spectator sport and a national obsession. Almost, though not quite, what Hockey (I am intentionally capitalizing the "H") is for Canadians. I probably first played chess with my father when I was five years old. I never took formal chess lessons. I played casually; I was never great at it, just an average intuitive player.

My son Jonah, who is now 19, started playing chess in kindergarten. Chess is something Jonah and I shared daily after dinner for years. In the beginning, he enjoyed chess and participated in and won some tournaments. But he lost his love for the game after I made the mistake of choosing a chess teacher who was wrong for him.

His teacher was a retired Russian engineer and ex-Moscow chess champion. A kind and all-round terrific human being, but not an appropriate pedagogue for an 11-year-old. His teaching style was remarkably similar to that of many Soviet teachers I encountered as a kid (which is why I was never a good student in Russia but blossomed in the US). He knew his subject incredibly well. He was tough, rarely smiled, and emphasized the negatives (when Jonah made a wrong move) and underemphasized the positives (when Jonah made the right move). He would have been a great teacher for a self-confident adult. But not for an 11-year-old child. He simply lacked kindness and playfulness.

I realize now that his job was not just to teach Jonah chess, but also to support and grow that little flame of love for chess my young son had. Jonah's lessons lasted about two years. Even after he stopped taking lessons, he still played in tournaments; but his opponents progressed as they dedicated themselves to studying chess, while Jonah just showed up.

If you asked Jonah today, he'd tell you that the part he enjoyed about tournaments was not the matches themselves but the lunch break. I was the one taking him to the tournaments (my wife stayed home with our daughters). Jonah and I had this little tradition where we'd go to a Japanese fast-food restaurant, where I'd let him get Izzy (a bubbly soda drink), and then we'd top it off with a visit to Dairy Queen, which was next door. I tell you, all my kids' best moments revolve around food. Though I have a feeling it was more than food; it was our spending time together.

Hannah is four years younger than Jonah. She never took formal chess lessons. I taught her chess when she was seven. After my experience with Jonah, I never pushed chess on her. If I am honest with myself, I am not sure if I subconsciously made this decision because of Jonah's difficult experience or because Hannah is a girl. I'll never know the answer because it was a mindless decision; I didn't give it much thought.

If I had subconsciously avoided nudging Hannah to pursue chess because she was a girl, then I could not have been more wrong.

Chess has historically been a men's sport. Intellectually, I was always bothered by the fact that there were men's and women's divisions. Unlike athletic sports such as running, soccer, or weightlifting, where differences in male and female physiology make a difference, chess is a sport of thinking. Putting men and women into different divisions somewhat implies different mental capacities of each sex.

One of my jobs as a parent is to instill in my kids that they can do anything they really want to do. However, I now realize that with my daughters I must work extra hard on this. I have to keep repeating to them that other than a very few biologically limiting tasks (like childbearing and breastfeeding), there is no such thing as a man's or woman's job.

The Queen's Gambit ignited a little flame of chess interest in Hannah. So we played chess. After we had played for a few weeks, I added a little bit of fuel to that flame and found Hannah a chess teacher. This time I was more careful. She is taking lessons from a 25-year-old Russian-born woman and chess master from Chicago (this is the beauty of online learning). Hannah absolutely adores her. She makes classes so interesting that Hannah went from taking lessons once a week to twice.

Interesting side effects from this: Hannah's younger, seven-year-old sister, Mia Sarah, seeing Hannah taking her chess lessons, expressed an interest in chess, too. So now both girls are taking chess lessons. And then last Saturday, I was reading a book and I overheard Mia Sarah teaching my wife chess moves. Soon we are going to have chess tournaments in the Katsenelson household – two feeble men against three strong women.

I have to tell you, though, that the best part about all this is that I am playing chess almost daily with my daughters. The beauty of this game is that I cannot lose: If I win, I win. If I lose, I still win as a father – I'm as happy for their win as they are. Of course, with my wife, the only way I can win is if I lose. Now I am looking forward to the days when my daughters will be beating their older brother, who is currently very smug about his game. Hopefully not for too long.

My Russian Book

OVER THE YEARS, my books have been translated into Chinese, Korean, Japanese, German, Polish, Romanian, and Russian. Usually, the publisher that published a book in the original language takes care of selling foreign rights; the author is not typically involved in this process. In fact, I only first discovered that my books had been published in foreign languages when my wife called me at work to inform me that a box of funny-looking books with my name on them had just arrived at our house. For a year or two, I kept getting boxes of books that had been translated into various Asian languages. I am not certain, but I may be as popular in South Korea as Psy (of *Gangnam Style* fame).

Anyway, as much as I enjoy my Asian fame, I really wanted *Active Value Investing* (my first book) to be published in Russian. Before I tell you why, let me tell you why I wrote *Active Value Investing.*

There are three categories of reasons why anyone writes a book (or does anything that requires a significant time commitment). The first category includes all the reasons you give in public interviews. They usually sound selfless and altruistic. Who wants to buy a book written by a selfish egoist?

The second type are the ones you tell your close friends or your spouse. These reasons are less altruistic and more selfish (nothing wrong with that).

But then there is the third category of reasons, the deeply personal ones. You may or may not even be aware of all of them on the conscious level, but they are sitting deep in your subconscious, driving your decision making.

So why did I write *Active Value Investing*?

When I did TV interviews I'd say something along the lines of, "I had an idea that I wanted to explore and share with other value investors," or "I wanted to develop a strategy for sideways markets," or "I wanted to know what I'd have learned when I was done writing this book." All these reasons were true, but they only scratched the surface of my true motivations.

I told my wife that sales from this book would not dethrone J.K. Rowling; after all, I was writing for a narrow niche of value investing geeks (seriously, that book had 75 charts and tables). But it could help my career. (And it did.) Then I'd say, "Wouldn't it be great if in addition to being married to this awesome guy, you were married to an author, and they were both the same person?" (Okay, I didn't say that, but I could have.)

And then there are the deeply personal reasons. These are the reasons that kept me going when I hit painful walls in my writing, which it seemed like I kept hitting every other day for a year and a half. One of the main reasons inadvertently slipped out of my subconscious onto the *Active Value Investing* dedication page: "For my parents. My father, Naum, and in memory of my mother, Irine. Thank you for always believing in me."

You will see this point made many times on these pages: My parents always unconditionally believed in me, even when I gave them no reason to do so. That belief gave me the fuel that kept me going through wall after painful wall. Writing this book was my way of repaying my father for all he had done for me. I wanted him to be proud of me. It was that simple.

I wanted *Active Value Investing* to be translated into Russian so my father could read it. He immigrated to the US when he was 58, and despite his significant efforts (he was still going to college in Denver to study English when he was 76), his control of English was limited. I put my soul into every word of my books, and I wanted to share this one with one of the most important people in my life.

I emailed my original manuscript to the largest publisher of foreign business books in Russia and asked them to publish it. They agreed, but asked if I'd mind "editing" the book. They would translate it, but I'd have to make sure that the translation was accurate. They'd still publish it even if I said no to the task, but they wanted to take advantage of my Russian background. I agreed.

A few months later, I received a Word document of the Russian version of my manuscript. I started reading it and went into shock: I understood every word, but I couldn't connect their meanings to make comprehensible sentences. It wasn't the translation – that was fine. It was me. My comprehension of business Russian was close to zero.

I left Russia when I was 18. I speak English to most of my friends. Even with my Russian friends, when the topic switches to business, we switch to English. All my business education was in English.

Back to "editing" the book. I didn't know what to do – I had given my word that I would edit it. I asked my father, who has a PhD and taught electrical engineering at the Murmansk Marine Academy for almost 30 years, to help. He knows little about investing, but he is very smart.

He grew up in a world where the government owned almost all private property. He had thought investing was a legalized form of gambling with other people's money. He could not believe that I could actually have a career in this investing thing. For a long time he insisted that I go into a real business, something tangible, like opening a bagel store or a donut shop. He even offered to help.

My father and I took the translated manuscript on our trip to South Africa in 2009 and discussed it for two weeks. Long (12-hour) flights suddenly seemed much shorter. He would read it and question everything; we had long conversations about investing, sideways markets, and my exploitation of Shalom Aleichem's characters (you have to read *Active Value Investing* or *The Little Book of Sideways Markets* to get that reference – sorry!).

After reading my book, he said he'd changed his mind about what I do for a living. While reading the book, he tried to relate investing to an exact science; and we had long debates about how investing is at the intersection of science, psychology, and art. As I look at this experience many years later, I realize that editing the Russian version of the book with my father was one of the highlights of my life.

After the editing work was done, I asked him if he would create a painting specifically for the book. I had borrowed another of his paintings for the cover of the English edition, but I wanted to be able to share something specifically created for the Russian version. Luckily for me, he agreed (you can see that painting among the other examples of my father's paintings in the middle of this book).

Share this chapter with a friend:
https://soulinthegame.net/dwp/

Parents of
La Mancha

A S MY KIDS grow up, I deepen my appreciation of the impact my parents had on me. I recently watched *Man of La Mancha*, a musical with Sophia Loren and Peter O'Toole, based on Miguel de Cervantes' *Don Quixote*. I read that book when I was a kid, but I don't think I understood its message until recently.

Now I get why this book is still read today, 400 years later. Don Quixote, though he is delusional, sees in people more than they see in themselves. He meets Aldonza, a farm girl (and a player of the "oldest profession") and, blinded by either love or insanity (probably both), he sees only a lady in her and treats her like one. He even goes as far as to call her by another name, Dulcinea.

She knows she doesn't deserve this treatment. However, she begins to believe, and this belief transforms her into a different person – she aspires to be the person Don Quixote sees in her.

When I was growing up in Russia, as a student I rarely received a grade better than a C in secondary school or even technical college. Teachers never believed in me; they thought I was a C student, and so I was. But my parents were like Don Quixote: They always saw a much greater person in me, though I rarely deserved it (they really had rich imaginations).

My mother passed away when I was 11 years old, but as I write this today, some 30-plus years later, I still remember how my mother had this incredible belief in me. My grades and other non-achievements gave her no reason for this blind faith. But she had it. And a year after we arrived in the United States, I overheard my father outside, talking with a neighbor, and he said, "Vitaliy, he'll achieve anything he puts his mind to."

It's not my intention to sound self-congratulatory. My point is that if it was not for my parents' faith in me and their constant encouragement, I'd still be what my teachers in Russia saw in me: Very little. Now that I'm a father of three wonderful kids, I try to do the same for them. The little things we say to our kids really do matter!

I watched an interview recently with Masayoshi Son. Mr. Son is not a household name in the US, but he built one of the largest companies in Japan, SoftBank, absolutely from scratch. Here is what he said:

> My father was always "brainwashing" me with praise. He'd say: "You are a genius." "You are number one in Japan." "There is no one better in your age group." "You are the smartest." "You are a big shot." He kept saying that. Like he was brainwashing me for any silly little thing. Even before I started elementary school I started to think, "Maybe I am the real deal."

Every Friday, before we sit down to have dinner, my wife and I bless our kids. My wife, a very religious person, puts her hand on each child's head and says a small prayer. I hug them and tell them how much I love them. I tell them that I know they'll grow up to be great people, and they'll be able to achieve anything they put their minds to – that they are special.

Share this chapter with a friend:
https://soulinthegame.net/egd/

Inhaling the World

Reflections and ideas,
born on the road.

I Left My Heart...

*"Each day of our lives we make deposits
in the memory banks of our children."*
— **Charles R. Swindoll**

Pier 39

I HAD A SHORT meeting in San Francisco. I absolutely hate traveling alone, so this time I was joined by 13-year-old daughter Hannah and my aunt Natasha. I always look for an excuse to visit San Francisco. We arrived on Sunday morning. I had a business lunch meeting in Sausalito and then we had the rest of Sunday and most of Monday to ourselves.

I've been to San Francisco half a dozen times, but discovering it through Hannah's eyes was an incredible joy. Every little detail that I'd taken for granted as an adult brought forth a fountain of joy and excitement from her. We watched how Boudin Bakery makes bread in different shapes, including large crocodiles. She was stunned. She also could not believe that Ghirardelli stores give out free chocolate.

She went wild when we saw sea lions on Pier 39. It is one thing to see them in the zoo and quite another to see them invade docks and surround boats. She was running around taking pictures. Then I hear, "Dad I just saw two sea lions kiss!" Hannah kept asking me, "Why it is called the Golden Gate Bridge? It's red!" Embarrassingly, I did not know the answer. I looked it up: It spans the Golden Gate, the strait that opens into San Francisco Bay.

I love mornings. I am an early-morning person. I especially love mornings in the city. I live in sleepy suburbia. IMA's office is in a sleepy office park. Suburban mornings don't have the morning energy of a city.

Hannah and I got up early, while the rest of the tourists were still asleep, and walked the streets of Fisherman's Wharf. We saw shops getting prepared for the army of tourists that were going to invade them in a few hours. Entrances to the stores were being washed and streets being swept. A fast-food place was accepting a delivery of boxes. Then there was the bay, with a few brave souls swimming in it, some of them halfway out to Alcatraz. The sun hit the Golden Gate Bridge stunningly. With every morning, we get to see the birth of another day.

I gave Hannah $20 before the trip and told her it was her spending money for San Francisco. She saw a homeless man sitting on the street at Fisherman's Wharf, went up to him, and gave him a dollar. (By that point she had already spent most of her $20.) Then she came up to me and said, "He had such kind eyes." Then she paused, smiled, and said, "Oh, and Dad, you owe me a dollar." I told her that's not how charity works.

Hannah and I stopped by the Boudin Bakery again. For breakfast we split a chocolate chip raisin baguette, with a cup of steamed milk for Hannah and an Americano for me. The best to-go breakfast I ever had.

These little moments. This hour I spent with my 13-year-old daughter I will remember for the rest of my life. I hope she does, too. Our whole trip lasted only a bit more than a day, but it implanted so many great memories that I feel as if it lasted a month. I guess life is not about quantity but quality.

A few years later, I visited San Francisco again. This time I was joined by both Jonah and Hannah.

Swimming in San Francisco Bay

Hannah was never afraid of anything. When she started skiing, she spent only a day on the bunny slope. Midway through day two she was conquering green slopes. She skied black slopes a month before she turned six. Jonah was the complete opposite; he was a timid skier. It took him a few days to get down a bunny slope, and it was another week or two before he agreed to get on the green slope lift. Skiing changed Jonah's life, as he learned how to conquer his fears.

Today he is an incredible skier without a fear in the world, at least when it comes to skiing. Both kids are better skiers than their middle-aged father. But Jonah still has a residue of past fears that he is trying to overcome. As we were strolling along Fisherman's Wharf, we saw people swimming in the bay in front of Ghirardelli Square. There were some serious swimmers doing laps, most (though not all) of them decked out in wet suits.

Jokingly, I challenged Jonah to swim. I said, "I'll pay you $100 if you swim to those boats" (Jonah responds well to financial incentives). The boats were 300 feet offshore. To my surprise, he happily agreed. Now, the water in the bay is 54 degrees. It was not dangerous for Jonah, but he would have to do something he was afraid of doing.

The next morning, we went on our usual early morning Fisherman's Wharf walk, armed with Peet's coffee and sourdough raisin bread from Boudin Bakery. As we were approaching the bay I have to admit I was expecting Jonah to back out. Instead he said, "Dad, today is your lucky day. I'll take $50 instead of $100 if you swim with me." To which Hannah added, "Dad, if you swim, I'll swim too; and I don't need any money, I'll swim for free."

Jonah was visibly upset; his heroism was about to be marginalized by his younger sibling, and a sister at that. Though initially I did not have any intention of swimming in the stunningly cold water, now I had to; I had a bargain on my hands – half-off and one free.

When it came time to actually go swimming, both Hannah and Jonah went in the water. When the water came up to his knees, Jonah stopped and launched into a stand-up comedy routine about what the cold water was going to do to his manhood. He was buying time and postponing the inevitable.

Hannah watched him and laughed, then realized that this might last a while. She was getting cold standing in the water, so she just started swimming. (I was on the beach filming them.) Jonah could not be outdone by his sister, who is five years younger and two feet shorter. Realizing that it was either now or never, his face turned serious, and I could see how every muscle of his body tensed up as he fought his fears and started swimming.

And swim he did. He had almost reached the boats when I called to him to turn back. The water was cold and Jonah, though he's a good athlete, lacks in the swimming technique department. He was getting a bit far from shore, so at this point I was worried. It didn't really matter to either of us whether he reached those boats or not; it was all about overcoming his fears.

After I could see that both of my kids were within a safe distance from the beach, I went in swimming, too. The first few seconds were a bit unpleasant, but then your body gets used to cold water and as long as you keep moving, you feel fine.

Now we have added swimming in the bay to the long and growing list of our San Francisco traditions.

Afterwards, I asked Jonah why he so readily agreed to do this. He said, "A few years ago you offered to pay me to go down a slide in a waterpark that I was afraid to do and Hannah did it easily. I chickened out and I've regretted it ever since."

As a parent, my job is to nudge my kids, hopefully with carrots but sometimes with sticks. When they are young, you bribe them with ice cream; when they get older, the bribes get more expensive. This was the best $50 I ever spent, and I could not have been more proud of Jonah.

Modern art

As I was growing up, whenever my family visited a new town with a decent art museum, my parents almost always made a point of taking me and my brothers there. Though my passion for music is greater than my passion for art, I still try to do the same with my kids as my parents did for my brothers and me.

This time we all went to SFMOMA. Modern art museums often push the limits of what we consider to be art. You might see a "painting," a Malevich square, painted in one color from side to side. That's it. A joke goes, "Every time Malevich's square was stolen, the security guards were able to recreate it before the museum opened the next morning."

I imagine the fellow who painted our house could do a few hundred of those paintings a day. This museum was no different. There was a pile of logs in a corner of one room. In another room, a bookshelf (which could have been bought at IKEA and probably was) faced a wall. That's it.

If these exhibits are so ridiculous, why do I keep coming back? In the past I would have answered that I need only one painting to touch me. Today I have an additional explanation.

When we walk into an art museum, we enter a different domain. We expect to see art – that is what you get in an art museum. When the curators put a pile of logs in the room, you cannot help but stare at those logs and try to find beauty or meaning.

We start asking ourselves, "What does it mean? Where is the beauty in this?" Sometimes these questions may lead us to see things that we otherwise would not see. Here is the punch line: If we train our minds to respond this way, then in other domains we may also see more beauty and meaning around us (which may or may not inhere in the IKEA bookshelf).

See, I just gave you another angle for your next trip to IKEA.

Santa Fe: "Remember This"

ANTA FE AND my family go way back to the early '90s. It all started with my father and my stepmother. My father had his paintings exhibited in a gallery on Santa Fe's famous Canyon Road. A few times a year, they would load up paintings in a minivan and drive them to Santa Fe.

My first experience with Santa Fe was in 1998 – it was not a good one. I went there with a girl I was dating. We got there. It was unbearably hot. We did not see much. Santa Fe fell flat with me (and I fell flat with the girl). I should have checked the weather before the trip.

Then eight years ago I wanted to do a road trip with my father and my then 12-year-old son, Jonah. My father suggested Santa Fe. This started one of my favorite Katsenelson family traditions of visiting Santa Fe in the summer.

Santa Fe is 400 miles from Denver. It is a gorgeous eight-hour drive through the Rocky Mountains – this beauty is worth every mile. We'd leave at seven in the morning, have lunch in Salida, Colorado, and arrive to Santa Fe by 4 p.m. We always finished our first day at our favorite restaurant, the India Palace.

We'd spend half a day walking Canyon Road – Santa Fe's gem. Canyon Road used to be just another residential street in a sleepy neighborhood. Then the houses were turned into galleries. There are about a hundred galleries along the road. Going from gallery to gallery is a bit like trick or treating – you want to make sure you stop by every house on both sides of the street (even if you don't get the Halloween goodies).

My father turned this gallery "trick or treating" into a four-hour art lesson. He is a phenomenal teacher and art guide. Though in the US he became known as an artist, he has a PhD in electrical engineering and taught electrotechnics theory for 27 years at Murmansk Marine Academy. He was one of the teachers most beloved by students at the Academy. Thus, in addition to being a scientist and an artist, he is a very gifted teacher. It doesn't matter what he teaches; you want to listen to him.

Anything and everything I know about art was taught to me by my father. As I have mentioned, our summer vacations were always accompanied by trips to art museums. Even when I was older and my father and I traveled to Europe, every city of size required a visit to an art museum.

This "trick or treating" through the galleries turned into a wonderful art lesson. My father was very gentle, not inflicting his thoughts on us, wanting to know our thoughts about the art. Our opinions mattered to him. He'd treat us as art equals. Obviously we were not, but it felt so good.

Student of life

In *Ego Is the Enemy*, Ryan Holiday makes the point that ego stifles our growth – we stop learning. What is the point of learning if we already know everything? Ego is a virus that is genetically programmed into all of us. It is sitting dormant and waiting to attack if we let it (usually triggered by failures and successes).

The best way to guard ourselves against our ego is by thinking of ourselves as evergreen students. Albert Einstein said, "As our circle of knowledge expands, so does the circumference of darkness surrounding it." We should welcome "the circumference of darkness" wholeheartedly.

As I think about it now, my father is the embodiment of the moniker that has become near and dear to me: *student of life*. He is an accomplished artist who has won national and international awards, and his art is in an art museum in Japan. He took masterclasses from artists he admired well into his 70s. There was always something he could learn from others.

After exhausting our "trick or treating" we'd go to our favorite restaurant, sit under a big tree, have lunch, and play cards. Then we'd go to the hotel. My father would take a nap. Jonah and I would take a dip in the swimming pool. Then we'd go out to dinner. Jonah always wanted to go back to India Palace. So we did.

Santa Fe Opera

We'd finish the evening with the Santa Fe Opera – the highlight of the trip, at least for me. I'd argue the Opera is the second (or maybe even the first) gem of Santa Fe. The Santa Fe Opera building is itself a work of art – it sits gorgeously on a hillside overlooking the Jemez Mountains to the west and the Sangre de Cristo Mountains to the east.

I've been to many operas, all over the world, but this was the first opera that had tailgate parties in the parking lot. And not your hotdog and beer football gathering. Opera lovers, dressed nicely for the occasion, brought their portable tables, with white linen cloths, and some even had flowers and candles. This was a wine, steak, and fine cheese kind of tailgate event with genuine wine glasses and fancy silverware – in the parking lot!

Saying that Jonah liked the opera is an overstatement, but he liked going there because I'd let him get Sprite during the intermission. He patiently suffered through the opera in anticipation of the intermission, when he'd have his Sprite.

On our third trip, in 2015, my father, and then 14-year-old Jonah, and I were joined by my then nine-year-old daughter, Hannah. We went to the Santa Fe Opera. This was Hannah's first time at the opera, and we saw *Rigoletto* by Giuseppe Verdi. After the performance, as we were walking to the car – this was five years ago, but I remember this conversation as if it happened today – I sheepishly asked Hannah what she thought. She said, "Dad, I know you really wanted me to like this opera. And honestly, what I am saying has nothing to do with what you want. I really, really liked this opera." My eyes are watering a little as I write this.

Santa Fe 2020

This year I went to Santa Fe with Hannah. My father and Jonah couldn't make it. It was a father-daughter trip.

The Santa Fe Hannah and I encountered this time, during the pandemic, was quite different from the Santa Fe I am used to seeing. It was a ghost town. The Santa Fe Opera was closed. It seemed like we were the only tourists in town during the virus outbreak. Though the galleries were open, we did not visit them. It was hot, and we'd have to wear our masks for hours to go trick or treating.

Instead, Hannah and I would get up at 6 a.m., arm ourselves with Starbucks, and walk the empty streets of Santa Fe for a few hours before it got too hot. We'd talk. Hannah would tell me about the fantasy novels she is reading (they sounded so good I wanted to read them too). She's been reading two books a week. We'd have breakfast, then find a bench under a big tree and read until dinner (we'd just snack for lunch). This was basically a reading trip.

The Martian

During our long drive, Hannah and I listened to the audio book of *The Martian*. Hannah has showed an interest in science since we watched Elon Musk's SpaceX rocket sending astronauts to the International Space Station. (Now I can understand how sending men to the moon in the '60s was so inspiring to the nation.)

After that we watched astronaut Chris Hadfield's *MasterClass*, and I could see Hannah's eyes light up. The movie version of *The Martian* was the next logical stop. The book was different from the movie in that it went so much deeper into how (fictional) NASA astronaut Mark Watney, stuck on Mars, deals with incredibly difficult problems thrown at him by using science, ingenuity, and the will to survive.

As a parent, it is so important to notice these little inklings that your kids have and nurture them and help them grow. Maybe Hannah will become a scientist – as long as she is happy, I'd be delighted if she did. (Jonah has expressed no interest in investing; nor has Hannah. My six-year-old, Mia Sarah, is my last hope for IMA to become Katsenelson &... Daughter.)

Hannah used *The Martian* on me before we even finished listening to it. In the book, Mark Watney needs to travel 1,300 miles over Mars in a vehicle. It will take him a few weeks. The only food he has left is potatoes. He bakes potatoes before the trip and then freezes them. He explains that he did this not just because it is easier and more pleasant to eat cooked potatoes, but because cooking breaks down the protein in potatoes, and thus they provide more net calories than uncooked ones.

A few hours after we listened to this episode in the book, we stopped for lunch in Salida. Hannah had an ahi tuna salad (mostly uncooked tuna). Thirty minutes later, after we've eaten and are driving again, she tells me she's hungry and could we stop and get a snack. I say, "You just ate!" She says, "Dad, you don't understand. That tuna was not cooked and thus the protein was not broken down and so I didn't get as many calories as you think!" How could I refute this well-constructed scientific argument?

Traditions

A friend of mine told me a story about the St. Louis Bread Company that is known today as Panera Bread. After they made their very first batch of sourdough bread, they took a lump of the dough and put it aside. The following day, when they made a new batch of sourdough, they added the lump from the day before. They did this every day thereafter – adding the dough from yesterday to today's dough. When they opened a new bakery, someone would bring a lump of yesterday's dough from another bakery. They have been doing this for 40 years.

Think about it; Panera has 2,000 restaurants today. Every piece of their sourdough bread has a little bit of dough from 40 years ago and every day in between. The history of the company has been strung together in its sourdough bread.

Traditions are like that. The connecting tissue (dough) of traditions are memories. We string them together when we do things together with our family. Going to Santa Fe is a tradition for my family. When Hannah and I were walking the streets of Santa Fe, we kept saying, "Remember this place? You were looking for Pokémon with Jonah here," or, "Remember this place? You played cards with Grandpa Naum and Jonah here."

That is what Santa Fe is for us now. It is full of memories strung together – it is our "remember this" place.

Inhaling Europe

I LOVE TO VISIT Europe. I've been to Europe probably a dozen times over the years, but every visit is special. Most things in the US are less than a hundred years old. Some tables in European coffee shops are older than that. Europe is old, and its long history stares you in the face with every cobblestone.

Americans often view Europeans as lazy – Europeans take longer vacations and have shorter work weeks. Europeans in return think Americans are too focused on making money. Okay, let the fight begin – but not here.

After every trip to Europe, I tell myself that I want to become more European. Slow down; inhale life more deeply; take long lunches, with a glass of wine or two (it's not like I'm operating heavy machinery at work); take longer walks, in the park or, even better, in the woods; or just go to a coffee shop and read. I've been trying and failing to become more European for years.

If you work on the assembly line of a Fiat factory, then hours worked has a direct relationship to your output – widgets per hour. But if you are in investing or any other creative profession, then the number of hours you spend in front of your computer has little to do with the quality of your output – your creative ideas. In fact, it may have an inverse relationship with your creativity. Ellen J. Langer writes, in *On Becoming an Artist*:

Mindfulness is an effortless, simple process that consists of drawing novel distinctions, that is, noticing new things. The more we notice, the more we become aware of how things change depending on the context and perspective from which they are viewed. Mindfulness requires, however, that we give up the fixed ways in which we've learned to look at the world.

Mindfulness is a huge component of creativity, and thus I looked at these trips to Europe as an opportunity to loosen some of my "fixed ways."

What follows is my record of two trips through Europe, from Zürich to Venice and from Zürich to Nice.

Zürich to Venice

On this trip to Europe my brother Alex and I were joined by my 18-year-old son, Jonah.

This was Jonah's first time in Europe, and I really wanted him to love it as much as I do. I wanted him to experience the enjoyment of just strolling the streets without a destination in mind, only interrupted by the occasional Americano or a meal. I wanted him to enjoy inhaling and embracing the rich European culture.

This ended up being a very packed trip. We took in eight cities (Zürich, Klosters, Lugano, Milan, Modena, Verona, Bologna, and Venice), four museums, and three classical music concerts. We visited the Kunsthaus – our favorite art museum in Zürich – and the Peter Paul Rubens exhibition in Venice. We saw the *Romeo and Juliet* opera at La Scala. I am still pinching myself that I was at La Scala; it had been one of my dreams. I explained to Jonah – for whom it was just another classical music detour, so he could hardly understand my excitement – that La Scala is to opera what Wrigley Field or Fenway Park are to baseball. Verdi's and Puccini's operas were premiered there.

In Modena we visited Luciano Pavarotti's house museum and the Ferrari museum. Ten or so years ago, I visited Graceland (Elvis' house in Memphis). It was fancy and luxurious. Pavarotti – this bigger-than-life person with a voice that makes me temporarily religious every time I hear it – lived in a large but quite modest house, similar to the houses around it. It was anything but a mansion. Visiting his home made him a bit more real to me. I got a glimpse into his life through the house where he lived.

In Venice we attended an opera and a Vivaldi "Four Seasons" performance. Vivaldi was born in Venice and was a monk there, thus his music is performed there regularly, especially the "Four Seasons" concertos. This was my third time in Venice. My wife and I went there in 2000 when she was three months pregnant with Jonah (so, as I explained to Jonah, it was really his second time in Venice).

To my surprise and great excitement, Jonah went patiently to the classical music performances and the museums. I know that at this stage of his life, in the battle between Puccini and Drake, Puccini doesn't have a chance. But my job as a parent is to gently keep exposing him to the art, planting little seeds. When he gets older, those seeds will get watered.

Jonah and Alex share a passion for Swiss watches. Alex collects them. They spent hours and hours walking from one shop window to another, discussing their finer points. I did not know that people could spend so much time talking about watches. Now I know. I don't share their passion, but my heart warmed as I watched two of my favorite people in the world sharing an interest dear to both of them.

While I patiently waited for Alex and Jonah to window shop for watches, I'd put headphones on, listen to music, grab a cup of coffee, and watch (more like observe) people. Life in the US is so fast that I never take the time to do that. I just sat and watched people walk by. I observed their interactions, their body language, their emotions. I tried to imagine what their lives and relationships were like. It was almost like reading micro stories about people I'd never see again. Doing this transports you from your over-familiar world into someone else's, which is what works of fiction do.

In Venice, we went to the Peter Paul Rubens exhibit at the Doge's Palace. Rubens was a 17th-century Flemish painter from Antwerp. I was never a big fan of this era until ten years ago, when my father and I visited the Rijksmuseum in Amsterdam. We were standing in front of Rembrandt's portrait of an old man (Rembrandt was Rubens' contemporary). I told my father that it did absolutely nothing for me; it lacked the vibrancy and the emotion that I love in the Impressionists. My father said, "Take a look at his tired hands. Look in his eyes. What is he thinking about?" We spent another hour in the gallery looking at Flemish painters, and I started to see what my father saw. These paintings offered glimpses into the human soul.

Now, as Jonah and I were standing in front of a painting by Rubens, I could sense that Jonah had the same struggle I had ten years ago. I told Jonah what my father had told me. Jonah usually springs through museums, but this time around he slowed down and went from painting to painting, trying to get glimpses into these (400-year-old) human souls. I guess a visit to an art museum is not that much different than people watching; we try to connect with other people and get out of our world (our head) and into the worlds of others.

Zürich to Nice

Another year, Alex and I were attending a conference in Switzerland organized by my friend Guy Spier.

Jeffersonian lunch

At the conference Guy introduced me to a concept I was not familiar with, but now I absolutely love: the Jeffersonian lunch. The first one was conducted in the early 1800s by Thomas Jefferson.

Before the conference, Guy invited a group of 12 of us, including yours truly, to a Jeffersonian lunch. We all sat around one table. The rules were simple: One conversation per table. No side conversations allowed. I knew only a few people at the table. To break the ice, Guy asked everyone to share positive and negative highlights of their life or something else on their mind, and then as an afterthought to tell everyone who they were. Each attendee was given one to two minutes.

Then Guy identified a few topics from this go-around, and we discussed these topics for about an hour.

The reason I love this Jeffersonian idea is that it eliminates the awkwardness from a dinner table discussion. You are not limited to learning just from the people sitting to your right and your left. You are exposed to a diversity of opinions, and you don't need to talk about the weather or other meaningless topics we subject ourselves to as icebreakers. It is a perfect instrument if you like to learn from others.

I do see the irony. I had to travel to Europe from the US to learn about a concept created by one of the founding fathers of the United States.

Lausanne and Charlie Chaplin

After the conference we rented a car in Zürich and went on a journey to Nice, in the south of France.

Our first stop was Lausanne. We arrived in the early evening as the sun was going down and were stunned by the beauty of Lake Geneva – one of the largest lakes in Europe, shared by Switzerland and France (the French call it le Léman).

Charlie Chaplin has always had a warm place in my heart since I was a little child in the Soviet Union. For American kids it was Mickey Mouse or some other cartoon character; for me it was Charlie Chaplin. You did not have to even speak a language to understand his movies (most of his classic films were silent movies). My oldest kids and I have watched *The Great Dictator* – the most anti-Hitler movie made during Hitler's lifetime – half a dozen times.

In 1953, Charlie Chaplin went to London for the premier of his new movie, *City Lights,* and was not allowed back into the United States. He was accused by Senator McCarthy of being a "communist sympathizer." This is when Chaplin moved to Lausanne. In 1972, five years before his death, Chaplin returned to the United States to receive the Academy Award for Lifetime Achievement.

Since then, MI5 has released its files on Charlie Chaplin, which showed that there was no evidence that Chaplin was a communist sympathizer or had any connection to the Bolsheviks (other than that little kids in Soviet Russia watched his movies with great admiration).

Charlie Chaplin's house in Lausanne was turned into a museum, which is probably the most memorable museum I've ever visited. I was sent down memory lane to the sets of *The Kid* and *The Great Dictator.* I bought my five-year-old daughter, Mia Sarah, a small figure of Charlie Chaplin, and to my surprise she did not know who he was. Now I get to relive my Charlie Chaplin journey all over again – that's the beauty of having kids. We started with *The Kid.*

Switzerland

Switzerland is an amazing country. Aside from the stunning beauty, I loved the food, the immaculate cleanliness of the streets (even the mountains look clean), and the fact that Switzerland has almost no crime or police officers.

The Swiss take traffic violations very seriously. A person who is caught driving 180 kilometers per hour in a 120-kilometer speed zone may have to pay a fine equal to 10% of their annual income (and may even go to jail). There is something to be said for the fairness of income-based punishment.

A friend of mine, who is also a legal resident, will have his village decide whether he can become a Swiss citizen. Yes, the village will hold a vote to see if he is a worthy addition to their community.

As I was talking to my friends about life in Switzerland, I was thinking about whether I'd want that life for myself. On the one hand, kids – five-year-olds – are walking to school on their own, without parents. In fact, my friend (a recent immigrant to Switzerland) was called to the principal's office and asked not to walk his child to school. But on the other hand, I was wondering whether I'd enjoy living in a society that is so strict and homogeneous.

The Alps and society

I live in Colorado. We go to the mountains a few dozen times a year. Mountains should not surprise me. I have to admit, though, that although this was not the first time I had been to the Alps, I was completely taken by the beauty of the Swiss Alps and Switzerland in general.

The Swiss Alps have this two-tone beauty – black, sharp, cold rock covered by gentle snow, with a pure blue sky magnifying the contrast.

And then there were the French Alps. Maybe it was just the weather we encountered (sunny days and low-hanging clouds), but the farther south (from Switzerland toward France) we drove, the less sharp and black and white the Alps turned. The cold black gradually morphed into warm blue; the sharpness gradually became more muted, and the two-toned Swiss coldness turned into multitoned and multilayered warmness.

This made me think about how societies are shaped by nature. I am generalizing and stereotyping here; but when you think of the Swiss people, you think well-organized, punctual, reserved, somewhat cold and unemotional. Their language is mostly based on German, and thus it is sharp and may sound a bit abrasive (sorry to all my German and Swiss friends).

Then you think of the French people, speaking a soft, rounded language, emotional and warm – "lovers, not fighters" – a lot less organized (their trains don't run as punctually as Swiss trains; but then again, no one's trains run as punctually as Swiss trains).

When you think about geopolitics, you have to think about geography – access to ports versus being landlocked, fertility of land, larger rivers flowing through the country allowing goods to be easily transported, being surrounded by hostile neighboring countries, etc. Maybe we also should think about how nature shapes society.

Provence and the French Riviera

After Lausanne, Alex and I drove to the beautiful French town of Annecy, often called "the Venice of the Alps." Sitting on Lake Annecy and surrounded by gorgeous Alps, this little town has preserved the architecture of the 15th century.

Our next stop was Lyon, the second-largest urban area in France.

Then we drove to Grenoble, birthplace of Hector Berlioz (you'll meet him in "Fantastic *Fantastique*") and home to the 1968 Winter Olympics. We took a cable car to the fortress on top of the mountain, overlooking the city. We spent the night at Avignon.

At our next stop, Arles, we felt we had been transported to ancient Rome. The Romans took over Arles in 123 BC. It has not just one but two Roman theaters.

Everywhere we walked in the old city of Arles, we saw signs pointing to the Fondation Vincent van Gogh Arles (the van Gogh museum). Vincent van Gogh spent over a year in Arles, and this is where he suffered his psychotic episode and cut off his ear. The town spent $15 million and turned an old hotel into the van Gogh museum.

The only problem is that during the winter Arles has very few visitors, and maintaining insurance on van Gogh paintings is very expensive. To our surprise and disappointment, the van Gogh museum doesn't actually have any van Gogh paintings. To which my friend Adam said, "That means I have a van Gogh museum in my house, as we have none too."

Our next stop was Cannes. I don't know if most Americans, including yours truly, would know where to find Cannes on a map if it was not for the Cannes Film Festival. Just like Monaco, which we visited the following day, it seems like a place for the rich and famous to park and show off their yachts.

My favorite places on the French Riviera were Nice, Eze, and Saint Paul de Vence. Eze is a small village a short drive from Nice, often dubbed a "village museum," because only 3,000 people live there. It is incredibly well preserved and a fun place to walk the streets.

Saint Paul de Vence is a picturesque little village very close to Nice as well, and on many levels it looks just like Eze. Unlike Eze, however, it houses a lot of art galleries; thus, in addition to walking ancient streets, you can look at beautiful art, which we did.

Saint Paul de Vence is also the place where Marc Chagall spent the last 20 years of his life. Marc and our family go way back. One generation before my father settled in Murmansk, my ancestors lived in Vitebsk, a small town in Belarus that happens to be the birthplace of Marc Chagall. My grandmother told me stories about how their neighbors, Marc's family, borrowed money and never paid it back. I always thought Grandma exaggerated a little, but I found the story adorable and enjoyed my hidden connection to a famous artist. Marc Chagall was buried in Saint Paul de Vence.

Nice was our final destination. Alex and I were walking in this city, down wide streets with beautiful but not very old buildings (by European standards), and it felt like another version of Cannes. Then Alex suggested that we make a turn to the right and go down a few flights of stairs. Suddenly we found ourselves in an old French city with very narrow streets and no cars, and I was teleported several hundred years into the past. This sums up the beauty of Europe – and it could happen anywhere in Europe. The old and new live so close to each other – just a few flights of stairs away.

One Day
at a Time

*A collection of small life tweaks that
have made a big difference in my life
– and might in yours, too.*

I Don't
Eat Desserts

A S I GOT into my mid-40s, I landed in my own version of a midlife crisis. Instead of getting a 20-year-old girlfriend or a red convertible, I started paying attention to my health. When you're young you think your future health will be simply a linear extrapolation from the past. And for good reason: Up to that point you have had a lot of data points to draw a straight line through. As you get older your body, as an older engine, starts to require higher-quality fuel (no more junk food) to run and requires more tuning up (exercise) just to maintain the same output of energy.

I realized that to feel good mentally, I had to work on feeling good physically. That meant I had to change my habits: Drop the bad ones and acquire good ones. There are two ways to give up bad habits: First, change your environment, and second, make a half-binary decision.

I discuss the importance of your environment in "Don't Let your Environment Control You." Making small but conscious decisions about our environment can influence our creative output and our ability to make good decisions. The other approach to dropping a bad habit is to make it a half-binary decision. After I read a wonderful book by Rolf Dobelli, *The Art of the Good Life*, I quit eating desserts (no more cakes, cookies, candy, ice cream). I told myself, "I don't eat desserts."

Bear with me here. If I eat dessert sometimes, let's say 2% of the time, despite that 2% being a minuscule number, it makes eating or not eating dessert a decision. But if you have a firm "I don't eat dessert" mindset, then every single time it's a non-decision decision. I call it a half-binary decision: Full-binary would be "Yes" or "No"; half-binary is just "No."

I've spent a lot of time thinking and reading about the relationship between the conscious and subconscious minds. The subconscious mind is an incredibly powerful computer that is running all of our bodily functions (breathing, pumping blood, digesting food, etc.). Think of the subconscious mind as having the processing capacity of a giant mainframe versus the conscious mind being an iPhone. The subconscious receives instructions from the conscious mind, and it obeys them.

The subconscious mind takes all instructions literally and doesn't understand irony. Therefore, if you consciously give the clear instruction "I don't eat desserts" to your subconscious mind, then your subconscious blindly and faithfully follows the instruction.

I am very aware of how this sounds, but willpower was never one of my greatest strengths. And sugar (desserts) was for me a substantial addiction. But since I made my half-binary commitment that I do not eat desserts, I've gone to birthday parties and dinners where people around me were eating desserts. And not eating dessert consumes zero willpower or energy. None! It is a non-decision type of decision. I also don't feel any less happy than I was before. I just did a blood test, and my cholesterol numbers showed a staggering improvement.

I've found that it is easier for me to give up bad habits than to acquire good ones. To start working out I needed external pressure, so I hired a trainer. My trainer, Sergey, is a Ukrainian-born world champion in weightlifting. Just imagine a Hollywood version of the stereotypical Russian "muscle" mob enforcer; that is exactly what Sergey looks like. He speaks slowly and very quietly, but when he tells you to do something, you do it. He trains my brother Alex and me twice a week.

Last time, at the beginning of our session, he was kind of thinking out loud: "Okay, so I am going to torture you for an hour, and then I have to return my car rental." Torture he does. I can barely walk out of the gym, and for an hour after our session I lose my ability to speak. I never thought I'd actually enjoy lifting weights, but strangely I do. Focus on each exercise, and pain redirects your thoughts from the stock market and kids – the outside world disappears for an hour.

I am not sure I have enough willpower to do weightlifting without Sergey. I know that I wouldn't push myself enough. So Sergey it is. In addition to feeling a bit more manly as my fat gradually turns into muscle, I also feel calmer.

So far my cardio workouts have been limited to riding my road bike to work a few times a week (seven miles each way) and walking. On a visit to London, one of my meetings was canceled and I suddenly found that I had four hours till my next meeting, which was six miles away. So I put my headphones on and I walked. I loved it. When I got to the meeting, which was with my friend Gary Channon (one of my favorite UK investors), as soon as he saw me, he said "Let's go!" We walked another four miles and talked.

The previous time I met Gary, two years before, we had breakfast that lasted well into lunch. But this walking meeting had a much livelier and more dynamic rhythm to it. Gary turns most of his meetings into walking meetings. I love this idea and will try to do the same. There is actually a lot of research that shows that walking and talking induces creativity. My goal is to do talking walks a few times a week.

The 8%

I GEOFENCE MY DIET.

Let me explain.

I stick with my diet religiously when I am in Denver, but when I travel I have no diet; I can eat anything my stomach (or brain) desires. I instituted this strategy because I found that it was often difficult, inconvenient, and frustrating to stick to my diet when I am not in Denver. Altogether, I travel about a month a year (this includes vacations). If I stick with my diet 11 months a year – that is, 92% of the time – then I'll achieve my goals of keeping my weight and cholesterol down.

My initial concern about the geofencing strategy was that I wouldn't be able to switch back to the diet each time I return to Denver. That has not been an issue – I match the diet to the environment. When I get on a plane or drive for at least two hours, no diet; but when I'm home, I make myself be good.

There is another benefit I've discovered with the geofenced diet. But first, let me tell you a story.

When I lived in Soviet Russia for the first 18 years of my life, I only had a soda (a Pepsi) once. I remember how much I loved the tingling sweetness of the magical drink. I was 12. But neither Pepsi nor Coke were to be had in Soviet Russia.

I did not have another Pepsi or Coke until I moved to the US in 1991. Here I discovered that sodas were sold by the gallon, just like water. And I drank them like water. In the first year in the US, my consumption of soda pop made up for all my non-consumption in the previous 18 years.

A few years later, when was 21, after asking for a third refill of Coke at a restaurant, I realized that I could no longer actually taste the tingling sweetness of the drink. Not anymore. I had drunk so many sodas that I had stopped enjoying them, and what used to be a special drink had turned into brown, high-calorie water.

At that point, I decided that I'd only drink a soda on rare occasions (e.g., when I went to the movies). There was no point in drinking so much of it and not enjoying it. My consumption went from a soda (or two) every day to just a few times a year. And an interesting thing happened. I only had one soda last year, but I tell you, I enjoyed every sip of it.

Abundance often devalues things we enjoy. There is a such a thing as too much of a good thing.

I did the same thing with food.

When I am in Denver – 92% of the time – I look at food very functionally: It is the fuel that powers me, and I want this fuel to be good for the engine. Just to be clear, I don't eat salad and quinoa and more salad all day. I just steer clear of food that isn't good for me, often passing on things I like (red meat, ice cream, pasta). But overall, I eat what I like and like what I eat.

When I travel – I eat guilt- and care-free and enjoy every bite; I don't care if the dish is loaded with carbs and dripping with fat. I enjoy that 8% of the time so much that it makes the 92% moderation worth it. So, when I am in Europe, in addition to inhaling Europe's slow beat and convivial company, I am looking forward to Swiss sausage and Italian pasta.

And one more thing on this subject. When I stopped casually drinking soda a quarter-century ago, I did not do it for health reasons – I was 21, and my health was not something I paid any particular attention to then. But in hindsight, just that one decision alone saved me 30 pounds of weight.

My Crash

"**Y**OU LOOK HORRIBLE. You have bags under your eyes, your face has no color. Are you okay?"

This is what my stepmother said to me one afternoon when I stopped by my parents' house after work.

I felt worse than I looked.

No, dear reader, I did not have a financial crash. Here is what happened.

It took me a month or so to write my mini-book on Tesla and the electric vehicle (EV) industry, *Tesla, Elon Musk and the EV Revolution*. I'd wake up a bit earlier than usual, at 4 a.m. (instead of 4:30 or 5), to write. I'd go to sleep later than usual, as I was researching what I was going to write the next morning. I was excited and incredibly energized by the topic. I was in the "zone." After I finished the Tesla book, I wrote a 20-page seasonal client letter, which took another two weeks. At that point I had already created a bad habit – going to sleep late and getting up very early.

I eat well. I exercise at least twice a week, sometimes three. I am in the prime of my health. However, the lack of sleep accumulated caused me to crash. Every afternoon I felt like I was hit by a truck – I was a walking zombie. In a normal conversation I could not recall names or facts. The irony is, I was so exhausted that I was not self-aware enough to recognize I had a problem.

This incident caused me to research the topic of sleep. I read a book called *Why We Sleep*, by UC Berkeley neuroscience and psychology professor Matthew Walker. This book dramatically changed my thinking on sleep. In our macho, workaholic society we glorify working long hours and getting little sleep. We value people who are the last ones to leave the office and the first ones to show up in the morning. We view sleep as an inconvenience that competes with the waking hours it doesn't occupy. The expression "I'll sleep when I'm dead" perfectly described my thinking (and, I suspect, society's).

I could not have been more wrong.

I had thought a lot about things that I have control over that impact my health. I had thought about diet, exercise, and lifestyle (relationships, stress), but never about sleep. *Why We Sleep* opened my eyes to the fact that sleep is an incredibly important part of the health equation, and one that is largely ignored today.

This is the punch line: We damage our brain during our waking hours, and it gets healed and repaired while we sleep. If you don't get enough high-quality sleep, your health will pay a substantial price.

Yes, it's that simple. If you don't sleep enough and sleep well, you cause both temporary and long-term damage to the most important organ of your body. But the damage doesn't stop at your brain: Poor sleep also demolishes your immune system (you are more likely to get the flu), doubles your risk of cancer, and is a key factor determining whether you get Alzheimer's disease. If this is not enough – and I am not going to go brain chemistry on you here – a weakened, sleep-deprived brain also causes depression, anxiety, heart attacks, weight gain, mood swings, and a lack of control over your emotions. I could keep going, but you get the point.

I realized that I had got off easy. Considering how exhausted I was, I could have had a real crash – a car crash. I was endangering not just myself but my family, who I drive to school, work, and social activities daily.[2]

Interestingly, Mother Nature did not anticipate that we humans would deliberately decide to sleep less. Our fat cells store energy in case we are stuck in traffic on our drive to McDonald's (or have to go a week or two between deer kills). But there is no reservoir of sleep that we can fill up and then draw upon. We need to get enough good sleep – at least eight hours, for most of us – on a continual basis.

Here is what you can do to improve your sleep life.

---

2 Sleep-deprived drivers are 15 times more likely to cause wrecks. In fact, more people die every year in automobile accidents caused by sleep deprivation than die by drinking and drugs combined. We should declare war not just on drunk drivers, but also on sleepy drivers.

Sleep in a cool room. We need to sleep in a room that is 3–7 degrees Fahrenheit lower than our normal room temperature. 65 degrees is the ideal room temperature for falling asleep.

Taking a hot bath or shower is a stimulant for a good sleep. This may sound a bit counterintuitive, but though your body temperature will rise in the shower, it will drop significantly as you head to bed.

Go to sleep and wake up at the same time every day (even on weekends). Mother Nature programmed into us a circadian rhythm – a roughly 24-hour physiological cycle that regulates the rhythms (including temperature) of our body. It is impacted by light and temperature (more on this later).

The circadian rhythm keeps going whether you sleep or not. To get good sleep we need to adjust our sleep to our personal circadian rhythm, which is different from person to person. I am an early-morning person – the temperature of my body starts dropping about 8 p.m., and thus it is easy for me to fall asleep relatively early in the evening, and I get up with ease early in the morning.

The person who has been sleeping next to me for 20 years – not going to mention names here – is not a morning person. If she tries to go to sleep at the same time I do, she won't fall asleep for hours. Her circadian rhythm is different from mine. She needs to go to sleep late and wake up late. If she wakes up too early in the morning, she has a headache.

You may or may not (I'd argue the latter) be able to change your circadian rhythm, and thus it is important to know if you are a morning or an evening person and to plan your life accordingly. However, there are a number of adjustments you can try to make.

Regulate the release of melatonin. Mother Nature programmed humans over millions of years in an environment where there were no alarm clocks or artificial light. The earth's rotation around the sun is what regulates our sleep. Light – actually, the absence of light – releases melatonin, "the hormone of darkness." If sleeping was an eight-hour race, melatonin would be the start pistol that tells your brain to start sleeping. It regulates the timing of your sleep, but it has little to do with the length or quality of your sleep. Melatonin is very sensitive to light.

There are a few things we can do to use Mother Nature's programming to our advantage.

Dim the lights a few hours before you go to sleep. I am planning to install dimmable lights around my house and turn them down an hour or two before we go to bed.

Sunglasses. Don't wear sunglasses in the morning, as the natural sunlight will help to fully wake you up. Start wearing sunglasses in the afternoon.

Limit electronic device use an hour or two before you go to bed. I am going to be switching to a Kindle device instead of reading Kindle books on my iPad. Also, I have started wearing blue-light-blocking glasses when I work on my laptop in the evening.

Drink coffee and alcohol strategically. Caffeine blocks signals to your brain telling you that you are sleepy. Your caffeine level picks up 30 minutes after you consume coffee. However, the half-life of caffeine is seven hours. This means that seven hours after you drink coffee, 50% of the caffeine is still in your body. It does not just keep you from falling asleep; it keeps you from sleeping well.

I drink a lot of coffee. But though I may drink my first cup for how it makes me feel, I drink the rest for the taste. I have started drinking decaffeinated coffee after 8 a.m. or 9 a.m., giving my body 12 hours to get rid of the caffeine. A warning here: Decaffeinated coffee is not caffeine-free; it still has 10–30% of the caffeine of regular coffee. Another caveat: The older you are, the longer it takes your body (mainly the liver) to cleanse caffeine from your system.[3]

Meditate. When we lie down in bed, we tend to relive our day in our head, and it often keeps us from going to sleep. Meditation may calm us down and help put the day to rest. I have had a difficult relationship with meditation. I found that it is hard for me to find time to meditate in the morning (as it competes with my writing). I'm going to try to meditate before I go to sleep. (I discuss meditation in greater detail in "Attend a Party in Your Own Head.")

Naps. Interestingly, we have to be strategic with our napping, too. A nap can actually recharge our battery during the day, but if we nap too long (longer than 10–15 minutes), or too close to the evening, it may hamper our ability to fall asleep in the evening.

---

3   Alcohol may help us to fall asleep, but it significantly erodes the quality of sleep. Most importantly, it impacts the REM (rapid eye movement) stage of sleep, when we dream. REM sleep is responsible for control of our emotional intelligence and creativity.

Read my books. I have been told that my books, especially *Active Value Investing*, are very soporific. On a serious note, don't read in bed. Your brain should be conditioned to think of your bed only as a place where you sleep.

It seems to me that the medicine most prescribed by doctors should be sleep.[4] But imagine going to medical school for a quarter of your working life and accumulating a few hundred thousand dollars of student loan debt just to say, "You need to sleep at least eight hours a day."

On top of all the health-related issues I wrote about above, there are other things to ponder here. As a parent, I really have to pay close attention to what time in the evening my kids watch and read on devices, and I also need to monitor how much sleep they get. I should not look at their sleeping in late as "being lazy" – I should let them sleep.

As a creative person – investing, writing, and life in general should be a highly creative adventure – I know that lack of sleep diminishes my creativity. As an employer, I need to figure out whether the people I work with are morning or evening people and let them schedule their work accordingly.

I realized that my days have to be planned from a day-before perspective. If I want to keep getting up at 4 a.m., then I need to be in bed by 7:30 p.m. This may prove to be impractical (I don't want to go to bed before my kids do); thus I have to settle for going to bed at 8:30 p.m. (and falling asleep by 9), and so my morning will start at 5. If I stumble on another interesting topic to write about, I should pace my excitement; and if it takes 45 days instead of 30 to finish writing, so be it.

We cannot repay the sleep debt we accumulate by sleeping more in the future – unfortunately, Mother Nature may need a few more millennia to fix this flaw.

I wish you good night and a restful sleep.

---

4   I highly recommend *Why We Sleep* – every insight above I drew either from an interview with Michael Walker or his book.

I Don't Eat Pork

THE CORONAVIRUS PANDEMIC has affected so many things.
Though I loved working from home, I now realize that it came at
a cost. In March and April 2020 I destroyed most of the good habits
I had worked very hard to build over the last few years. I stopped working out
with my trainer for social distancing reasons, and thus stopped working out (I
really need external pressure).

I did not write much in April. During the market-crazy volatility in March,
I worked super-long hours, and when April came I wanted to make sure I got
enough sleep. I let myself get up at 7 a.m. instead of 5 a.m. Since I usually write
early in the morning, my writing habit was interrupted.

As my good habits were slipping, it got to the point where I made a conscious
decision to proactively restore old good habits and create some new ones.

I dusted off my favorite book on habit building: *Atomic Habits*, by James
Clear. Here are a few thoughts from this terrific book.

There are three layers of thinking on changing habits.

First, the most superficial layer: Setting goals or focusing on results. If you
look at successful and failed athletes, they had the same goals. Goals do not
set us apart; our systems do. (By the way, the same applies to investing.) In fact,
goals often can be at odds with our long-term success and happiness. Once
you accomplish a goal, then what? We should enjoy the journey more than
the destination. Goals (destinations) do still have value, as they set a direction.

This brings us to the second layer of thinking: Systems, creating an
environment and processes that help us achieve our goals. As James Clear

writes, "You do not rise to the level of your goals. You fall to the level of your systems."

For me to start writing, I need to get up early. I go to sleep early. I stop drinking coffee at noon. I have an earlier, light dinner. I take a hot shower before I go to sleep. I set my alarm clock for 5 a.m.

That is a system that gets me to write for two hours a day. After a break, waking at 5 a.m. is painfully difficult in the first week. I have to force myself to wake up – that is the cost of having interrupted a system that worked. Then, in the second week, it gets easier. I wake up, splash water on my face, make coffee, put on my headphones, hit play on my Spotify playlist, and write until 6:30.

One trick I learned from James Clear is stacking one good habit on top of another. After I finish writing, I go for a three-mile walk in the park for an hour. I love these walks; I listen to books, music, and podcasts. By waking up at 5 a.m. and writing for two hours, I then get to enjoy my walk in the park afterward.

And finally, we have the third layer of thinking on changing habits: Our identity. Your identity is your self-image, your worldview.

Clear writes, "The more you repeat a behavior, the more you reinforce the identity associated with that behavior. In fact, the word identity was originally derived from the Latin words *essentitas*, which means being, and *identidem*, which means repeatedly. Your identity is literally your 'repeated beingness.'"

I am a person who writes. I am a healthy person. I am the person... you fill in the blank. Eating cheeseburgers and washing them down with milkshakes is contrary to the identity of a healthy person. So, lunch at Sonic Drive-In is out if I want to be healthy (sorry, Sonic lovers).

I have a good friend – an orthodox rabbi. He was at my house and he told me that he had gained a lot of weight. He said, "I eat too much bread." I told him that he needed to change his identity to that of a person who doesn't eat bread. He was puzzled. I said, "Well, how much energy does it take you not to eat pork?" He said, "None. I don't eat pork." Do the same with bread, I said. He did. He called me a few months later, thanking me for the weight he had lost.

Another way to look at these three layers of thinking is that systems are what you do, outcomes are what you get, and identity is what you believe in.

The beauty of this three-layered framework is that you can completely rewire your identity (your perception of who you are) by setting goals, designing a system that is easy to follow and that works for you, and then faking it until you make it. Yes, you may be faking it. If you are 350 pounds and can barely walk up a flight of stairs, you're faking if you're telling yourself that you're a healthy person. However, once you embody the behavior of a healthy person and start losing weight, it will be easier to convince yourself that you're healthy once you get to 280, then to 250 and 200, and you're moving with ease.

When writing is a habit, I do not have to force myself to write. Writing is part of my identity. I am a person who gets up every morning and writes. After *not* writing for a month, I realize that without it my brain is complete chaos. Just like working out is exercise for my body (I feel mushy when I skip workouts), writing is exercise for my brain. It is not something I do in addition to investing. No, it's a necessity for me; it's how I keep my brain tuned and how I connect and organize my otherwise chaotic thoughts.

For every habit I am trying to instill, I create a "meaningful measuring unit" or "minimum measuring unit." Either way, I just call it an MMU. It must be meaningful – big enough that if you keep repeating the MMU long enough (it takes about a month or two to form a habit), you'll feel the impact and have a sense of accomplishment. But not so big that you can't stick with it. It must also be measurable, in that you mentally (and physically) check off that you did this.

When I started walking daily, my MMU was three laps in the park by my house (almost three miles). My MMU for writing is to get up at 4:30, put headphones on, and stare at a laptop screen for two hours while my hands are resting on the keyboard. I am just making myself available for the subconscious to take over.

An MMU may increase or decrease over time. When I rode a road bike, my MMU started out at 20 minutes daily. Then it was "ride at a cadence of 60 rotations per minute for X minutes," and so on. When I hurt my back, my daily walking MMU was "just get out of the house for as long as you can bear the pain."

I now realize that we need to treasure and protect our good habits and not take them for granted. Though I did not appreciate it at the time, it is clear to me now that going to the office provided structure. When I stopped going to the office, I should have mindfully created a new structure that helped me maintain my habits or at least replace one good habit with another. For instance, even though I stopped working out with the trainer, I could have walked in the park and done push-ups, sit-ups, and squats instead.

It is time to treasure and rebuild old (good) habits and forge new ones. I am looking forward to it. I wish the same for you.

Attend a Party in Your Own Head

*"It isn't what you have or who you are or where you
are or what you are doing that makes you happy or
unhappy. It is what you think about it."*
— **Dale Carnegie**

GOOD THOUGHTS BRING you happiness; bad thoughts poison you
with anxiety and pain.

Our brain is invaded by thoughts nonstop. In fact, *invaded* does
not correctly describe this, because it implies that thoughts are foreign entities
and not occupants of our brain to begin with. The reality, as strange as it
sounds, is that we are a guest in our brain. Yes, we are a guest at the party of
thoughts that is happening nonstop in our own head. Though we believe we
have control over what we think, we really do not. Most of the time we are not
even aware of what we are thinking.

This brings us to meditation. It allows us to mindfully attend this party and,
like a well-intentioned chaperone, examine all the guests (thoughts) and *their*
intentions.

There are many meditation techniques. The one I've been practicing is
mindfulness.

I sit in a comfortable position and focus on my breath. I am attempting to have no thoughts other than the awareness of my breath moving through my body. When I catch myself thinking about something other than my breath, I lightly acknowledge that thought without judgment, and poof – it disappears. This technique is called *noting*.

My goal is to become a calm, reliable observer of my thoughts. There is a significant hurdle I have to clear here, and keep on clearing: To focus only on my breathing. The first time I attempted to practice meditation I gave up after only a few weeks. I got frustrated with my inability to *not think*. I was constantly interrupted by thoughts barging in. I felt I had failed at meditation. It took me a while to understand that this "failing" is not a bug, but a feature of meditation.

The benefits of meditation

I did not understand the true benefits of meditation until I started meditating again, after the first failed attempt. I thought it was just something you do to calm down, but I was wrong. Though it will calm you down, it is so much more than this.

Here are some benefits I've discovered.

Meditation reduces suffering. The poisonous, negative thoughts are either reevaluations (judgments) of our past or worries about the future. Our thoughts are chronically stuck in the past or the future, but ironically, life happens in between – in the now.

It is difficult for us to sustain negative emotions. Dwelling on them adds fuel to flames that would have died out otherwise. By meditating, we can identify these negative thoughts; and by *noting* and recognizing them, we cut off the fuel to the smoldering fire.[5]

Sam Harris, meditation guru, sums it up perfectly: People who don't meditate experience unnecessary suffering. Imagine reducing your (unnecessary) suffering from days or hours to less than two minutes.

---

5   Dr. Jill Bolte Taylor, neuroanatomist, in her book *Stroke of Insight*, discussed what became known as the 90-second rule: "When a person has a reaction to something in their environment, there's a 90-second chemical process that happens in the body; after that, any remaining emotional response is just the person choosing to stay in that emotional loop."

Meditation focuses on the present. Meditation transports us back to the present, interrupting our habitual tendency to be either in the past or the future. Meditation trains our brain to be right here. I have found that being present is – wonder of wonders! – starting to spill into my daily life.

Here is an example. I've been working out with a personal trainer for almost three years. I have a complex relationship with working out. I don't always look forward to it. But I am always happy when it is over. I do it purely for health reasons and because I get to spend time with my brother Alex – we work out together.

Before I started meditating, with every exercise I was impatiently waiting for the torture to be over. My mind was always counting down toward the future. However, after a few months of mindfulness practice, I noticed that while weightlifting, I was much more in the moment. As I lifted the weight, my mind was following the tension in each and every muscle in the same way it had got used to following my breathing as I meditate.

Living in the future was a default setting for me, and not only with regard to things I hated.

My father and I were in Vienna in 2010. He remarked to me one afternoon as we were walking down the street, "You always want to be in the next place." He was right. Whenever we'd get to a museum or some other attraction, I was in a hurry to go to the next one. Inhaling the moment was not my default setting.

Now, being present, not goal-focused, has become my goal. (Yes, I do get the irony of this sentence.) Meditation has helped me with that. I have been inhaling life more lately – be it as I walk in the park, or spend time with my kids.

I keep reminding myself what Master Oogway teaches in *Kung Fu Panda*: "Yesterday is history, tomorrow is a mystery, and today is a gift... that's why they call it the present."

Meditation increases emotional intelligence.[6] It's about those

---

6   There are a lot of other benefits of meditation that I have yet to observe in myself. Harvard conducted a study, "Eight weeks to a better brain," and discovered that an "eight-week mindfulness meditation program appears to make measurable changes in brain regions associated with memory, sense of self, empathy, and stress. ... Participant-reported reductions in stress also were correlated with decreased gray-matter density in the amygdala, which is known to play an important role in anxiety and stress." In other words, after eight weeks of meditating an average of 27 minutes a day, participants' brains had become rewired for the better. Other studies have shown similar results.

few extra seconds. You know, those few seconds that you need in order to take a deep breath before you respond to a stressful event. Meditation gives them to you.

One of my employees called me to say that he had unintentionally deleted a database that, at the time, I was unsure we had backed up. I vividly remember the anger rising in me. But then I found myself the dispassionate observer of that emotion. This bought me a few seconds, and thus my response was, "Well, let's figure out a solution." Since I had noticed the negative emotion, it was difficult to stay angry; and surprisingly, just a few minutes later, I found myself laughing.

Part of daily life

I wish I had started meditating 30 years ago. I think my perception of meditation was ruined by a poster. A beautiful, trim woman with a ponytail was sitting in a yoga posture with her eyes closed at the edge of a cliff overlooking a gorgeous mountain landscape, the sun's gentle rays bathing her perfect skin. That is what meditation was to me – and it didn't work.

But what I have discovered since is that meditation is probably the least space- and environment-demanding exercise you can do. I don't have to get up at 4 a.m. and drive to the mountains to meditate. I can literally do it anywhere.

I have linked my meditation to my walks. I usually do it at the end of my walk in the park, on my favorite bench. But I've also meditated in my office, hotel lobbies, my back yard, and lying in bed (though this one knocks me out very quickly). I am new at this and need quiet to succeed, but I have read that it is possible to meditate to the noise of a jackhammer or people chattering. Here is the key: Meditation is an exercise for your brain, and just like any exercise it requires consistency.

Everyone I know who meditates does it daily. I do, too. I am at it for ten minutes once or twice a day, and am starting to experiment with 20-minute meditations. I use an app, *Waking Up*, created by Sam Harris. There are other good apps, too. At some point, as I get more experience, I may be able to meditate without training wheels. There are meditation sessions you can listen to on YouTube or Spotify.

When I meditate during my daily walk, after I am done with the meditation itself, I sit on the bench and listen to classical music, gaze at the trees, and try to hear and follow the sound of each instrument and every note and try to *not think*. This type of meditative listening changes music from background noise into a compelling immersive experience.

I have a dear friend who I thought would benefit from meditating. I sent him a draft of this essay. His reaction was, "Meditation sounds like a magic fix-it-all tool. I hope it is as helpful for me as it was for you." Mulling over his remark, I realized that meditation requires faith and patience. Yes, faith. Faith in your own mind. Faith that by gently spending time alone with it, you'll be better able to harness and direct the power that is already there.

During meditation we are rewiring our brain, each ten- or 20-minute session at a time. Your brain, my friend's brain, and my brain are different from each other. We have different personalities and so the process of learning to meditate will be different for each of us. Set expectations low – that way you won't be disappointed.

Meditation requires patience, too. Meditation *practice* (key word here) is not unlike going to the gym and lifting weights. Even if you and I lift the same weight the same number of reps, we have different bodies and so our results will differ. One thing is guaranteed: When we lift weights, we are going to experience some pain from muscles breaking down before we grow them bigger and stronger. It's much the same with meditation. We must put in the work, and be patient about it, if we want to grow. Again, faith is important here. Some people enjoy feeling that pain more than others. (Yours truly is not one of them.)

How much should you meditate?

In "I Don't Eat Pork," I discussed minimum measuring units (MMU). My MMU for meditation when I tried it the first time was not to have thoughts – a set-up for failure. Today when I do a ten- or 20-minute meditation, I am aiming for a perfect minute. At the very end of a meditation, the *Waking Up* app alerts you that this is the last minute. I try to make this minute as good as I can. I still cannot *not think* for a minute, but I am improving a millisecond at a time. I don't really have a destination; my goal is to enjoy the journey.

Share this chapter with a friend:
https://soulinthegame.net/mvn/

Dale Carnegie –
Better Late than Never

"Before you speak, let your words pass through three gates.
At the first gate, ask yourself 'Is it True?' At the second gate
ask 'Is it Necessary?' At the third gate ask 'Is it Kind?'"
— **Rumi**

I READ DALE CARNEGIE'S *How to Win Friends and Influence People* several times since I came to the US. I have much greater appreciation for this book now than when I read it the first time in 1990.

I was living in Russia; the Cold War had just ended. Capitalist American books suddenly became very popular. Carnegie's was one of the first to be translated into Russian and was "the book to read." Everyone wanted to be a capitalist, and this book was supposed to make me a better one. I decided, however, that it was stuffed with disingenuous fluff – that it taught the reader how to not be authentic; it turned you into a fake.

Thinking back, at the time I read it, that book had no chance of getting through to me. I was a product of the Soviet system. We were Seinfeld's Soup Nazi "No soup for you" nation. Teachers who were kind and inspired students were considered weak. I remember two teachers in my school who were considered virtuosos. Neither one smiled. They rarely praised and were never afraid to insult their students for getting an answer wrong. But they were highly regarded because they knew their subjects well and thoroughly subjugated their students.

Here is how Carnegie puts it: "When dealing with people, let us remember we are not dealing with creatures of logic. We are dealing with creatures of emotion, creatures bristling with prejudices and motivated by pride and vanity."

If we were computers and had no emotions, then my Soviet teachers would have been right that knowledge is the only thing that matters. Then teaching (communicating) would be just data transfer from teacher to student. But if you have something you think is worth uploading to others, they have to be willing to download it. This is where the wisdom of Carnegie comes in. If we were computers, the way data was packaged would be irrelevant – the content would be all that mattered. However, because we are human, the way we package our content is paramount if the other side is to be willing to receive it.

Criticism is futile because it puts a person on the defensive and usually makes him strive to justify himself. Criticism is dangerous because it wounds a person's precious pride, hurts his sense of importance and arouses resentment.

There is a person I work with. She has a task she does for me on a regular basis. She is a very diligent and hardworking person, but occasionally she makes a mistake. Pre-Dale Carnegie, I would criticize her. Not anymore. Now I start with praise – how she does a great job, how sometimes I wish I could match her attention to detail – and only then do I lightly mention her mistake. Everything I say about her work is absolutely true – she'd detect a lie. The data upload is the same – she made a mistake – but I package it differently. The result is that over time she has made fewer mistakes and the quality of our working environment has improved.

As an investor, I am constantly involved in arguing and debating with others. I debate ideas with my partner, Mike, and with my value investor friends. Mike and I often disagree – which is awesome, because if we always agreed, one of us would be extraneous. But this quote from Carnegie's book changed how I debate:

You can't win an argument. You can't because if you lose it, you lose it; and if you win it, you lose it. Why? Well, suppose you triumph over the other man and shoot his argument full of holes and prove that he is non compos mentis. Then what? You will feel fine. But what about him? You have made him feel inferior. You have hurt his pride. He will resent your triumph.

Carnegie provides this advice:

Our first natural reaction in a disagreeable situation is to be defensive. Be careful. Keep calm and watch out for your first reaction. It may be you at your worst, not your best. Control your temper. Remember, you can measure the size of a person by what makes him or her angry. Listen first. Give your opponents a chance to talk... Look for areas of agreement. When you have heard your opponents out, dwell first on the points and areas on which you agree.

I used to feel I had to win every argument. I patted myself on the back when I did. Now I wish I hadn't.

Twenty-five years later, I wish I could turn to my 17-year-old self and say, "Read this book slowly; pay attention; this is the most important thing you'll ever read. It will change your life if you let it." Unfortunately, due to my lack of a time machine, I can't do that, but I can encourage everyone around me, including my kids, to read this very important book.

Carnegie's book will turn anyone into a better businessperson or capitalist because it will help you to understand other people better. But more important, this book will make you a better spouse and a better parent.

You Are Responsible for What You Have Tamed

"At the end of your life, you will never regret not having passed one more test, not winning one more verdict or not closing one more deal. You will regret time not spent with a husband, a friend, a child, or a parent."

— **Barbara Bush**

IHAVE A CLIENT. Her husband was a second-generation American; a Yale-educated lawyer who worked in the family business that was started by his father, a Russian immigrant. Four years ago he was diagnosed with cancer. He put up a great fight, but cancer won and a year later he was gone, at 66.

He left $100 million, which went to his wife, son and daughter (the kids are in their late 20s). I had a meeting with the family recently. The son's wife was a few days away from giving birth to a baby girl. As the son and I were talking about his upcoming fatherhood, I asked him what kind of father he wants to be. He said, "I don't want to be like my father." I was a bit surprised and asked why.

He said:

After my father passed away, his friends would tell me how he was this larger-than-life, gregarious man. I never saw that man. My father worked 16-hour days, seven days a week. He worked in the basement – he'd come up for dinner and go back down. He never spent time with me or my sister. My mom did everything, from driving us to school to taking me to football practice. I always felt like I was raised by my mother. I don't want to be like that. I want to be there for my kids.

He went on:

My father thought till the last moment that he'd beat the cancer, and so he never expressed his true feelings to me or my sister. A year later my father's friend told me that my father confided in him that he wished he'd spent more time with us kids.

Listening to him, I felt a sudden urge to run home and hug my children. I also felt enormous sadness. I was thinking, "What if he had worked eight or maybe even ten hours a day instead of 16 and left his kids $10 million rather than $100 million? Would it really have made a difference to his kids' lives?" They are wonderful, thoughtful young adults who don't have pretentious lifestyles. His son would probably trade all his money for a father who was there for him.

I was deeply impacted by this story because, as a father who runs a business, I was asking myself, "Am I doing the same thing to my kids?"

And then, a few days later, it came time to drive my 18-year-old, Jonah, to the airport. He was taking a gap year after graduating high school and will spend the next two semesters in Israel. He'll be taking classes at American Jewish University, doing internships, touring Israel, and discovering himself.

When your kids leave for college, you somehow get to look back at your life through a different lens. You start asking yourself, "Did I spend enough time with them?" Before Jonah boarded the plane, we exchanged letters (it was his idea); my wife and I wrote a letter to him and he wrote one to us and his sisters. There was a paragraph in his letter that put tears in my eyes:

Thank you for using your time to create great memories with me while still balancing everything else that you do. ... A while ago you read a book about Warren Buffett. In this book it talked about how Warren wished he had spent more time with his kids. You were worried that you weren't spending enough time with me. Don't worry, I can happily say that you were and are a great father. I have never in my life felt that you didn't spend enough time with me.

This stands above anything else I have accomplished in my life. Everything else feels somehow temporary and insignificant.

I remember when Jonah was a few years old. I held his tiny hand and I was thinking, "What will he be like when he grows up?" I was trying to picture him as an adult – I could not. Now I see an adult, standing at 6'3", with a deep voice, a great sense of humor, curly hair, and a kind heart.

Today I look at my two girls and try to imagine them growing up. Just like with Jonah, I cannot. But they will. I have only five years and 13 years left, respectively, before Hannah and Mia Sarah leave home. And though it feels far off, the time will fly, just like it did with Jonah.

After we hugged Jonah and put him on the plane, my wife looked at my daughters (Hannah is 13, Mia Sarah is five) and said, "You are not going anywhere; you'll be home-colleged!"

I share my wife's sentiment. Intellectually, you know that your kids will grow up, but you want to slow down the process as much as possible. Still, you know this day will come and the only thing you can do is spend as much time as you can with them while they still live under the same roof. And when the time comes for them to leave, you just don't want to let them go.

Tim Urban estimated that by the time you finish high school, you have spent 93% of the total time you'll ever spend with your parents. Today I spend at least six hours a day with my kids and another 20 hours on weekends. When kids live in your house they are completely dependent on you, especially younger ones.

Let's take Mia Sarah and Hannah, for example. Neither one drives, of course, and my wife won't let them past the porch without adult supervision (she'd put a leash on Mia Sarah if she could). When they go to college, get married, and have their own offspring, we'll be lucky to see them six hours a month (though I hope it will be more than that).

Now I want to set a new, higher standard for myself when I spend time with my kids. I recently read that "attention is the currency of time." I want to make sure that when I spend time with my girls, I am there with them 100% – not thinking about a stock or a book I just read, but giving them my full attention.

One more thought.

As an entrepreneur, you always want to grow your business. Your current revenue and profit are never enough; they just set the bar higher for next year. We always want more. But this "more" has a hidden cost: time with our family. It's my core responsibility to provide for my family, but at some point I (and maybe some of my readers) might say that *more* is not worth it.

Sometimes work for us is a game – a real-life version of *Candy Crush*. Where money is not a currency that buys us material stuff, but chips that we never intend to spend. These chips are just there to keep count of our successes – they are the currency that move us to the next level, and the next level. Just as we can mindlessly spend tens of hours playing *Candy Crush*, our work can turn from being something we do to live into an addiction.

My own father often quoted from *The Little Prince*, by Antoine de Saint-Exupéry: "*You* become *responsible*, forever, for what *you* have tamed."

Share this chapter with a friend:
https://soulinthegame.net/wrp/

Set Your Egg Timer
to Six Months

"Think of yourself as dead. You have lived your life.
Now, take what's left and live it properly."
— **Marcus Aurelius**

A T THE END of a trip to Europe, where I visited Switzerland and Venice, I bought my wife and daughters bracelets at Venice airport on my way back to Denver. When we changed planes in Frankfurt, I realized I had left the bracelets in the airport gift shop. I was upset for about five seconds, then I remembered a story from *The Last Lecture*, the book I was rereading for the third time on the flight home. It's the first-person story of Randy Pausch, a 46-year-old (same age as me) professor who has only six months to live – he has been diagnosed with pancreatic cancer.

Here is an excerpt:

Once, about a dozen years ago, when Chris was seven years old and Laura was nine, I picked them up in my brand-new Volkswagen Cabrio convertible. "Be careful in Uncle Randy's new car," my sister told them. "Wipe your feet before you get in it. Don't mess anything up. Don't get it dirty." I listened to her, and thought, as only a bachelor uncle can: "That's just the sort of admonition that sets kids up for failure. Of course they'd eventually get my car dirty. Kids can't help it." So I made things easy.

While my sister was outlining the rules, I slowly and deliberately opened a can of soda, turned it over, and poured it on the cloth seats in the back of the convertible. My message: People are more important than things. A car, even a pristine gem like my new convertible, was just a thing.

Though we don't think of ourselves as being in Randy's situation, we all are – we have an expiration date. Randy's egg timer had been set for six months by his doctors (he actually lived for 11 more months). Others of us have our lives suddenly interrupted, like Kobe Bryant, or greatly extended, like Kirk Douglas. We don't know.

How would you live your life if you knew you had just six more months to live? Would you *let* yourself care about the same things? Would you *let* yourself be upset about leaving some tchotchkes at the airport? Would you *let* a stained back seat or dirt on your car upset you? Think about it. Randy died 12 years ago. Where is his car today? Does it have clean back seats? Does it have dents? Does it really matter? The truth is we make a choice when we allow ourselves to value things that are so fleeting and unimportant.

I keep saying *we*, but when I say *we* I really mean *me*. Before I left for our 10-day European trip, I asked my wife to please not park my brand new shiny Tesla Model 3 close to other cars, so it wouldn't get scratched. My wife loves to play a game of finding the closest parking spot to the door of the grocery store, which means she often parks too close to other cars. She was texting me pictures of my car parked alone on the outskirts of parking lots, with the caption, "Your car is scratch-free."

If I knew I had six months to live, would I still have asked her to do this? We objectify things, cars especially. If we had our egg timer set on six months, we'd prioritize what really matters: relationships, inhaling life, walking in the park. We'd reset what we care about, and it wouldn't be things.

I don't know when the buzzer on my egg timer will go off, but I'll be trying to keep it mentally set on six months (and at some point it will be). And honey, if you are reading this, you can park that piece of metal anywhere you want.

Share this chapter with a friend:
https://soulinthegame.net/abc/

Personal Finance Advice That Changed My Life

WHEN I GOT married in 2000, one of the best gifts given to my bride Rachel and me was lunch with my friend Mark Bauer. Mark and I became friends when we studied at the University of Colorado – he was always my dependable study partner. He is ten years older than me, which at the time of that fateful lunch meant he had double my maturity (I was 28).

A few months before our wedding, Mark asked if he could have lunch with Rachel and me. At lunch, Mark explained that many marriages come to ruin over money issues.

Mark told us:

A tool that has been very helpful for me is a family budget. On the surface it sounds easy – you project your revenue (for your family that would be your combined salaries) and then subtract your expenses, and that gives you your net income. If you have money left over then you have savings, and then you can afford to spend money on whatever your hearts desire.

At that point, I was a bit disappointed in Mark's wisdom. I was a few months away from completing the Chartered Financial Analyst (CFA) designation, and that was on top of my master's degree in finance. The simplicity of his advice was frankly a little insulting to me.

Mark read my unimpressed facial expressions, but continued:

> The problem with a normal budget is that though it captures well ongoing daily expenses like a mortgage, the cable bill, groceries, etc., it ignores future expenses. Let's take your car, for example. It's paid for, which is great. But in five years this car will need to be replaced and "suddenly" you'll discover that you have a one-time $20,000 expense, which should not be sudden and is actually anything but one-time unless you are planning to drive this car for the rest of your life. But the car is just the beginning – you'll take vacations, buy furniture, your kids will go to college, and then there's retirement.

Now this discussion was starting to get more interesting:

> Sit down together and identify all of your expenses, current and future. Once you have identified your future major expenses, create a sinking fund for each one of them.

He explained about sinking funds:

> Think of "sinking fund" as synchronizing the future to the present.
> Let's take your car as an example. If in five years you'll need to buy a new car for $20,000, you'll probably be able to get $5,000 for your present car, and thus you'll need $15,000. That means you need to save $3,000 a year or $250 a month. This $250 a month should become a line item in your budget, and the $250 should go into a separate account. Or you can use one savings account and track sinking funds on a spreadsheet, but some banks will allow you to create separate savings accounts. You can get fancy and start assuming rates of return, but unless I am dealing with an expense that is at least five years out, I ignore compounding. Take the vaguely right approach rather than the precisely wrong one.
> Once you've identified your future expenses, create your budget; and I guarantee that you'll discover that your true income is much lower

than you thought. Just because these expenses are going to happen in the future doesn't make them less real.

What happens to a lot of families that don't plan for future expenses is they get surprised by them and are forced to borrow. Borrowing makes everything exponentially more expensive, because compounding interest turns from being your friend to your enemy – you start paying interest on interest and the rat race begins.

I could not wait to go home and fire up Excel and start budgeting. As Rachel and I were guesstimating our monthly and future expenses, we had to make calls to her and my parents. We had both lived with our parents and were oblivious as to how much things cost. Once we figured out how much we'd spend on recurring items like utilities, groceries, car insurance, clothes, etc., we started to think about our future big-item expenses. Suddenly a lot of unexpected things showed up on the list: furniture, car insurance deductibles, a new TV (that was when big TVs cost a lot of money)... and this was all before we had kids.

As I am thinking about this almost two decades later, I see that Mark's budgeting advice turned our spending from a mindless, often impulsive endeavor into a mindful one. It was a great prioritizing tool. Rachel and I intentionally allocated our limited income to the things that mattered to us the most, at the expense of things that mattered to us less. By bringing all current and eventual expenses into our monthly spending budget, we got rid of unwelcome surprises. Also, when unexpected things happened – a car accident, a significant repair to the house – since money had been saved in the "emergencies" sinking fund and it came out of a different savings (and mental) account, writing a check was a lot less painful.

I realized over the years what Mark saw then: That our wants are unlimited and will always exceed our income. No matter how much money you make, without a system your insatiable wants (if not controlled) will always outpace your income.

You think if you double or triple your income you'll be happy, you'll have enough? Unless you keep your expenses the same, which most us of will not do, then you won't have enough. As we make more money, we seem to develop a taste for finer wines, more luxurious cars, and larger houses in pricier neighborhoods.

"Wealth consists not in having great possessions,
but in having few wants."

— **Epictetus**

We'll always have neighbors and friends who have fancier things than we do. If we allow our internal compass to be magnetized by them, we're guaranteed a life of misery, as our income will always lag behind our envy and we'll be destined for the never-ending rat race. Warren Buffett says that envy is the stupidest of all the deadly sins – at least you get some pleasure from the other ones.

As you can imagine, in the investing industry, where you rub shoulders with multi-multi-millionaires and billionaires (be it your clients or colleagues), it is very easy to let your internal compass get out of whack. Over the years, when our (mainly my) impulses were getting the worst of us, my wife and I would go to the budget and see what we'd have to give up if we were to opt for a new car or a bigger house. Was the new house worth a winter without skiing or a Florida vacation?

We realized that material things – houses and cars, etc. – were on the lower end of our priority list. We found that four categories were important to us: health, experiences, time, and education. It's not that we don't have a budget for these categories, it's just that the budget is larger and much looser.

Let's start with health: Without health, nothing else matters. A personal trainer may look like an unnecessary luxury, but without him every attempt I have made to work out has failed. Food fits into this category as well. We simply don't pay attention to the price of tomatoes or meat at the grocery store.

Education: On top of paying for the education of our kids and their after-school activities, we put no limits on how much money they (and we) spend on books. The same applies to our own education, be it for seminars or coaches.

Experiences: As my kids are growing up, I have become acutely aware that we'll have only a limited time with them. Family vacations, skiing in the winter, and day trips are very important to us. Whenever I travel for business, I always try to take a family member with me.

And then there is time: My thinking on this topic has changed over the years. I was always bothered when my investment friends used assistants to schedule calls with me or their assistants replied to emails I sent them. I incorrectly perceived that it was their way of telling me that they were more important than others. However, I realized as I got older that instead of time buying money, money should be buying time.

The time I save by not doing low-value tasks (e.g., going through my inbox, replying to emails that my assistant can respond to, scheduling calls, making doctor's appointments, or booking airline tickets), I can spend doing research, talking to clients, and yes, hanging out with family and friends.

I realize that this may sound a bit pretentious, so here is another example. I used to spend an hour on the phone, calling some credit card company to dispute an erroneous $6 charge. Today, I would not do that.

Health, education, experiences and time are categories of spending that are important to my family, and as a consequence, our budget for them is very loose. But just because they are important to us does not mean that they should be important to you as well. Not at all. We are all different. We have different values, different financial situations, and are at different stages of our lives. My categories were examples of my family's conscious (key word) choices.

Here is another example.

I have a friend. He is divorced and has a 21-year-old daughter he is very close with. He is a personal trainer and chooses to work 20 hours a week. He lives in an apartment that is slightly bigger than his car, which he shares with a roommate (his daughter lives on her own). He doesn't eat out much and generally leads a very modest day-to-day lifestyle. But he loves traveling. A couple times a month he takes a three-day trip with his daughter to a new place in the US. They stay in cheap, $60 motels. I get the feeling that spending time with his daughter is the main reason why he loves to travel. He also enjoys the experience of driving and, despite his modest income, leases a new car every two years.

I doubt that he intentionally sat down and wrote out a budget. But he made a budget through intentional prioritization of his spending – elevating things he values and enjoys like travel and driving – and deemphasizing things that are less important to him, like food and size of his dwelling. At this point in his life, he chooses to work just enough to cover his very limited needs. And here is the best part – he is incredibly happy. Our personal budget should follow our values. We need to figure out what matters to us (our values) and calibrate and prioritize our spending accordingly. After all, money buys the most when it buys things we actually value.

I am not sure if money can actually bring happiness, but I am sure that the lack of money is a source of a tremendous amount of unhappiness. On the surface, this sentence may fail a test of logic as it lacks linearity, but it's true just the same. Oxygen doesn't make you happy, but a lack of oxygen will make you unhappy very quickly. So it is with money. Although we'll all disagree on what *a lack* means.

Just as a reminder: happiness = reality minus (properly calibrated) expectations. When you control your budget, you control your expectations.

When you constantly spend more money than you earn, after you chew through your savings (if you ever had any), you're getting deeper into debt. Therefore, to maximize health, education, experiences, and time and still live within our means, Rachel and I had to give up things that were less important to us – a huge house and brand-new cars.

By living within our budget (and, I am sure, thanks to plenty of good luck), Rachel and I have never had to argue about money (we had plenty of other topics), because we were on the same page, since we both created that budget.

I was lucky to have Mark as a friend who, with just one lunch, made my life richer and easier. I hope that with this essay I'll do the same for others – and Jonah, Hannah, and Mia Sarah, I hope you're reading this!

Stoicism –
The Philosophy
for Life

S TOIC PHILOSOPHY HAS had a life-changing impact on me. I wish I had learned about the Stoics when I was a teenager; I would have been spared a lot of unnecessary pain. I hope you'll see what I see in the Stoics and that they'll brighten both your good and bad days.

I divided this section into two parts. The first part, "Operating System," introduces Stoic concepts that I have found to be extremely useful in daily life. They include dichotomy of control, negative visualization, reframing, and dealing with insults, among others.

The second part zooms in on a subject that is dear to me – goals and values.[7]

---

7   In this essay I will not touch on the Stoic cardinal virtues: wisdom, justice, courage, and moderation. I am taking this tack because I don't want to pay lip service to something I could not internalize. The same goes for another Stoic principle, "living in agreement with nature," which sounds great, but I still don't understand what it really means.

Stoicism: Part 1 – Operating System

WE ENTER MINDLESSLY into life, born almost as a blank piece of hardware. Mother Nature equipped us with a very rudimentary hunter-gatherer operating system. Then our parents start programming us and the external environment slowly kicks in. We get programmed by family, friends, co-workers, the media (and now social media), and, simply, by circumstances.

If we are lucky and we get the right parents, siblings, and friends, read the right books, and the road of life nudges us into the right direction, we may end up with better programming. But the reality is that most of our programming is random and happens without our direct intervention.

Life kind of just happens.

This is where mindfulness comes in. Mindfulness is thinking about thinking, or being aware of making decisions. It is being fully present. Mindfulness requires you to take a step back from yourself, to become almost an outside observer of yourself and your programming. Meditation is helpful in this regard; it allows us to get into the thinking about thinking mode. (Read more about meditation in "Attend a Party in Your Own Head.")

Once we tune ourselves into the "mindfulness mode," which programs do we activate and which do we stop? Each one of us comes equipped with unique hardware, and thus we need to create and maintain the programs that work for us.

I feel like I had enough luck to qualify as a life lottery winner – great parents, relatives, friends, family, career; lucky to be born in Russia and also lucky to have moved to the United States. But until I started to write about life, I did not have much in the way of introspection, or self-awareness. I lacked mindfulness.

I realized I needed to consciously program myself (and my subconscious), with a program that worked for me (religion was not the answer for *me*).

Stoic philosophy was that program.

What you are about to read is not an academic adventure, but an exploration of a practical operating system that I am writing as much for me – and (hopefully) my kids – as for you.

Knowing
and Doing

An introduction to the Stoics

MY INTRODUCTION TO Stoicism happened very slowly – one quote from Seneca or Epictetus at a time. And then it was very fast, and I found myself reading about Stoic philosophy nonstop. Stoic philosophy offered *to me* what religion could not – an operating system for *this* life without any promises of an afterlife, no relationship with a friend[8] up in the sky, no leaps of faith required; just a very logical and practical way to approach life. This works great for me. If you are religious, Stoicism doesn't compete with any religious teachings and only complements them with insights on the human psyche.[9]

Before we dive in, let's talk about Stoic philosophy and the Stoics.

Philosophy in its literal translation from ancient Greek is love of wisdom.

---

8 I respect the fact that religious people don't view God as "a friend up in the sky." I am writing this strictly from my perspective, which I may or may not change when I grow up.

9 Several of my religious friends (of different faiths), after reading an early draft of this book, pointed out to me that a lot of Stoic wisdom resembles the teachings of religious texts.

To me, philosophy is a thinking framework; a framework full of interconnected mental models.

But Stoicism has gotten a bad rap (it needs a better PR agent). It is a common perception that to be a Stoic is to have as much emotion as the ancient marble statues that commemorate Stoicism's founders. A common definition of the word "stoic" is someone who experiences no feelings of pain, pleasure, joy, or grief.

Dear reader, you may not know me well, but I am a volcano of feelings. A philosophy that advocates having no feelings would not work for me. Though that may be a definition of the word, that is not what Stoicism – the philosophy – is. Stoicism seeks to minimize *unnecessary* negative emotions, which in turn amplifies positive emotions.

The less your mind is preoccupied with unnecessary negative emotions, the more room it has for positive ones. No, I am not going to turn into a Greek marble statue by the time I am done writing this, and neither will you by the time you finish reading.

Nassim Nicholas Taleb put it so well: "A Stoic is someone who transforms fear into prudence, pain into transformation, mistakes into initiation, and desire into undertaking."

Stoicism was started in ancient Greece around 300 BC by Zeno, a wealthy merchant who lost all his wealth in a shipwreck and barely made it out alive himself.

Throughout this book I constantly make this point: Pain often unlocks creativity. It must have been a devastatingly painful experience for Zeno to lose everything overnight. Nevertheless, he later wrote: "My most profitable journey began on the day I was shipwrecked and lost my entire fortune."

For a while Zeno's philosophy was called Zenoism – but maybe because Zeno did not want it to become a cult of Zeno, he named it after a place in Athens where he and his students gathered, the *Stoa Poikile* ("painted porch"). A few millennia later, this tradition was borrowed by the hedge fund industry in the US, which named their companies after places where the founders grew up, had their first kiss, etc.

Three Stoics whose writings have survived to this day are Epictetus, Seneca, and Marcus Aurelius (I'll refer to him as *Marcus* for brevity; yes, we are on a first-name basis). It is through the eyes of these three Stoic giants that we see Stoicism today.

I want to warn you, I'll be quoting them extensively in these pages. There is so much beauty, clarity, and wisdom in their original writings, and I want to bring you as close to the source as possible.

As I've been reading books by and about these great men, I have been shocked at how little people have changed over the last 2,000-plus years.

Epictetus

Let's start with Epictetus (50–135 AD). We don't know much about him, other than that he was a slave. Epictetus was not even his real name – it translates from ancient Greek as "acquired." In his late teens, he was granted his freedom and proceeded to teach philosophy. Epictetus did not leave any writings behind. Luckily, his lectures were transcribed by his student Arrian into a series of eight books, titled *Discourses*, of which only four have survived. Epictetus's dichotomy of control framework is so simple yet so brilliant (we'll discuss it soon).

Marcus Aurelius

And then there is Marcus Aurelius (121–180 AD) – a Roman emperor, a general, a philosopher, and a practicing Stoic. He was the one who impressed me the most.

Let me clarify this. It is not his status as emperor that impressed me, but the fact that while being an emperor he remained a good human being. If you want to destroy a person, give him absolute power and unlimited wealth. History is littered with rulers destroyed by power and money. Marcus is a rare exception. Just imagine the Roman Empire in the second century AD. It controls every territory that touches the Mediterranean Sea. Marcus's word is law. He can have anything he wants. He could have taken shortcuts through life. But he did not.

During his 19 years of ruling the Roman Empire, Marcus did not abuse his power; he governed with justice and civility. He promised that he would not prosecute any of his political opponents, and he kept that promise.

The only piece of writing Marcus left us is his private journal, which he called *Meditations*. This journal was written *not* to be published but for Marcus to privately reflect on his life.

He wrote, "Waste no more time arguing about what a good man should be. Be one." And, "Never esteem anything as an advantage to you that will make you break your word or lose your self-respect." And, "A man's worth is no greater than the worth of his ambitions."

Seneca, to whom we shall turn next, remarked, "No man was ever wise by chance." Marcus was no accidental genius but a person who applied Stoicism to all aspects of his life and carefully cultivated, through deliberate practice, the person he became.

All that said, Marcus lived 2,000 years ago, and we'll never really know if the image I painted above is overidealized or not. Epictetus said, "Imagine for yourself a character, a model personality, whose example you determine to follow, in private as well as in public." To me, Marcus is the "personality" I am trying to become, knowing that it's unlikely I'll ever get there. However, just constantly striving to be more like Marcus will elevate my life.

Seneca

And finally, there is the Spanish-born Lucius Annaeus Seneca (5 BC–65 AD), or just Seneca. A true Renaissance man (15 centuries before the Renaissance), in addition to being a philosopher, Seneca was an investment banker, a playwright and writer, a senator, and advisor to Roman emperor Nero. Seneca was the most prolific writer of the three.

Seneca's wisdom is often stunning in its simplicity. My favorite quote from Seneca is only three words long: "Time discovers truth." It epitomizes a lot of things in life, for instance, it slices to the core of what investing is. As an investor, my goal is to discover the truth (what a company is worth) before time does.

If you keep this quote in the back of your mind when you have a conversation or debate with someone, the objective of the conversation may change from one ego prevailing over another to a search for truth. After all, eventually time will discover the truth. And if the conversation doesn't change your mind, maybe you shouldn't have the conversation. What's the point? (Read more about intellectually honest debate in "Abracadabra.")

Seneca is the most controversial of our three Stoics – he's full of contradictions.

He writes that wealth must be acquired in an ethical way. Here is the first contradiction: Seneca became one of the richest men in Rome at the service of the truly evil Emperor Nero, who assassinated his own mother and later ordered Seneca to kill himself. We don't know Seneca's true intentions. Nero was a despot, but Seneca may have felt it was his civic duty to provide him guidance for the benefit of Rome and its citizens. We do know that Seneca acquired a lot of his wealth by serving Nero.

Here is another contradiction. Seneca wrote, "Wealth is the slave of a wise man. The master of a fool." And, "He is a great man who uses clay dishes as if they were silver, but he is equally great who uses silver as if it were clay." It seems that at times Seneca was a slave to his own wealth, as he obsessed over material things[10] – the high polish of his furniture, his exotic slaves, the age of the wine he drank, and the earrings he sported.

Seneca epitomizes the saying, "In theory there is no difference between theory and practice; in practice, there is" (which has been ascribed to that great American philosopher Yogi Berra). Seneca literally wrote books on the theory of Stoicism, but often struggled to practice that theory. He self-admittedly did not live up to his own ideals. If you're listening for notes of judgment on my part here, there are none. Quite the opposite. Seneca's struggles make me appreciate that though theory is a prerequisite, it is not enough; success comes from practice.

In other words, my spilling of ink on these pages means absolutely nothing for me (other than that you are reading it) if I don't practice Stoicism every day. There is an Asian proverb:[11] "Knowing and not doing is not knowing!" Therefore, my goal is to be a practicing Stoic who both *knows* and *does*.

---

10   Emily Wilson, "Seneca, the fat-cat philosopher," *The Guardian* (27 March 2015).

11   A term we use when we do not know the origin of a saying; there are multiple contradictory sources; we are just too lazy to look it up; or it really is an Asian proverb.

Dichotomy
of Control

"**S**OME THINGS ARE up to us and some are not up to us." This is how Epictetus introduced the dichotomy of control framework.

He continues: "Within our power are opinion, aim, desire, aversion, and, in one word, whatever affairs are our own. Beyond our power are body, property, reputation, office, and, in one word, whatever are not properly our own affairs."

So what is up to us? Opinions we hold, our actions, our feelings, goals we set for ourselves, our values, our desires. These things are internal – we have complete control over them. Everything else is external to us, and thus we have little control over those things. This is the framework that attracted me to Stoicism in the first place. It changed how I interact with people. Yes, people are probably the biggest source of negative emotions for me.

Unless I decide to spend the rest of my life with monks who have taken a vow of silence, I have to accept this reality of life: People I love (friends, relatives) or hardly know (the lady at the rental car counter, a telemarketer) will sometimes disappoint me. They'll say something I don't like or do something I don't care for. I am not joining a monastery anytime soon. Therefore, though I may not be able to control what people do or say, I can control how I respond to them. There is absolutely no reason to get worked up about things you cannot control (externals).

You can worry all you want whether the sun will come up tomorrow. The sun, however, is not aware of your existence or your worrying. It will either come up or it will not. As Epictetus so beautifully put it: "The more we value things outside our control, the less control we have." This worrying about something over which you have absolutely no control increases the frequency and amplitude of unnecessary negative emotions. Negative emotions compound upon each other – a lot of little worrying results in big stress. If you worry about things you cannot control, you always suffer an extra time. Epictetus said, "No person is free who is not master of himself." Our goal is to become masters of ourselves.

Let me tell you a story (I'll be telling you a lot of stories here). In the late 1990s I studied to become a CFA. The CFA is a three-year program; it is like a super MBA program for investment professionals. As I like to explain to my accountant friends (poking fun at them, a little), it is like the Certified Public Accountant program but more difficult. You buy books and a study guide in January. You study on your own or with a study group, then take the exam in June. If you pass the exam, you move to the next level (there are three levels). If you don't pass, you just lost a year. You must wait till January and try again.

I did not want to fail and wait a year. I studied incredibly hard – probably twice as hard as my friends. The CFA Institute said that it would send out results at least a month and a half after the test, in late July or so. Starting in mid-July, I was stalking the mailman daily. At 11 a.m., I was right there at the mailbox. Being around me in mid-July and into August was not much fun. My results arrived in mid-August (and I passed). For those months from January to August each year, the test results were all I could think about.

Looking at this 20 years later, my approach to the whole thing was completely wrong. I tied my happiness and my self-worth to something I could not completely control – passing not just one but three exams. William Irvine, in his terrific book on Stoicism, *A Guide to the Good Life,* took Epictetus' dichotomy of control and turned it into a trichotomy of control. There are things that are completely up to us – our values and goals, our emotional responses (internals). There are things that are completely not up to us – the sun rising tomorrow sort of things (externals).

And then, Irvine added, there are things over which we have *some* but not complete control.

Let's apply this framework to my CFA exams.

Passing an exam has externalities. There could be questions on the test that are poorly phrased. I could have a headache while taking the test. I could inadvertently miss a section of questions (which I actually did and discovered 20 minutes before the end of a six-hour exam).

Therefore, passing the exams was partially but not completely under my control. Instead of setting a goal to pass the test, I should have set a goal to do the best job possible studying for each exam. This is a process-based goal where I design and execute the process. We want all our goals to be process-based, with short-term feedback loops so we can make course corrections. The best part is that the process is completely under my control.

Stoics would say that my passing the test should be a preference, not a goal. If I pass, I am happy. If I fail, I will not be upset about it – no negative emotions. I like this asymmetry of emotion. I put my absolute best effort into studying. I am proud of the effort I put in and what I've learned. If I fail, there is next year. (As I am writing this, across the table from me is my 19-year-old son, Jonah, diligently studying six hours straight for a statistics exam. I realize I really don't care what grade he gets – that is external to him; but I am so proud of his focus – that is internal.)

Once I left the exam room, I had absolutely no control over the result. At this point I should have just let it go and enjoyed my summer, telling myself that at this point it was not up to me. Any anxiety I'd experience would not change the outcome.

In our relationships we should set a goal, not for someone to love us, but to behave according to our values (to be worth loving) and to be a good, caring partner. We cannot control whether people will love us, but we can control our actions and our behavior.

I could not figure out for a long time why so many actors and musicians ended up having horrible lives. It's clear to me now; happiness linked to adulation by others is like an addictive drug, and thus you want a constant flow of it and you want an increasing dosage. These people also tie their happiness to external forces over which they have so little control. Your fans may love you today and move on to another louder and shinier object tomorrow.

I am not the Lady Gaga of writing, but I get a lot of emails from my readers. They come in spurts. Emails showing up in your inbox carry little hits of dopamine. They can, if I let them, indicate to me that I matter. If I am not careful and I tie my happiness to them, I'll increase the volatility of my emotions, getting little in return. Now, my readers' emails come into a separate mailbox that I check only a few times a week.

Also, if I write with the goal of getting more emails (likes) from readers, eventually my writing will suffer. I'll start writing what my readers care about, which may come at the expense of what is meaningful to me. I'll trade my long-term happiness for bits of dopamine. I should just focus on writing (I can control that) and pay little attention to what others think of it.

The more we tie our happiness to things that we cannot control, the more we subject ourselves to the negative volatility of the outside world. Therefore, we need to be mindful in setting our goals. They should be internal to us, under our control, and process-based.

Labeling

In my daily life, as things that trigger negative emotions arise, I label them *internal or external* (a trick I learned from practicing meditation). One day, my wife said something I didn't especially like, and instead of mentally labeling, I labeled it out loud. "Honey, you are an external!" I exclaimed. She gave me a look that suggested the couch in the living room was all mine. Lesson learned – don't label out loud.

I view Stoicism as mental Aikido. Aikido is a Japanese martial art that was born in the 20th century and is loosely based on Jujitsu. It tries to protect both practitioner and opponent. Instead of doing hard blocks of an opponent's attack (as in traditional martial arts), it uses the opponent's energy to redirect the opponent's moves away from the practitioner's body. To some degree, this is how I view the dichotomy of control framework: Once I recognize that whatever is bringing me negative emotions is external, I mentally let them fly by me.

Marcus says, "You have power over your mind – not outside events. Realize this, and you will find strength." I don't want to disagree with a Roman emperor, so I'll just add that in addition to strength you'll find happiness. Removing negative emotions from your life is like adding a small pinch of salt to a dish when you are cooking – it brings out flavor and enhances happiness.

Share this chapter with a friend:
https://soulinthegame.net/eag/

Event, Judgment, Reaction Framework

A RENTAL CAR COUNTER clerk had the audacity to tell me that the SUV I ordered was not available and I could only have a minivan. (I know, I can feel your blood boiling, too.) In the past, my reaction would have been completely random, most likely based on what I had for breakfast (it was a subconscious response).

Dichotomy of control opened my eyes to the fact that I cannot change others' behavior, which is external to me – but I can change how I respond to it. Easier said than done. I am an emotional person. If left unchecked, my negative triggers lead to automatic, negative responses, and later to enormous guilt for these responses. Let's be honest, that is a horrible way to lead a life.

Stoics have this wonderful concept: pre-emotion (*propatheia*). Pre-emotion is an innate, unjudged, unevaluated feeling. My initial feeling of anger at the car rental counter is pre-emotion. I cannot control it. It is programmed into me by Mother Nature. In our cavemen days, when a leopard jumped in front of us out of the bush, Mother Nature did not want us to philosophize; she wanted us to react and react fast.

Without judgment, pre-emotion automatically converts into an emotion and then into a reaction. But judgment can convert this pre-emotion into a more positive emotion and then into a more effective reaction. Viktor Frankl, Holocaust survivor and psychologist, said, "Between stimulus and response there is a space. In that space is our power to choose our response. In our response lies our growth and our freedom."

Judgment lives in that brief space Frankl described, between stimulus (event) and response, and between pre-emotion and emotion. This is why the concept of pre-emotion is so wonderful: I can blame Mother Nature for it. But I cannot shift the responsibility for my emotion.

What is correct judgment? The rational me has a core value: Leave the world a better place than I found it. Add to the lives of people I come into contact with, rather than subtracting from them. But my emotions often don't let me live up to this ideal. The judgment step is when I ask myself one of these things: "If I look at my behavior an hour from now, will I be proud of it? Am I following my values?"

I cannot control whether the rental company has the car I want; nor can I change the world. Yes, the world will disappoint me at times, but I can control how I respond.

This basically sums up the event, judgment, reaction (EJR) framework: There is an event which triggers pre-emotion; then you have a space where you insert your judgment, which in turn calibrates your emotion and reaction.

One more thought. Though pre-emotions are innate feelings programmed by Mother Nature, by practicing EJR for a while we are able to reprogram them. I treat mini-incidents like these as little Stoic quizzes that give me an opportunity to practice the EJR framework, helping me reprogram my pre-emotions into healthy emotions.

Epictetus sums it up for us: "Remember, it is not enough to be hit or insulted to be harmed; you must believe that you are being harmed. If someone succeeds in provoking you, realize that your mind is complicit in the provocation. Which is why it is essential we do not respond impulsively to impressions; take a moment before reacting, and you will find it easier to maintain control."

Negative
Visualization

MY COMPANY, IMA, is an investment advisory firm. We are long-term value investors. We analyze companies as any intelligent businessperson would, with the intention of owning them for years. When we find undervalued companies (stocks), we buy them, but we have no idea how the stock market will price them tomorrow or a few months from now.

When IMA was small, we were hired by a large client. We told him up front what we did, and he also read our 30-page brochure. It seemed like a match made in heaven – until a few months into our relationship, when I realized that he was measuring our performance on a weekly basis. (Remember, we were looking years out.)

Today, I'd have a conversation with this person and explain that what we do is likely not for him, and I'd gently ask him to reevaluate his time horizon or his relationship with us.

Then, we could not afford to be too choosy. But I instinctively started practicing negative visualization (though I didn't call it that at the time). I visualized how we lost this client. Most importantly, I managed the firm as if this client was already gone. I did not have to visualize for very long – he left after four months. When he left, the pain did not sting as much as it might have. I was mentally and financially prepared.

This is what negative visualization is: Imagining and contemplating bad

Discussion, Jerusalem, Naum Katsenelson, oil (1994).

Flowers, Naum Katsenelson, oil (1995).

London, Naum Katsenelson, oil (c. 1999).

In the Park, Madrid, Spain, Naum Katsenelson, oil (2002).

Karlovy Vary, Czech Republic, Naum Katsenelson, oil (2002).

Remembering Rome, Naum Katsenelson, watercolor (2003).

Flamenco, Spain, Naum Katsenelson, pastel (2005).

Paris Flower Market, Naum Katsenelson, watercolor (c. 2005).

Paris, Naum Katsenelson, oil (c. 2005).

Brighton Beach, Brooklyn NY, Naum Katsenelson, watercolor (c. 2006).

Central Park, New York, Naum Katsenelson, watercolor (c. 2006).

Mexican Fisherman, Acapulco, Mexico, Naum Katsenelson, watercolor (2007).

Naples, Italy, Naum Katsenelson, watercolor (2008).

Foggy Morning, Naum Katsenelson, watercolor (2008).

Spring Time, Murmansk, Naum Katsenelson, watercolor (2009).

New York Stock Exchange, Naum Katsenelson, oil (2010).

things happening before they happen. It is like being vaccinated against an adverse future. You already visualized it, and your mind has had a chance to pre-adapt to it. As Seneca explains, "He robs present ills of their power who has perceived their coming beforehand."

There is another reason to practice negative visualization – it enhances your appreciation of what you have. I wrote in "Born in Russia, Made in America" how after my mother's death I inadvertently, out of fear and trauma of recent experience, visualized losing my father. This increased my appreciation of my father from a young age and made our relationship stronger and more meaningful.

Since my mother passed, I have never practiced negative visualization when it comes to the deaths of friends or family (it's simply too painful). I did visualize my kids growing up and going off to college, and that helped me appreciate the limited time I have with them under the same roof. Once you realize that everyone (and everything) around you is transitory, you value people and things a lot more. This may improve the relationships you have with people you love, by encouraging you to treasure those relationships.

I want to make one point clear – negative visualization does not mean we constantly dwell on negatives, thinking about bad things happening to us. For instance, I do not dwell on the fact that my kids will grow up, leave home, and have their own lives. Instead, negative visualization tells me that I need to free myself from the computer screen and refocus my attention (the currency of time) on them – be it going for a bike ride, a trip to a bookstore, skiing, or simply having a dinner conversation without constantly looking at my smartphone. Then a potential negative becomes a real-time positive.

Negative visualization can spur us to positive action, helping us to deal with stress and reduce suffering in real time. Imagine this. You are driving home, there is dinner waiting for you on the table, and you find yourself stuck in traffic. You are doing positive visualization as your mind is comparing two activities: sitting in a metal box on wheels, idling in the traffic, versus eating dinner. Idling in the box is less appealing than the alternative. You get stressed – unnecessary negative emotions spike and your happiness declines. I am sure this did not require much imagination. All of us go through this all the time.

This is when the EJR frameworks kicks in. Stuck in traffic – the event. Judgment – we have several options. We can do negative visualization. Instead of doing positive visualization, comparing our idling in traffic to the warm meal and glass of wine that awaits us, we can visualize that things could have been so much worse. We could have been driving back from a doctor's appointment after he told us we only have two weeks to live. Suddenly, arriving home 30 minutes late doesn't feel so bad.

Here are a few more examples. I had a conversation with a friend. He is a widower who had recently started dating. A woman he really liked had broken up with him. He said he was depressed and lonely. I told him, think about it. You are in your 70s. You have good health. You have kids that love you, and they are all healthy and have good lives. You have a lot of friends. You are financially independent: you may not be flying on private planes, but you don't have to worry about the price of tomatoes at the grocery store. Even your football team did well last year. Imagine that you lost all that. Is your life now so bad? He paused and really thought about it, then said, "Yeah, not so bad." I saw glimpses of a smile on his face. (Note to self – it is easy to dispense advice to others; I need to remember to follow my own advice.)

Another friend told me a story. He was at the airport, standing at the airline service counter. There was a man in front of him who looked like a soldier coming home from a tour in the Middle East. My friend overheard the airline representative telling him that the airline had lost his bag. The soldier calmly and quietly replied, "Well, that's okay, nobody died." It is not difficult to imagine how trivial losing a bag might be when you have faced death in combat; when you have seen your friends blown to pieces by roadside bombs. This soldier did not have to theoretically practice negative visualization; he had lived it. It was seared into him. And it gave him a clear, strong perspective on what is important and what is trivial.

Speaking of trivial. I've been practicing negative visualization for years with my wife and did not even know it. My wife is not a big spender. Whenever I buy something that she did not ask me to buy, she gives me a questioning look and says, "How much was that?" If it was $100, I triple the price and say $300. Her eyes widen and she says "$300!?! That's too much!" Then I say, no, it was actually just $100. I anchored and tricked her mind to negatively visualize $300 just for a second, and suddenly $100 seems like a bargain. I know that with this little piece of advice I just saved thousands of marriages. You're welcome.

Last point.

Now we can explain, from a Stoic perspective, why social media makes us miserable, while watching reality shows about dysfunctional people makes us happy (shows about hoarders, family feuds, or cheating spouses come to mind here).

Social media results in positive visualization (longing for things we wish we had). People don't put their miserable moments on social media – those moments when they have a fight with their spouse, their kids are throwing tantrums, or their house looks like a hurricane went through it. No, our friends share their best picture- and video-perfect moments, when their houses look like model homes, their kids are adorable, and their spouses are smiling and loving.

You'd think seeing your friends' happiness would brush off on you and make you happy. Wrong! Your subconscious kicks in and starts comparing your ordinary life with your friends' never-ending smiley paradise. You feel like you don't measure up.

Reality TV featuring dysfunctional people, on the other hand, fires up the negative visualization. We realize that our lives could have been so much worse, like those people on TV.

What would the Stoics say about social media and reality shows?

Seneca would probably remind us of the preciousness of time (as he will in a few chapters). He would not be a fan of social media or reality TV. Epictetus would quote himself: "Most of us would be seized with fear if our bodies went numb and would do everything possible to avoid it, yet we take no interest at all in the numbing of our souls [and minds]." Marcus would meditate on this in his journal and decide that there is no point engaging in activity that ultimately makes us miserable.

None of them would suggest that we start gulping reality TV as an antidote to social media. Instead, they'd suggest we'd learn to appreciate what we have by imagining our lives without it.

I'll let Marcus finish this chapter: "Do not indulge in dreams of having what you have not, but reckon up the chief of the blessings you do possess, and then thankfully remember how you would crave for them if they were not yours."

Share this chapter with a friend:
https://soulinthegame.net/ovr/

Last Time

*"One day you ordered a Happy Meal for the last time
and you didn't even know it."*

— McDonald's.

NO, THIS MCDONALD'S was not an ancient Roman contemporary of Seneca. This was a tweet by the McDonald's Corporation that appeared in my browser right when I sat down to write about this topic. It perfectly summarizes a type of visualization that William Irvine, in *A Guide to the Good Life*, called "Last Time."

For everything we do, there will be a last time. Yes, there will be a last time we'll take a breath, but that is not the focus of this exercise. There was a last time I changed Mia Sarah's diaper (though my wife will insist I did not change it enough); there was a last time I drove Jonah to school; there was a last time Hannah needed me to lull her to sleep with a story; there was a last time I saw my mother; and yes, there will be a last time I buy a McFlurry at McDonald's (I'm not a Happy Meal-type person).

The Last Time negative visualization is there to ignite the appreciation that time, though infinite, is given to us in limited amounts to spend. This negative visualization of the finite nature of the personal time granted to us can help us increase the value of the present moment.

"It is not that we have a short time to live, but that we waste a lot of it. Life is long enough, and a sufficiently generous amount has been given to us for the highest achievements if it were all well invested." This excerpt from Seneca's *On Shortness of Life* is very appropriate here, but here is the punch line:

"But when it is wasted in heedless luxury and spent on no good activity, **we are forced at last by death's final constraint to realize that it has passed away before we knew it was passing**. So it is: We are not given a short life, but we make it short, and we are not ill-supplied but wasteful of it... Life is long if you know how to use it."

We, yours truly included, are often not here, not in the present; we are daydreaming away in the past or in the future, while time does what time does, turning future into past. As the great Freddie Mercury put it, "Time waits for no one."

When we go to graduations or funerals, we recognize the shortness of life, we contemplate it on the drive home, and then we forget about it.

I am writing this on Wednesday before Thanksgiving, at 5 a.m. We are in Vail for a few days of skiing. In about two hours my kids will wake up; my wife will make breakfast; she'll worry that the kids are underdressed for the weather (that is what mothers do); and we'll get ready to go skiing.

I'll put my laptop away and not think about this book till tomorrow morning. I'll focus on inhaling life with my kids – helping Mia Sarah (6) put her cute ski boots on; reminding Hannah (14) not to forget her gloves; and being in awe of Jonah (19) as he teaches Mia Sarah how to ski.

Some of the things I do today I may be doing for the last time. The kids will grow up. Mia Sarah will not need help with her ski boots. Though I doubt Hannah will stop forgetting and losing her ski gloves, at some point her husband will be the one reminding her. Mia Sarah will not need Jonah's ski lesson, and Jonah will be teaching his own kids to ski.

Yes, there is something I'll be doing today for the last time. I don't know what it is and will only recognize it in hindsight. I want to be present for it. I need to keep reminding myself of this daily and not wait for funerals and graduations.

William Irvine writes: "By contemplating the impermanence of everything in the world, we are forced to recognize that every time we do something could be the last time we do it, and this recognition can invest the things we do with a significance and intensity that would otherwise be absent."[12]

---

12   W. Irvine, *A Guide to the Good Life* (Oxford University Press), p. 84.

I am not a big fan of religion (blame the Soviets for that), but religion did figure out daily repetitions. The Last Time visualization is a useful daily repetition (or prayer, if you like). Just remind yourself every morning that there is a good chance there is something you'll be doing for the last time – the past is already past; the future lies forever in the future; we have only now.

Seneca puts it beautifully: "Let us prepare our minds as if we'd come to the very end of life. Let us postpone nothing. Let us balance life's books each day. The one who puts the finishing touches on their life each day is never short of time." Seneca's Eastern counterpart, Confucius, appropriately pointed out 500 years earlier: "We have two lives, and the second begins when we realize we only have one."

Share this chapter with a friend:
https://soulinthegame.net/rzq/

Reframing

REMEMBER HOW I told you that Stoic philosophy is just a tool set of interconnected mental models? The EJR model is interconnected with another tool called *reframing*. When you are in the judgment state, you get an opportunity to reframe an event in a way that turns it from negative to positive. Epictetus sums up reframing nicely: "It is our attitude toward events, not events themselves, which we can control. Nothing is by its own nature calamitous."

In 2010, my family – my wife and I, the kids, and my aunt – were driving through a large park. I was driving my wife's minivan and didn't notice that we were low on gas and... we ran out of gas. The car stopped dead in the middle of this large state park.

My wife was initially upset that we were stuck in the middle of nowhere. The normal me would have been upset, too. But the parent (and future Stoic) in me thought, "What would my father say and do?" I put a smile on and said to my family, "Think about it: If we drove through the park and nothing happened, it would have been just another time that we drove from point A to point B. Now we have a little adventure that we'll remember. Our lives are not threatened; we are all safe. Let's just make the best of it."

This story lacks drama and suffering (thank God). We simply called my father and asked him to bring us some gasoline. In the meantime, we played soccer and walked in the beautiful park. An hour later my father brought us the gas.

My kids and I filed this little misadventure as a happy memory of when we ran out of gas in the park and did fun things. My wife put it into the mental file of when I forgot to check if we had enough gas in our (her) car before we started driving.

I wasn't a practicing Stoic then, but I did manage to avoid blaming either myself or my wife for not putting gas in her car. Once we were out of gas, nothing we could do would change that fact – it was an external. What I could control was my response to the situation. I chose to look at the situation as an adventure rather than a calamity. I reframed it. Though I didn't know it at the time, I was taking a Stoic quiz – and I passed that one with flying colors.

In case you haven't noticed, we just connected EJR, reframing, and the dichotomy of control. Event: out of gas, stuck in the park. Judgment: choosing to reframe it. Reaction, now reframed: Instead of treating the event as being stuck in the park, seeing it as an opportunity to spend time in the park with people I love. I could have added negative visualization, too! Instead of the weather being sunny and warm, it could have been freezing cold.

My son Jonah had to do some reframing in his senior year of high school. Jonah's first car was going to be my wife's Honda Odyssey minivan. We were going to buy my wife an SUV and Jonah would drive her 11-year-old car. I loved this idea because I wanted Jonah to be surrounded by a lot of metal in his first few years of driving.

Jonah attended Cherry Creek High School, which is not just another high school – it's the "90210" public high school of Denver, attended mostly by kids of wealthy parents. Jonah's minivan (also known as a soccer mom's car) would have been parked next to a lot of fancy German cars (none of them minivans).

Having a car of his own was a big win for Jonah, but then he started to consider what his friends would think of it. My solution was to change his attitude toward the minivan. I showed him a movie. Not just any movie, but my favorite movie of all time, *Get Shorty*. As you'll probably recall, it stars John Travolta, who plays a Miami mobster, Chili Palmer, who comes to LA to collect from a guy who owes money to the Mob. He thinks he's rented a mobstermobile – a Cadillac. But when he gets to the airport, it's pouring rain and all the cars are rented out. There is only one car left – a minivan. Travolta's choice is to either take a taxi or get the minivan. He chooses the van.

Once in LA, Travolta decides he wants to become a movie producer. He projects this image of a cool mobster (this role is the highlight of the movie). There is a scene where Travolta meets a famous actor (played by Danny DeVito) who is smitten by Travolta's coolness and the mystery of Travolta being a mobster. As DeVito walks him outside to his car, the camera zooms in on Travolta's minivan. DeVito asks, "Chili, is this your ride?"

Travolta doesn't skip a beat; there's no hint of embarrassment, no excuses about the car rental company screwing up his reservation. None of that. He says "Yeah, yeah, I like to sit up high, check everything out. It's the Cadillac of minivans." And then he says, "Check this out," clicks the remote, and the rear passenger door opens. DeVito's eyes light up, as if Ferrari had just come out with a new model, and he says, "Mind if I take it for a spin?" Fast forward to the last few shots of the movie, where we see a Hollywood studio parking lot filled with minivans.

After I showed *Get Shorty,* and that scene in particular, to Jonah, his attitude changed (it was reframed). If you act like you've got the coolest car in the school, then it will be the coolest.

Jonah was one of the most-liked kids in school. He stands at 6'3", is handsome (I'm as objective as any father can be), always smiles, and is happy to help anyone in need (he has a good heart). If anyone could spin this, it would be Jonah. He named his car Oksana (something to do with a Borat movie; I am afraid to ask) and started driving it with pride (just like Chili Palmer), telling his friends that this is the BMW of minivans. (Cadillac doesn't have the same cachet that it used to.)

Problem reframed and solved!

A few months later, Jonah's problems got more difficult and he had to do some major reframing again.

In his junior year of high school, Jonah had a girl problem – and ended up with a broken heart. His grades suffered, and his cumulative GPA was ruined. Now all of his friends were going to good universities, their first or second choices. Since Jonah was a little pup, I had taken him once or twice a year to Colorado Buffaloes games at University of Colorado (CU) Boulder. Jonah fell in love with that campus and going to CU was his dream.

Now this dream had crashed. He'd have to go to community college for a semester or two and then transfer to CU Boulder. He was very upset for a while, and then he reframed his problem. Instead of looking at his situation as "not getting into CU Boulder," Jonah decided to look at it as an opportunity to study abroad.

He went to Israel for a year. While there he took classes at American Jewish

University, did an internship at a fintech startup, and played tourist. He got perfect grades at American Jewish University.[13]

Ask him today and he'll tell you that *not* being accepted to CU Boulder was the best thing that ever happened to him.

When you are stuck in traffic you can *choose* to feel miserable for 30 minutes thinking about warm food waiting for you. Or you can reframe your situation as an opportunity to catch up on your podcasts, or even as a rare opportunity to be alone with your thoughts.

As Epictetus said, "Men are disturbed not by the things that happen, but by their opinion of the things that happen." We just need to remember that *opinion* is completely up to us. We can reframe it in a way that minimizes our suffering.

You can also reframe what is happening to you as a story. As any writer knows, a story requires conflict. I, as a writer, have an advantage over a person who doesn't write: I always look for stories. When you write, your mind is always on high alert for stories. Everything going smoothly and according to plan makes for very uninteresting tales.

When Jonah got his first speeding ticket, he was visibly upset. But when we

---

13   Warning: Proud parent here. Jonah did reapply to CU Boulder again. I have never seen him more determined to achieve anything. He spent a month working on his entrance essay (I provided only very superficial feedback), and he was accepted with an academic scholarship.

There is another postscript to this story. After Jonah was accepted to CU Boulder, the world was hit by the coronavirus pandemic. Jonah realized that if he went to CU Boulder, he'd be taking classes online and not getting to enjoy dorm life. This was not part of his childhood dream. Jonah did the Jonah thing. He enrolled for online classes at the local community college. The money he saved on CU Boulder tuition he used to go to Hawaii for a few months with three of his close friends. The beauty of online learning was that he was able to both surf and take classes from 3,000 miles away. The next semester the CU Boulder campus was still closed. Jonah continued taking classes at the community college, lived at home, and skied almost every day. He maintained a perfect GPA.

In fall 2021 the CU Boulder campus reopened. Jonah transferred his community college credits and enrolled in his childhood dream school.

It may be redundant of me, but I'd like to stress a very important point. When CU Boulder initially rejected him, he was devastated. At that point, going to community college seemed liked a nightmare. A year later he chose (twice!) to go to community college. What before seemed horrifying turned into a dream come true. The difference between a nightmare and a dream come true is that Jonah *chose* to go to community college. Life will throw adversity at us. If we behave like victims, we'll be destined to have a miserable, sorry life. If we decide to *choose* adversity, the color of life will change.

discussed it, he was not upset at the $200 he had to pay with his own (earned) money (part of our agreement when he got the car) but because, in his words, "Getting this ticket was so boring and uneventful. There was no drama. I got no story to tell." I am only slightly sad that he did not get a story out of this speeding ticket, but I am proud that he was looking for a story.

Misadventures give us the opportunity to turn (reframe) them into stories where we are the heroes, and thus to be a good hero we should behave like one. Life gives us plenty of chances to be the heroes in our stories.

Life often will not go according to our plan. If it always did, it would be boring. Things will happen to us. We may initially perceive them as bad, but remember, *bad* is just how we choose to frame something, and most of the time it is in our power to reframe it.[14]

Seneca said, "A good person dyes events with his own color ... and turns whatever happens to his own benefit."

---

14 Stoics would say all the time. I, personally, have a hard time reframing the death of a loved one.

Temporary Insanity

HADRIAN WAS THE Roman emperor who preceded Marcus. In one of his angry spells, Hadrian poked out the eye of a poor slave. Once he came back to his senses, Hadrian asked the slave if there was anything he could do for him. The slave said, "All I want is my eye back."[15]

Though anger is just another emotion, the Stoics singled it out because the damage it can do often cannot be undone.

Marcus writes, "How much more harmful are the consequences of anger... than the circumstances that aroused them in us."

The venom generated by anger, when allowed to spill into others, is always followed by regret. We get angry because we feel we've been harmed – anger is an emotional shortcut to communicate our frustration. However, if your goal is to be master of yourself, anger is the easiest way to derail that goal as you give an outsider free rein to run your kingdom.

Seneca calls anger "temporary insanity." When we are angry, we temporarily lose control over what we say and what we do. We lose the ability to think clearly. We hurt people – often people we love. I cannot stand the angry version of myself. When I am angry, I feel like an imposter has taken over my body.

There is also another anger. At times we deliberately use anger as an

---

15   D. Robertson, *How to Think Like a Roman Emperor* (St. Martin's Publishing Group), p. 83.

expedient shortcut to secure a desired result. For instance, we use anger to express our discontent with the rental car company that screws up our reservation, hoping that will lead to an upgrade. Seneca, in his book, *On Anger*, argues that you should not use anger in this way: "The best plan is to reject straightway the first incentives to anger, to resist its very beginnings, and to take care not to be betrayed into it: For if once it begins to carry us away, it is hard to get back again into a healthy condition, because reason goes for nothing when once passion has been admitted to the mind and has by our own free will been given a certain authority. It will for the future do as much as it chooses, not only as much as you will allow it."

In other words, anger is like a wild beast that ultimately you cannot control. You think you can, but every time you intentionally use anger as a tool you give up a little bit of control, and eventually the beast turns on you.

Seneca also argues: "Anger has no ground to stand upon, and does not rise from a firm and enduring foundation, but is a windy, empty quality, as far removed from true magnanimity as foolhardiness from courage... anger brings about nothing grand or beautiful."

Anger is a negative emotion, but it is a negative emotion on steroids. If a garden-variety negative emotion is a wave, anger may reach the proportion of a tsunami. Stoics saw the distinction and addressed anger separately. Seneca wrote a full book dedicated to it, entitled *On Anger*.

The EJR framework may or may not be useful when anger threatens to strike, depending on the time available for judgment between event and reaction. If you manage to conquer yourself and have time for judgment, then you may be able to treat anger just like any other negative emotion. You also have the dichotomy of control framework (and other frameworks we have discussed) at your disposal – you cannot control the outside world, but you can control how you respond to it.

Seneca believes that doing nothing is the best course when you are possessed by anger. He writes, "While you are angry, you ought not to be allowed to do anything. 'Why?' you ask? Because when you are angry there is nothing that you do not wish to be allowed to do." Marcus agrees: "The best answer to anger is silence."

A good thing about anger is that you usually don't stay angry for long. When we are angry, we just need to buy time. Count to... whatever it takes.

Twenty-five years ago, I would not have needed to write this, but in the 1990s, if you were angry at someone, you had to use a landline to make a phone call, and you might or might not have reached that person. It took time, often enough time for you to calm down. Today, everyone has a mobile phone in their pocket, and you are a few seconds away from letting the beast destroy a relationship.

Today, you can also destroy your career and reputation by replying to an email or posting on digital media while angry. I have a rule not to respond to emails, texts, phone calls, or posts on social media while angry.

Once you come off the peak of anger, Marcus has a lot of advice for you. In *Meditations*, Marcus provides a number of strategies to deal with anger. In *How to Think Like a Roman Emperor,* a wonderful book, Donald Robertson, a psychologist by training, unwraps them for us.

We are social animals designed to help each other. We should accept meeting people who we know will push our buttons. If it were not for them, our lives would be boring – we should look at these interactions as our "Stoic quizzes." I often remind myself that one of my values is to leave the world a better place than I found it. My reacting angrily to people I don't especially like or agree with doesn't help with that.

Consider a person's character as a whole. Imagine people that offend you living their daily lives – eating dinner, driving their cars, sleeping in their beds, etc. Once you consider them as a whole, it is harder to get angry with them. If it's a person you know well, a person close to you, remind yourself of the good moments you've had with that person.

Nobody does wrong willingly. Marcus writes, "You should view others' actions in terms of a simple dichotomy: Either they are doing what is right or doing what is wrong. If they are doing what is right, then you should accept it and cease to be annoyed with them. Let go of your anger and learn from them. However, if they are doing what is wrong, then you should assume it's because they don't know any better."

Marcus says that whenever you believe someone has wronged you, you should first consider what underlying opinions they hold about what's right and wrong. Once you really understand their thinking, you'll have no excuse for being surprised at their actions, which should naturally weaken your feelings of anger.[16]

Nobody is perfect, yourself included. Remind yourself how many

---

16   D. Robertson, *How to Think Like a Roman Emperor* (St. Martin's Publishing Group), p. 236.

times you were wrong. When someone cuts me off while driving, before I get out my weapon of choice (the middle finger), I remind myself that I too am guilty of bad driving at times. If I allow myself to express anger at that person, I should be angry at myself first for all the times I did the same thing to other people.

It's madness to expect others to be perfect. Do we really expect to go through life and only meet perfect individuals living in perfect bliss? Life happens. We should not be surprised that we'll meet good people on their bad days or bad people on their average days. That's life; we should be prepared for it. Marcus believed that in reality someone who is capable of exercising gentleness and kindness in the face of provocation is stronger and more courageous than one who gives in to their anger.

We cannot be certain of other people's motives. Start with the assumption that people are not evil and go from there. Anger assumes an unwarranted certainty about the motives of other people. Donald Robertson explains that cognitive therapists call this the fallacy of *mind-reading* – leaping to conclusions about other people's motives although they are always somewhat veiled from us. You should always remain open to the possibility that the other person's intentions are not in the wrong. Consider that other plausible interpretations of their actions exist. Keeping an open mind will help you dilute your feelings of anger.

My wife is an eldest child; she has a younger sister and brother. Her father always wanted to have a son, but he got two great daughters first and then, when he got a son, the kid was treated like a little prince. My wife always harbored a slight feeling of jealousy toward her brother, as he was spoiled rotten by their father.

Ten years or so ago, our house was being repainted and we moved into my in-laws' house while they were on vacation. My wife and I were staying in her parents' bedroom. The first day we were there, I walked into the bedroom and found my wife sitting on the bed very upset, on the verge of crying. What happened? I asked. She said, "See this painting on the windowsill? My brother painted it when he was eight. It is not a very good painting. I painted so many paintings that are better than this, and I don't see any of them here." I told her that her parents love her dearly. How could they not? I set the painting on a nearby dresser.

A few hours later we went to sleep. I was awakened by a light shining right into my face. Then I realized what had happened. When it gets dark, the streetlight comes on and shines right through the window. That painting by my wife's brother was on the windowsill to block the light from the street. I don't think my in-laws even paid attention to what painting it was and who painted it; they just needed a large object to block the light. After I told my wife about my revelation, we had a good laugh.

Don't assume the worst.

Remember, we will all die. Remind yourself that you and the person you are angry with will eventually die. This will put your anger in the right, temporal, transitory perspective.

It is our judgment that upsets us. Here we go again with Epictetus's dichotomy of control. Marcus writes, "If you are distressed by anything external, the pain is not due to the thing itself but due to your estimate of it, and this you have the power to revoke at any moment."

Anger does more harm than good. Buddha said, "Holding on to anger is like grasping a hot coal with the intent of throwing it at someone else; you are the one getting burned." Marcus reminds himself that the vice of another man cannot penetrate your character unless you allow it to do so. Ironically, anger does the most harm to the person experiencing it, although he has the power to stop it.[17]

Nature gave us virtues to deal with anger. This one is my favorite. When someone sends me an email that offends me, once the anger inside me subsides, I smother that person with kindness and politeness, often disarming him *and* myself. It is very difficult to be angry at another person when you are extra nice to him. I really look at such moments as Stoic quizzes, and it is amazing to see how kindness transforms both the other person and you.

I'll wrap up with this recommendation from Warren Buffett:[18] "You can always tell someone to go to hell tomorrow."

Share this chapter with a friend:
https://soulinthegame.net/ezp/

---

17   D. Robertson, *How to Think Like a Roman Emperor* (St. Martin's Publishing Group), p. 242.
18   Buffett was quoting Tom Murphy, former CEO of Capital Cities/ABC.

Each Day Is a Separate Life

W E ARE HORRIBLE with our time. Our initial reaction is to blame it on Netflix and Facebook. I get it – but at the same time, I don't. Seneca lived almost 2,000 years ago. Then, pictures of friends were carved in stone, not posted to Instagram. History was written in real time in the Roman Colosseum so it could later be dramatized on Netflix. But even then, according to Seneca's first letter in the book *Moral Letters,* "The largest portion of our life passes while we are doing ill, a goodly share while we are doing nothing, and the whole while we are doing that which is not to the purpose."

Even then, Seneca was really upset about how people wasted their time: "What man can you show me who places any value on his time, who reckons the worth of each day, who understands that he is dying daily? For we are mistaken when we look forward to death; the major portion of death has already passed. Whatever years lie behind us are in death's hands."

His advice: "Hold every hour in your grasp. Lay hold of today's task, and you will not need to depend so much upon tomorrow's. While we are postponing, life speeds by."

Think about this when you waste your next hour on cat videos on Facebook: "Nothing is ours, except time. We were entrusted by nature with the ownership of this single thing, so fleeting and slippery that anyone who can will oust us from possession."

Seneca struggled with managing his time, too, and he admits it: "I cannot boast that I waste nothing, but I can at least tell you what I am wasting, and the cause and manner of the loss..."

And this is the part I really want my kids to read. Seneca writes:

"I advise you, however, to keep what is really yours; and you cannot begin too early."

After reading Seneca, it is impossible not to want to retake control of the most important, irreplaceable gift you are given as a birthright – time. But how do you do this? I borrowed my practical solution from Seneca: "Begin at once to live and count each separate day as a separate life."

"Each separate day as a separate life." What a brilliant idea. A life bookended by sunrise and sunset. A day is a perfect, meaningful measuring unit. I can look at each day and evaluate how I spent it. If I achieve mostly perfect days, then they'll spill into a perfect life.

Every January most of us set New Year's resolutions. Though we don't think about it that way, we really treat each year as Seneca's separate life. Except that a year is so long that we forget about our New Year's resolutions by March.

Each day as a separate life has many advantages. Every single day you have feedback that allows you to make micro course corrections. It focuses you on process versus outcome. If you want to lose weight, instead of setting a New Year's resolution to lose 30 pounds, set daily resolutions – eat so many calories per day, exercise so many minutes per day, etc. (I can see that setting a goal to exercise so many days a week may be better, and that is okay.) None of us knows how long we have been given on this Earth. But I am certain we will be given more days than years.

The perfect day doesn't depend on stoplights turning green on my way to work, or a rental car company giving me the car I ordered, or great weather, or the people I come in contact with bending to my will. Epictetus provides great guidance here: "Don't hope that events will turn out the way you want; welcome events in whichever way they happen: this is the path to peace."

This gives you an opportunity to live this day as if it was your last (and one day it will be). Imagine if this day was your last day. What would you pay more attention to (your loved ones) and what would you pay less attention to (a rental car mix-up)?

The goal is not to change our activities but to change our state of mind as we carry out those activities. You don't want to stop thinking about or planning for tomorrow; instead, as you think about tomorrow, remember to appreciate today.[19] Or as Seneca puts it, "Hurry up and live."

At the end of each day, as the sun sets, I evaluate the day.

Did I spend my time wisely on good problems? When I was with my family and friends, was I present; did I pay attention to them? Was I kind? Did I leave the world better than I found it? If life presented Stoic quizzes (red stoplights, rental car problems etc.), did I pass them? How close did I come to practicing tranquility in motion? (I'll discuss this in a bit.) Did I interrupt any habits I am establishing? Did I incur any new bad habits? (I am looking for a pattern here. Ordering nachos twice in a row could be the beginning of a new bad habit.)

This brings me to the daily journal. We can examine our *separate life* at the end of each day.

Here is what Seneca wrote: "When the light has been removed and my wife has fallen silent, aware of this habit that's now mine, I examine my entire day and go back over what I've done and said."[20]

He took this opportunity to reexamine that day's life, see if he made mistakes, forgive himself for these mistakes, and prescribe himself a corrective course of action. "I conceal nothing from myself, I pass nothing by. I have nothing to fear from my errors when I can say: 'See that you do not do this anymore. For the moment, I excuse you.'"

Reviewing your day presents an opportunity to learn from your mistakes and correct them. For instance, today I debated politics with a friend for an hour. As I look at that hour, the time was completely wasted, and I won't get it back. Neither of us changed the mind of the other. In fact, we got a little bit annoyed with each other. The next time the topic of politics comes up, I should let my friend speak his mind and not offer a rebuttal, hoping that the conversation will take a better turn. If it doesn't, I'll let him know that I don't talk politics.

Daily journaling – in the morning, evening, or both – can be a life-changing habit. In addition to being a record of your day and thus your life, the journal provides a canvas for self-reflection and self-examination. I promise you it is a lot cheaper than a therapist. It is a safe place for you to be honest with yourself.

---

19   W. Irvine, *A Guide to the Good Life* (Oxford University Press), p. 71.

20   "The Art of Journaling," Daily Stoic.

Just like meditation, it allows you to identify and address thoughts that are spinning around in your subconscious.

This has another benefit: If you do this before you go to sleep, you'll sleep better (it worked for me).

Seneca was not the only Stoic who kept a diary. Most of what we know about Marcus came from a personal diary he wrote to himself, which he called *Meditations*. This was a safe place for Marcus to have a conversation with himself – being an emperor is a very hazardous occupation.

How much to write? Do your best. If you struggle, one sentence may be enough. Just as in creating any new habit, consistency is more important than quantity or even quality.

You can also use your daily journal to time travel. Penn Jillette of Penn & Teller started keeping a journal when he was 30, and at the time he felt that it was already too late to start. He has kept the journal for 35 years without skipping a day. Every day he writes about important conversations he's had, and reviews books he's read and movies he's watched. He writes about things that happened that day. But most importantly, he looks at what he wrote a year, ten years, and 20 years ago on that day.

As Socrates said, "The unexamined life is not worth living."

Share this chapter with a friend:
https://soulinthegame.net/nxj/

What Others Think

WE ARE SOCIAL animals, programmed to care what other people think of us. Marcus is bemused by this: "It never ceases to amaze me: We all love ourselves more than other people, but care more about their opinion than our own."

Epictetus writes, "Never depend on the admiration of others. There is no strength in it. Personal merit cannot be derived from an external source. It is not to be found in your personal associations, nor can it be found in the regard of other people. It is a fact of life that other people, even people who love you, will not necessarily agree with your ideas, understand you, or share your enthusiasms. Grow up! Who cares what other people think about you!"

Richard Feynman, Nobel laureate physicist, said, "You have no responsibility to live up to what other people think you ought to accomplish. I have no responsibility to be like they expect me to be. It's their mistake, not my failing."

Again, it comes down to dichotomy of control. We really cannot control what other people think of us. Therefore, if you put a lot of weight on what they think, you'll always be trying to satisfy elusive ideals of others, which are a moving target. This will bring you a lot of disappointment and anguish. We should live according to our own values and judge ourselves based on those values.

Warren Buffett – as I keep discovering – in addition to being the Oracle of Omaha, is also a Stoic from Nebraska; and he agrees with Epictetus on dichotomy of control: "The big question about how people behave is whether they've got an Inner Scorecard or an Outer Scorecard. It helps if you can be satisfied with an Inner Scorecard."

But the Stoic of Nebraska doesn't stop there; he takes it up a notch: "Would you rather be the world's greatest lover, but have everyone think you're the world's worst lover? Or would you rather be the world's worst lover but have everyone think you're the world's greatest lover?"

I'll let Marcus deliver the punch line: "If any man despises me, that is his problem. My only concern is not doing or saying anything deserving of contempt."

Insults

O N THE ROAD of life we sometimes encounter people bearing pernicious gifts: Insults. Insults are really just people's thoughts expressed in a way that offends us.

Insults, as we all know, can trigger negative emotions, including anger. If we succeed at training ourselves to deflect them in the event phase, even before we reach the judgment state, then we'll reduce negative emotions.

Stoics, of course, have plenty to offer in this department, too.

This is the dichotomy of control at its core. Epictetus opines: "If someone tried to take control of your body and make you a slave, you would fight for freedom. Yet how easily you hand over your mind to anyone who insults you. When you dwell on their words and let them dominate your thoughts, you make them your master."

We cannot control what other people think or say; insults from others are outside of our control. Marcus says, "You have power over your mind – not outside events. Realize this, and you will find strength."

Insults are just words to which we give meaning; we have the freedom to interpret them any way our Stoic mind desires. Epictetus explains: "Remember that the person who taunts or hits you does not insult you, but your opinion about these things as being insulting does. So whenever somebody upsets you, know that it is your own opinion that upsets you. Accordingly, first strive to not be carried away by the appearance. For if you take the time and pause, it is easier to control yourself."

I write, and my writings are read by hundreds of thousands. I get criticized and insulted plenty. If I let insults get to me, I would have quit a long time ago.

We need to consider the source of the insult or criticism. Don't take criticism from someone you wouldn't take advice from.[21] Or, as Epictetus put it, "If they are wise, do not quarrel with them; if they are fools, ignore them." I'd add, they don't have to be a complete idiot – just unversed when it comes to the subject at hand.

Here is another example. My wife has never skied a day in her life; she hasn't ever taken a ski lesson. But that doesn't stop her from giving skiing advice to my kids when we watch their skiing on home videos. I smile.

Stoics recommend responding to insults with self-deprecating humor. Seneca writes, "No one becomes a laughingstock who laughs at himself." Epictetus adds, "If someone speaks badly of you, do not defend yourself against the accusations, but reply, 'You obviously don't know about my other vices, otherwise you would have mentioned those as well.'"

Seneca has a suggestion for us less witty ones: ignore the insult. "It is a sort of revenge to rob the man who has sought to inflict an insult of the pleasure of having done so. 'Oh dear me!' he will say, 'I suppose he didn't understand.'" Here is the punch line: "Thus the success of an insult depends upon the sensitiveness and the indignation of the victim." By ignoring the insulter, we devalue him, which is an even greater insult in itself – an Aikido master type of response.

Marcus sums up the most important thing we need to keep in mind when we are insulted: "The best revenge is not to be like your enemy."

---

21   I read this somewhere but cannot remember the source.

In Beta

SOFTWARE DEVELOPERS HAVE a concept called the beta version (or *in beta*) – a software program that is almost ready for prime time but still has some bugs to be identified and fixed. That is how I look at myself; I'm perpetually *in beta*.

This *in beta* attitude is liberating, as it gives you the chance to constantly improve yourself; to learn and grow. This doesn't mean that you need to be buried in self-help books. You just need to have this *in beta* (student of life) attitude.

We are constantly given opportunities to learn, not just from books (which are an incredible source of wisdom and role models), but, as Ralph Waldo Emerson said, "In my walks, every man I meet is my superior in some way, and in that I learn from him." We can learn from our friends, acquaintances, and even people we've never met.

Let me give you a few examples.

My brother Alex and I were in Dallas, Texas for a day and had the pleasure of spending four hours with John Mauldin. John is an economist, a thinker, and an incredible writer. He has written a dozen books and pens a newsletter read by millions. Unlike most financial writers, he writes with incredible warmth – you feel as if he is writing just to you. He is never boring and likes to share glimpses of his life.

There are two things I've learned from John that have had a long-lasting impact on me.

First, he is authentic. The John you like through his writing is the real John.

Yes, the real John is not as well-polished as the writer John – very few writers are. He may speak with a slow Texas drawl – and print destroys accents (believe you me)! – but it is impossible to fake the real you in print when you write once a week for years. John takes complex, often boring, economic concepts and reveals them through stories you can relate to. He treats writing as a continuous conversation with his readers; therefore people who have read him for years feel they know him. John had a tremendous impact on me as a writer.

The second thing I learned from John on that visit in Dallas: Be kind to everyone, all the time. John treats you like you're the most important person in the world to him. I felt very special being around him. I noticed that this is his default behavior. Our visit with him started in John's apartment in downtown Dallas and continued in a three-hour conversation in a bar at a nearby hotel.

When John and I walked into the bar, he gave a warm smile and a hello to every person in our path. When he talked to the waiter, it was as though he'd known him all his life. He committed 100% of himself to that conversation.

Comparing my behavior, when I talk to waiters, my mind is often elsewhere. I sometimes look at a waiter and don't actually see him or her. I've caught myself a few times being unable to describe the waiter I just talked to. John, on the other hand, is totally into whomever he's talking to at the moment, and the person can sense it. When I interact with other people, I ask myself, "How would John do this?"[22]

As Seneca puts it: "Wherever there is a human being, there is an opportunity for a kindness."

---

22 How someone treats a waiter tells a lot about a person. When I interview people for a job at IMA, at times I take them to lunch and ask a waiter to mix up their order. Then I carefully observe their reaction. If they talk down to a waiter, then they'll treat their subordinates the same way.

My 19-year-old son Jonah worked as a caddy at Cherry Hills Country Club in Denver for a few years, a very ritzy golf club in Denver. Here is what Jonah told me about his experience there: "Being someone's servant is not what I want to do. But I learn how to deal with different people – a skill that is going to be important for me in life. At times I meet interesting people, and quite often I learn how to interact with drunken a-holes. I look forward to every trip around the course because I am curious what kind of people I'm going to meet. If I meet an interesting person, I'll learn something good from him. If it's a drunken a-hole – it is going be a learning experience on how to handle them. Being on the receiving side of this, I have learned how to treat and not treat other people, especially when they are below you in social status." There is a lot I can learn from my son, too.

Another writer, Ben Thompson, writes a technology newsletter with the funky name *Stratechery*, which I read daily. I learned from Ben to be your own harshest critic. When you write daily, you'll spew out a lot of opinions and analysis. You won't always be right. Ben constantly goes back to his past analysis and brutally points out his faults. When I find a flaw in my past writing or thinking, I ask myself, "What would Ben do?"

Then there's Ian Bremmer, who runs the Eurasia Group political risk research and consulting firm. There are two things I have learned from Ian. First, he constantly seeks out people he disagrees with so he can learn from them. Second, he has the ability to approach every issue without pre-existing bias. When I analyze a political topic and I notice my bias (hard not to in politics), I ask myself, "How would Ian approach this?"

You are an average of your five closest friends.[23] The people you surround yourself with will either pull you up or sink you to their level. Seneca warns that vices are contagious. They spread, quickly and unnoticed, from those who have them to those with whom they come into contact.[24] I've been careful and lucky to surround myself with friends who elevate me.

There is always something we can learn from our friends. Each of my good friends has qualities I'd like to copy.

My friends Darren and Matt are both nonjudgmental and incredibly positive people. I call Darren the Moses of Denver, and Matt the Jesus of Seattle (for quasi-religious and geographic reasons). They never allow themselves to speak negatively of others; rather, they go out of their way to find neutral words to describe negative qualities in other people. This positivity colors their personalities. As Marcus says, "Your soul takes on the color of your thoughts." When negative thoughts about others come to me, I ask myself, "What would Darren or Matt do?"

My friend Barry is always calm and logical with his kids. Chris is constantly trying to self-improve. For Daniel and Jeff, the world outside ceases to exist when they are with their kids. Ethan is in complete control of his emotions (he'd make Epictetus proud). Alan cares deeply about people in need. We had dinner at a restaurant in Tel Aviv, and we had some bread left over. Alan asked for a to-go bag. On our walk to our hotel, he found a homeless person to give

23   Google says this saying is attributed to the motivational speaker Jim Rohn.
24   W. Irvine, *A Guide to the Good Life* (Oxford University Press), p. 135.

this bread to. I can keep going, but hopefully you get the point. There is a lot we can learn from our friends, so we should choose them carefully and pay attention to what we can learn from them.

You can also learn what *not* to do from your friends and others. There is a person I have great admiration for as a thinker. But he has another side: When people disagree with him or he perceives they have wronged him, he eviscerates them in public, then continues to stomp them into dust. On the one hand, he is a source of incredible wisdom, and on the other, he teaches me how not to behave. He would benefit from Warren Buffett's advice: "Praise in public, criticize by category."

Of course, my most important teacher is my father, and you see glimpses of his wisdom in various stories throughout this book. Every time I face a really difficult situation, I ask myself, "What would my father do?"

The Stoics were *in beta*. Marcus' *Meditations* were continuous reflections of lessons he learned from others and from life. Seneca continued to write, and thus to learn, well into his old age.

Never behave as if you've reached the prime time; always be *in beta* or, as Seneca wrote: "As long as you live, keep learning how to live."

Go Ahead, Covet Your Neighbor's Wife

I HAD A DEEP, existential, meaning-of-life type of conversation with a friend of mine, another value investor. I asked him, "Do you want Warren Buffett's success?"

He was somewhat stunned by the question, and asked: "Is that a rhetorical question?"

It was not.

I told him about a nugget of Jewish wisdom my wife shared with me. But first, let's revisit one of the Ten Commandments: Don't covet. Or more precisely, don't covet your neighbor's wife. To be even more precise, I am not talking about outright adultery here, but rather about thoughts you may have about the desirability of your neighbor's wife. And to make it even clearer: Not *my* neighbor's wife (I don't want my neighbor reading this and getting any ideas).

Here is that practical Jewish wisdom (severely paraphrased by me). Go ahead and covet your neighbor's wife, but don't just covet her beautiful eyes, her soft voice, and her stunning figure. Covet her in her entirety. Don't forget about her mother who would insist you kiss her on the lips every time you see her and who loves to dispense unlimited quantities of unsolicited advice. Or her brother, who needs to get bailed out of jail every other week. Don't forget about the hours that the neighbor's wife spends in front of the mirror (forgetting about her hubby and the kids).

Covet away! But covet the whole package. The antidote to coveting is holistic coveting.

So when you covet Buffett's success, do it holistically, too. Not just the empire he built and the billions he accumulated (that he'll give away anyway), but also the life he led. When I read Alice Schroeder's *The Snowball,* the main point I got out of the book was *not* to be like Buffett. I was lucky I read it when my kids were still young. Buffett's obsession with the stock market was anything but healthy. He got tomorrow's newspaper delivered to him the evening before. He spent every living moment in his study, completely neglecting his wife and children. His wife, the love of his life, could not take this anymore and left him. So, do you still covet what Buffett has?

Would Buffett have achieved the degree of financial success that he has without sacrificing his marriage or neglecting his children? We will never have an answer to this question. Maybe he could have, but he would have been a billionaire with a small *b* and would not have the global adulation that came with his capital *B* wealth.

My gut sense tells me (though I could be completely wrong) that if he was given a do-over and could make some changes to his earlier life, Buffett would not choose to change something about his investing approach – for example, embracing investing in tech companies earlier in his career (he only made first significant investment in a tech company when he was in his 80s) – but he would tweak how much attention he paid to his wife and kids.

We have a lot of power within us to get rid of suffering if we make the decision not to want the wrong things. This message constantly resonates through Stoic philosophy and Seneca explained it perfectly: "No person has the power to have everything they want, but it is in their power not to want what they don't have, and to cheerfully put to good use what they do have."

The bright side of coveting

Coveting is a lot less interesting to me than its more toxic cousin, envy. Envy is coveting (desiring) what another person has *and then* resenting the person for that. Envy poisons people's lives. But if we learn how not to covet, we may be able to kill envy in its tracks.

Buffett nailed it when he said, "As an investor, you get something out of all the deadly sins – except for envy. Being envious of someone else is pretty stupid. Wishing them badly, or wishing you did as well as they did – all it does is ruin your day. Doesn't hurt them at all, and there's zero upside to it."

Charlie Munger made an interesting contribution on the topic of envy:

Mozart ... here's the greatest musical talent maybe that ever lived. And what was his life like? It was bitterly unhappy, and he died young. That's the life of Mozart. What the hell did Mozart do to screw it up? Two things that are guaranteed to create a lot of misery – he overspent his income scrupulously – that's number one. That is really stupid. And that other thing was, his life was full of jealousies and resentments. If you overspend your income and be full of jealousy and resentments, you can have a lousy, unhappy life and die young. All you've got to do is learn from Mozart.

Stoics have an interesting approach to coveting (and thus envy). They apply Epictetus' dichotomy of control to it. The neighbor's wife and Buffett's wealth are externals (actually, Buffett's wealth would fall into *positive preference*: nice to have but not necessary).

But this is where things get interesting. Stoics would recommend that you look at Buffett and desire his virtues that you admire – make them internals (echoing our discussion in "In Beta"). I just talked about what I have learned from Buffett's mistakes, but there is so much more I've learned from him.

Here are just a few examples.

The newspaper test. How would you feel about any given action if you knew it was going to be written up the next day in the newspaper? Reputation takes a lifetime to build and five minutes to lose. In other words, always behave honorably. Always!

Buffett's definition of *success* (he probably came to it later in life). Behave in a way that makes people you care about love you. He said, "If you get to my age in life and nobody thinks well of you, I don't care how big your bank account is, your life is a disaster."

Buffett has a friend who survived the Holocaust. When she looks at people, she only asks one question: Would they hide me? Buffett said, "When you are 70 and you look back at your life, and you have a lot of people who would hide you, then you'll have had a very successful life."

"Praise by name, criticize by category." I mentioned in a previous chapter that you'll never hear Buffett speak negatively about anyone in public, and at the same time he is generous with his public praise of specific individuals.

Buffett had a tremendous impact on me as a writer (I discuss this in "On Writing"). And of course, he had an immense impact on me and millions of others as an investor.

Seneca was a big believer in internalizing qualities of people you respect: "Choose someone whose way of life as well as words, and whose very face as mirroring the character that lies behind it, have won your approval. Be always pointing him out to yourself either as your guardian or as your model. This is a need, in my view, for someone as a standard against which our characters can measure themselves. Without a ruler to do it against you won't make the crooked straight."

The False
Sophistication
of Sophists

I N ANCIENT GREECE and Rome, parents took their kids to study oratory skills from teachers called Sophists (the word *sophisticated* has *sophist* in its root). Sophists focused on the art of persuasion through *both* emotion and reason, and kids were taught to argue both sides of an argument. Stoics, on the other hand, put the emphasis mainly on reason (not emotions) in their communications.

The Sophist's oratory skill was like a spear; it was a powerful weapon that could be used for good or for evil. Thus students needed morality taught by philosophy to know where to point it.[25]

Stoics were extremely cautious about the Sophists – they thought the words you use to persuade others matter, since in persuading others you may impact your own thinking.[26] In the attempt to persuade others through an appeal to their emotions, we use colorful metaphors; we dramatize the words we use. If we had two brains, one to talk to others and one to talk to ourselves, we'd be

---

25   W. Irvine, *A Guide to the Good Life* (Oxford University Press), p. 21.

26   D. Robertson, *How to Think Like a Roman Emperor* (St. Martin's Publishing Group), p. 70.

fine. But that is not the case; thus our words may turn on us and impact our own emotional state.

It is almost as though Stoics would not want to use the colors available in the rainbow to express their opinions, but resort only to black and white. However, I see the value of their thinking. We need to examine the words we use when we communicate with ourselves. When something stirs up negative emotions inside us, we need to be careful when we describe the problem to ourselves. We want to make sure we are not being Sophists against ourselves.

The best way to do this is to write it out. When you lay each word on the paper, examine it. Instead of "My husband drives me insane," write, "My husband says the following ... that upsets me." (I am not quoting from my wife's journal; I am reading her mind.)

Instead of "The stock market collapsed," write, "The stock market declined X%." Epictetus said something along the same lines. Instead of saying "Our ship is lost far at sea; we'll never get home," he suggested we go with, "We are at sea, and we don't know where we are."

We take fancy words, string them together, and add dramatic, superfluous colors. Instead of calling a dish, "Basil Honey-Glazed Wild Alaskan Salmon," Marcus might suggest we describe it as "the dead body of a fish, with herbs and honey." He writes, "where there are things which appear worthiest of our approval, we should lay them bare and look at their worthlessness and strip them of all the words by which they are exalted."

We need to pull the fancy outer layer off our problems and strip them to their bones. Instead of "My life is horrible," create a list of things in your life that bother you, spelling them out as plainly as possible (don't use big, colorful words; leave those for the Sophists).

Here is an example of breaking things down. I was a sophomore in college; I was taking five or six classes and had a full-time job and a full-time (more like overtime) girlfriend. I was approaching finals and had to study for lots of tests and turn in assignments; and to make matters worse, I had procrastinated until the last second. I felt overwhelmed and paralyzed.

I whined (I am sure I was using big, colorful Sophist words) to my father about my predicament. His answer was simple: Break up my big problems into smaller ones; create a list and then figure out how to tackle each item separately. It worked.

I listed every assignment and exam, prioritizing them by due date and importance. Suddenly, my problems, which all together looked insurmountable, one by one started to look conquerable. My father didn't have to tell me to use plain English, because my academic problems, broken down to bare facts, didn't even require that; they all simply had due dates.

The beauty of the Stoic advice of reducing our problems by analysis is that our subconscious doesn't sense or understand sarcasm or humor. If you keep telling yourself you're a loser and will never amount to anything (even jokingly), you'll sooner or later be right.

This point is extremely important and has a lot of implications of its own; thus it requires another analogy. Look at the conscious mind as the captain of a ship and the subconscious mind as the ship's engine room. Those in the engine room don't see what the captain sees, and thus if the captain says to go forward, in reverse, to port, or to starboard, they just follow the command without questioning. Is this command good for the ship? The engine room doesn't know, nor does it care. Our subconscious doesn't exercise that judgment.[27] The words you use to talk to yourself matter, so be careful with them.

To illustrate my next point, I'd like to share a story from my favorite book of all time: *Fooled by Randomness,* by Nassim Nicholas Taleb.

Around 155 BC, Athens sent Carneades, a philosopher, to Rome to plead with the Roman Senate for a favor. Athens had been levied a fine by the Romans, which Athens desperately wanted removed. Carneades delivered a brilliant speech. The audience was swayed by his passionate delivery. However, this was not the message Carneades wanted to convey. He felt the audience had been swayed by his delivery, not by the logic of his brilliant argument.

So the next day, Carneades came back to the same square and delivered another impassioned speech, making the opposite point from the day before. He managed to persuade the audience all over again! Unfortunately for Athens, Cato the Elder was in the audience this time; and enraged at Carneades' oratorical antics, he convinced the Senate to send the ambassador packing.

Though Taleb was trying to make a different point with this story, the lesson I got out of it was: Beware the Sophists. A great speaker can bend logic with emotions and exert undue influence on your decision making.

In my day job, investing, I talk to executives who run the companies we are analyzing. I also listen to dozens of conference calls each month. To become a senior-level executive at a publicly traded company, you need to be a good

---

27   I borrowed this from Joseph Murphy's book, *Beyond the Power of Your Subconscious Mind.*

communicator. After I am done listening to a call or after a conversation with them, I often want to mortgage my house, pawn my wife's car, and turn all our money over to them.

Just to be clear, I don't want to imply that all executives with great oratory skills are frauds – not at all. We just need to have a Sophist filter – we need to reduce the emotional content of their messages down to the core. Remove the emotional content of the message, identify the important points the CEO made, and break them down to their essence. The better someone speaks, the more discriminating your Sophist filter needs to be.

Your Sophist filter should also be on when you deal with cynics. Not the ancient Greek Cynics (with a capital *C*), just plain old cynics; people who paint negative pictures. They always sound smarter than optimists, but they are not always right.

You also want to be aware of arguments made through jokes, especially at the expense of your own argument. By getting people to laugh, your opponent brings them over to their side of the argument. This doesn't make them more right though.

Finally, be careful with people who advertise their virtues of their own volition: "I am honest"; "I never steal." Odds are that by advertising their virtues they are overcompensating for that void in their character. A fellow I know was beating his chest, boasting about the strength of his word and his character. He borrowed a large sum of money from another friend of mine, skipped town, and never paid it back.

I'll let Seneca conclude this discussion: "A sword never kills anybody; it is a tool in the killer's hand."

Share this chapter with a friend:
https://soulinthegame.net/ohr/

Creating Stoic Subroutines in the Subconscious

I WAS ALREADY WORKING on this book when my son Jonah started driving, four years ago. (And if you read later in the book that my daughter Mia Sarah got married, it means one of two things happened. Either it took longer to write the book than I expected, or Mia Sarah fell in love and married a nice Jewish boy at an extraordinarily young age, because she is six as I am typing this.)

Back to Jonah. In the beginning, Jonah's driving was completely managed by his conscious mind. He had to consciously think about how he placed his hands on the wheel and how hard he pushed the gas and brake pedals; he had to pay close attention to the distance between his car and the car in front of him; and he had to look hard for traffic signs.

In the beginning, his conscious mind was so overwhelmed with all the new driving tasks that it couldn't handle any additional ones. A small task like lowering the volume on the radio while he was driving would overwhelm his conscious mind, and the car would start to slip into the adjacent lane.

However, after a month or two, tasks that had been processed solely by Jonah's conscious mind were slowly relegated to his subconscious. He stopped thinking about the gas and brake pedals, the mirrors, his hands on the wheel. The almighty subconscious now processed these tasks with incredible ease, freeing up the conscious mind to change the volume on the stereo or debate with me the choice of music we listen to while he drives.

If we do something long enough, it becomes a routine. Our human operating system acknowledges the superior processing power of the subconscious mind, and when a task becomes routine to the conscious mind, it is offloaded to our subconscious.

If I practice dichotomy of control, EJR, reframing, or negative visualization for long enough, at some point my subconscious will be running the show and I won't have to consciously think about these Stoic techniques.

I have to warn you, it may take a while to change the old subroutines of your subconscious. Often Stoic practices require us to replace an old habit or a behavior we've been doing all our life (unlike Jonah's driving, which was a brand-new activity for him). This remove and replace may require long practice.

Cold (and Warm) Showers

I TAKE COLD SHOWERS. This is not because I am a Russian-born bear, though that is part of it. In their 40s, my father and mother swam in a frozen lake in Murmansk while it was minus 30 degrees Celsius outside. My father copied his father, who swam in the Moscow River in the middle of the Russian winter. I remember hearing a story of my grandpa threatening to divorce my grandma in his late 70s when she hid his swimming trunks. Grandma called him "old fool" in a vain attempt to prevent him from swimming in the sub-zero weather.

I guess that to some degree taking cold showers must be a hereditary activity and I was destined to follow in the "foolish" footsteps of the preceding generations.

I started taking cold showers because I liked how I felt completely refreshed and reborn after them. However, once I started studying Stoic philosophy, I realized that they can also be part of my Stoic exercise.

Let me explain.

Let's divide the process of taking a cold shower into three time periods. First, before you take a shower and are staring at the cold water. Second, the first minute under the cold water, breathing heavily with your heart racing. Third, once your breathing normalizes and you decide how long you choose to stand under the cold water (I usually stay a minute or two). The third part is not important to this discussion, but there are studies (there always are) that cold showers are good for your health.

Let's focus on time periods one and two.

I turn on the cold shower. I am engulfed by fear and hesitation. Fear of what? There is no health risk in being exposed to cold water for a few minutes. This is not skydiving, where the fear of death is at least substantiated by risk, though it's a low-probability one. Nobody gets hypothermia from taking a cold shower.

What I am really afraid of is the temporary discomfort caused by cold water. In fact, I instinctively (automatically) visualize this temporary discomfort. This is where a practicing Stoic looks at this as an opportunity to practice visualization. I visualize how good I am going to feel after I leave the shower. This exercise trains me to replace one visualization with another.

Now I am under the cold, chilling water.

Cold water is an external stressor. During the first minute of taking a shower it is almost like I get an adrenaline injection – my heart races, my body tenses, and I breathe heavily. This is when I train myself to relax. I practice dichotomy of control. An airline losing your bag, a rental car company screwing up your reservation, cold water causing discomfort – they are all externals. How I react is completely up to me – that's internal.

I know I am repeating myself, but this point is very important. Event, judgment, reaction. Event: cold water. Judgment: how I interpret it. Marcus would remove any adjectives and say that rivulets of seven-degrees Celsius water are falling on my body. Reaction: Relax, divert attention to the sound of the water; focus on slowing breathing; focus on finding joy in the experience.

These daily exercises help me to train and develop the skills of negative visualization, Last Time visualization, and putting to work the EJR framework.

After I am done with the cold portion of the shower, as a reward I take a long warm shower. These 15 minutes are important, too. This is when I do my best creative thinking. The sound and feel of the water (and not having access to any electronic gadgets) shift my brain to a different, tinkering track, helping me make mental connections I would otherwise not be able to make. These long showers do wonders for my creativity. (A lot of concepts in this book were born during my long showers.)

If you are still hesitating to take that cold shower, remember what Seneca said: "It is not because things are difficult that we do not dare, it is because we do not dare that they are difficult."

You Want to Be? Do

I WAS OBSESSED WITH the Stoics. I'd go around telling my friends and kids about them. But I could not bring myself to sit down and write about them. I was waiting for motivation. Then I stumbled on a quote by Epictetus that spoke directly to me: "If you wish to be a writer, write."

A popular author, Mark Manson,[28] echoes Epictetus: "Action isn't just the effect of motivation; it's also the cause of it."

I sat down and started working on what you are reading now. The act of writing brought on inspiration, which was then followed by motivation. So instead of motivation being the instigator of action, we need to flip the sequence – action leads to inspiration which leads to motivation.

I discuss the MMU in "I Don't Eat Pork." When it is hard to get into doing something, set the MMU to a very small value. James Clear writes about this in *Atomic Habits,* too. One of his readers, who wanted to start working out, would literally go to the gym for five minutes every day for weeks, just to form a habit. And then he gradually increased his time at the gym.

Setting MMU to a small number helps us overcome inertia and establish a habit. My MMU for this book was just sitting down and writing. This is not an exaggeration – it took four weeks of getting up a few hours before sunrise and a modicum of frustration and self-doubt to get into a flow.

As Yoda said: "Do or do not. There is no try."

---

28 Mark wrote a fantastic book, *The Subtle Art of Not Giving a F*ck*. If you can overcome the "F" word, I highly recommend it. A lot of content here has been influenced by Mark's book.

Stoicism: Part 2 – Values and Goals

THIS SECTION ON values and goals is very dear to me. I've been practicing a lot of the concepts I'll discuss here for years (long before I learned about Stoicism). They have made my life much richer and less anxious. Stoics have helped me put my practices into a wonderful framework.

Values are our internal measuring system. We use them to measure progress toward our goals and to internally interpret whether we are happy. A person who values everything values nothing, thus what we value determines where we focus our thoughts and our energy. This is what we use to measure ourselves against, and thus it is what determines our happiness. Marcus said, "A person's worth is measured by the worth of what he values."

We need to think about what is important to us, and then we'll be able to filter whatever the external environment tries to shove down our throats. We need to be mindful in setting our values and our goals.

Here is a very real example. I run what many would consider a good-sized investment firm in Denver. We are growing; we generate enough revenue to pay our employees and principals well. I don't fly on a private jet, and Warren Buffett doesn't need to worry about being displaced on the *Forbes* list by yours truly, but we are not constrained by any financial resources from doing great investment research and providing excellent customer service for our clients.

Recently I was reading a *Denver Business Journal* article that listed asset management firms in Denver ranked by their size – that is, by assets under management. I noticed that we didn't quite make the cut to be among the top 20 firms *by asset size* in Colorado. I caught myself thinking that it would be nice to boost our assets under management to make that list.

Here is the irony: I didn't know the list existed until I randomly stumbled upon it. If I then added being among the top 20 asset managers in Colorado *by size* as one of my goals, I'd be adding another thing to care about that had absolutely zero calories for me – none! It would add nothing to my happiness and likely subtract from it.

But I had almost let the external environment barge in and set values and goals for me.

More importantly, doing this would contradict my values and my goals – which are focused around building a great firm that I'm proud of. (I discuss this in "Soul in the Game" (on page 26). Paradoxically – and as anti-capitalistic as it may sound – size (assets under management) becomes a secondary factor above a certain threshold.

Unfortunately, we (including yours truly) do this sort of thing all the time. Often mindlessly (on autopilot), we let the external environment set the goals that drive our lives – and bring us eventual disappointment.

Since our values are our internal filtration, evaluation, and measuring system, if we get our values right, then a lot of problems in our lives will take care of themselves. This is the path to happiness.

Before we discuss good values, let's invert and start with the bad ones.

Material Success

Let's start with the most alluring bad value – material success.

> *"Money is not a substitute for tenderness, and power*
> *is not a substitute for tenderness. I can tell you, as*
> *I'm sitting here dying, when you most need it, neither*
> *money nor power will give you the feeling you're*
> *looking for, no matter how much of them you have."*
> – **Morrie Schwartz, *Tuesdays with Morrie***

MY FAMILY AND I were vacationing in Ft. Lauderdale. My older kids and I took a boat out to go snorkeling. As we were cruising through the intercoastal waterway, the captain of the boat would point to a fancy house or a yacht and tell us how much this or that celebrity paid for it and when. There we were, passing the house where Al Pacino lived when he was filming a movie; there was Steven Spielberg's yacht; there was a mansion owned by windshield wiper magnates (I kid you not). None of these mansions were architectural marvels, and these people had not landed on the moon or cured cancer.

The captain was doing his job, and in playing his role as he was reciting price tags, you could hear notes of admiration in his voice. All I was thinking during this tour was that he was sending the wrong message to my kids, who were absorbing all this with their eyes and ears wide open. They were getting the typical message that you encounter not just on a boat tour in South Florida but on any TV channel: Money and things equal happiness. After we got back on land we discussed this, and I told them what I'm about to tell you (without ever mentioning the word *Stoics*).

The Stoics viewed money as an external advantage. The goal, however, is not to acquire as many external advantages as possible but to use them wisely.[29] When we think of wealth, the word that usually comes to mind is *more*. But the Stoics flipped traditional wisdom upside down: Their insight is that (once our basic needs are satisfied) the easiest way to create wealth is to want less.

Epictetus said, "Wealth consists not in having great possessions, but in having few wants." And, "He is a wise man who does not grieve for the things which he has not, but rejoices for those which he has." (I discuss this topic in greater detail in "Personal Finance Advice That Changed My Life.")

After we meet our basic needs, more money brings little incremental happiness.

Ray Dalio, billionaire, who runs the largest hedge fund in the world, wrote the following in his book, *Principles:*

Having the basics – a good bed to sleep in, good relationships, good food, and good sex – is most important, and those things don't get much better when you have a lot of money or much worse when you have less. And the people one meets at the top aren't necessarily more special than those one meets at the bottom or in between.

Being in the investment industry has provided me the interesting opportunity to meet people who have hundreds of millions and even billions of dollars. Their poodles may be getting fancier haircuts; they may drive swankier cars and take posher vacations; but money alone has not brought them hundreds of millions of dollars' worth of happiness.

In fact, I have found that for some of these people money has been more of a curse than a blessing, often because of the constant anxiety involved in growing it. If money is your goal, you'll never have enough. With every additional hundred million or billion, you'll be graduating into a new financial circle occupied by people who have even more.

---

29   D. Robertson, *How to Think Like a Roman Emperor* (St. Martin's Publishing Group), p. 40.

I remember talking to an acquaintance who had built several companies from scratch and assembled a half-billion-dollar nest egg. We were having lunch and he was complaining about how he was stressed and losing sleep over one of his large positions in 30-year US government long-term bonds (he was betting that interest rates would decline). I wasn't sure whether he was treating investing as a game to pass the time, or he desperately wanted to join the billionaires' club. When he asked my advice, I told him to bring the position down to a size where he wouldn't lose sleep over it.

Seneca's advice would help this acquaintance: "It is not the man who has too little, but the man who craves more, that is poor."

I understand the irony of your hearing this story from an investment guy. But just as a sculptor doesn't have to be in love with the rock from which he creates a sculpture, an investment guy doesn't need to be in love with money. It's just a basic material with which I help my clients build their dreams, and provide for their retirement and the college educations of their kids. And yes, some use it to buy intercoastal mansions in South Florida. I don't judge.

I'll let Seneca have the last word here: "If what you have seems insufficient to you, then though you possess the world, you will yet be miserable."

Always Being Right

I WAS SICK WITH the always being right disease for a long time. I am almost cured of it now, but it cost me friends and a girlfriend. Though my relationship with the girlfriend was going downhill for other reasons, I remember that the penultimate moment that led to its collapse was a debate about which is better, tariffs or quotas – I kid you not.

We were both taking macroeconomics classes, though at different universities. I don't remember how this seemingly harmless debate got started, but I could not let it go – I wanted to prove to her that I was right. My ego took over. I don't remember if I convinced her that I was right (probably not), but in trying to win this argument I lost a relationship. There are several issues here.

Again, Epictetus' dichotomy of control comes in handy. We can only control our views. The views of others are external; and thus if we set our goal to change them, we'll dump ourselves into a sea of disappointment and negative emotion.

But even if you win that argument, you lose. You make that person feel inferior. You've injured their pride. They'll resent you. We – and this is the royal we in this case – have to accept the fact that other people don't have to see things the way we do.

An always being right attitude is also contradictory to continuous learning and personal growth. If you always focus on being right, then you'll have a fixed mindset. As Epictetus said, "It is impossible for a man to learn what he thinks he already knows." The best way to not let ego take over is to look at yourself as a student; yes, a student of life.

Finally, you're not going to have many friends if you're a know-it-all. Who wants to be friends with a jerk who has the answers for everything, who never changes their mind, and who isn't interested in learning from you?

Marcus had the right attitude, which I suggest to both you and (especially) the younger me: "If someone can prove me wrong and show me my mistake in any thought or action, I shall gladly change. I seek the truth, which never harmed anyone: The harm is to persist in one's own self-deception and ignorance."

"If This, Then..."

WE SHOULD NOT attach our happiness to "If this, then..." statements. If only I got this job ... this house ... this girl ... then I'd be happy.

Jonathan Haidt, in *The Happiness Hypothesis*, has done a terrific job explaining why "If this, then..." doesn't lead to happiness. First, pleasure comes from the journey (which is often a struggle) toward a goal, not from actually achieving the goal. Arriving at the destination doesn't bring us more pleasure than we get by overcoming micro and macro struggles during the journey itself.

And second, Haidt writes, "The human mind is extraordinarily sensitive to changes in conditions, but not so sensitive to absolute levels." In other words, we adapt. We adapt to bad things and good things. If pleasure is our *core value*, then it will ultimately lead to our unhappiness, because our minds will adapt to each new absolute level of pleasure. And then ... well, we'll need a constant increase in the level of pleasure to stay happy, but each increase of pleasure will make us less and less incrementally happy.

Psychologists call this *hedonic adaptation*, and it has the power to reduce our enjoyment of life.

"If this, then..." thinking is deeply encoded in our human DNA; it is often the default setting for our thinking. In attaching our happiness to externals (things we cannot control), we may find that once we get what we want we may experience a temporary feeling of happiness and *then* find ourselves in hedonic adaptation hell. Logan Pearsall Smith wrote, "There are two things to aim at in life: first, to get what you want; and after that, to enjoy it. Only the wisest of mankind achieve the second."

Practicing negative visualization neutralizes (hedonic) adaptation. William Irvine writes, "One key to happiness, then, is to forestall the [hedonic] adaptation process: We need to take steps to prevent ourselves from taking for granted, once we get them, the things we worked so hard to get."

The easiest way to deal with hedonic adaptation is to set our goals so that we don't even need to deal with it. This is why my goals for IMA are not to get to *this* level of assets under management, so that *then...* I am not even sure what that *then...* is.

Our goals at IMA, just like our values, are process-based. We can control our investment process (though not always its outcome); we want to provide great service to our clients – we can control that; our goal is for the company's operations to run with the precision and ease of a Swiss watch – we can control that; we can control the culture we create and how we treat our employees. Our final goal is to have fun while we are doing this.

Let's zero in on investing. Investing, too, is a process-based endeavor. Though no two stock analyses are identical, the systematic way of approaching them is the same from stock to stock. Unless you are in love with the process, you'll subject yourself to a life of misery, because the causal chain between a well-thought-out process and a good outcome often takes years to unfurl.

My investment friends will agree with me on this point: If you are investing solely to get rich and don't enjoy the struggle, the ups and downs of the process, then you are destined for unhappiness.

I write a few hours every single day. When I'm done writing I have a similar feeling to the one I have after I work out at the gym. When I've worked out hard, the micro-tears in my muscles leave me with a feeling of fullness and growth. Despite the pain and struggle, writing gives a similar satisfaction, except not in my arms or abs but in the muscle between my ears. I receive satisfaction not just from finishing an article or a book, but from the journey itself.

My father's best and oldest friend, Alexander, is a brilliant mathematician and an incredibly gifted teacher, loved by everyone who ever came in contact with him. Alexander and my father both taught at the Murmansk Marine Academy. Alexander had a younger brother who, when he died, left him several books. One of those books was Solzhenitsyn's *Gulag Archipelago*. The book was banned in the 1970s in Soviet Russia.

One of Alexander's guests must have seen Solzhenitsyn's book at his apartment and reported him to the authorities, because one day he got a knock on his door from the KGB. They searched his apartment and found the book. His superb reputation saved him from imprisonment, but he lost his job at the Murmansk Marine Academy.

The Academy faculty held a vote over whether to keep Alexander or kick him out of the Academy. The vote was almost unanimous: Yes, fire him. The only person who voted against was my father, risking his own career.

For 15 years Alexander's goal was to get his teaching job back – that became the focus of his life. Then, in the 1990s, after the Soviet Union collapsed, the Academy took him back with open arms; he was reinstated. What happened next came as a great surprise to everyone: Alexander fell into a deep depression. His goal had so occupied him that achieving it sucked the meaning out of his life – now he was goalless and his life was empty.

This story has a happy ending, because his depression lasted a year or two, but then he found a new joy in writing books and teaching high school kids mathematics. In other words, what he valued in life had changed.

When I started studying for the CFA exam, I should not have tied my happiness to an "If this, then..." trap. After I passed the test (on the first try), I looked around, and nothing had changed. I had got through the *if this....* part and *then...* there was nothing. Absolutely nothing. Nobody cared (maybe my parents and my brothers did). I got a raise at work, but that is not why I had done it. Luckily, I did not run out of good problems. I found a new challenge in teaching investing at CU in Denver, and I also started writing.

When you are constantly trapped in "If this, then..." thinking, you are ignoring the present. You may not even be aware of it, but life just slides by you. Paraphrasing the Stoic of Nebraska, constantly thinking about the future, being stuck in the "If this, then..." thinking, is like saving sex for old age.

We should heed Seneca when he says, "True happiness is to enjoy the present, without anxious dependence upon the future ... The greatest blessings of mankind are within us and within our reach. A wise man is content with his lot, whatever it may be, without wishing for what he has not."

Share this chapter with a friend:
https://soulinthegame.net/bdk/

A Twist: Applying "If This, Then..." to Form Habits

BEFORE WE MOVE on to good values, let's take a small detour. I have discovered that there is an interesting twist to "If this, then..." thinking, which can turn it from a negative to a positive.

"If this, then..." can be a great habit-forming and behavior-enforcing tool. I used it to quit smoking and to achieve perfect attendance when I was an undergraduate and in graduate school.

I started smoking at the embarrassingly early age of 13. I was a product of my environment – my father and my brothers smoked. I also have a very addictive personality – if you put a bag of candies in front of me, I won't stop until the bag is empty.

Cigarettes were not much different; I was a cigarette addict, smoking two packs a day. My father, being the great father he is, tried everything to get me to quit, including forcing me to smoke a pack of cigarettes at one go. He was hoping that light tobacco poisoning would force me to hate cigarettes. He even took me to meditation classes and to an acupuncture guru who promised to cure my bad habit. Nothing worked for a simple reason – I did not want to quit.

And then...

I was 21. I had a mild crush on a girl. The girl mentioned in passing that she did not like men who smoked. I quit. This was before nicotine gums and patches, when quitting smoking was even more difficult. I told myself, if I smoke just one cigarette then I'll start smoking again. I pictured *then*.... as not getting the girl, which was horrifying to my young mind. I'd wake up in the middle of the night in a cold sweat because I'd had a dream that I smoked. This little "If this, then..." calculation changed my life.

The irony of the story is that the girl dumped me two weeks later, but till this day I am very thankful for that little crush. There is a bonus to this story: My father – not wanting to be a hypocrite – quit smoking a week after I did. Neither of us have touched a cigarette since.

I was never a great student and actually not even a good one (no false modesty here). Then, in my second year at CU at Denver, after two years of not-so-great grades, I began to mature. I realized that learning and good grades were a big deal if I didn't want to spend my whole life unloading boxes at Walmart. Come to think of it, this was around the time I quit smoking, too. Yes, this flower bloomed late.

I became a bit more mindful and started to examine why I was getting bad grades. I found that the problem was twofold: First, I did not study well by myself. I dealt with that by finding study partners in each class. The second reason was that I missed too many classes. I had a job and thus my classes were all early in the morning. A lot of times I chose sleep over school.

I told myself that if I missed even one class, I'd end up missing a lot of classes, so I couldn't go there. It worked. During my last two years as an undergraduate and then in graduate school, my attendance record was perfect. My grades improved tremendously. This was another situation where "If this, then..." thinking worked for me.

I call this a half-binary behavior and discuss it in greater detail in "I Don't Eat Desserts." Stoics would have been proud of me. I could not completely control which grades I'd get, but I could control how I studied and how often I made it to class.

Good Values Start with Good Problems

I F WE LIVE our lives in constant avoidance of pain, we will lead very empty and meaningless lives. This may seem to contradict what I've said many times, that Stoicism should help us avoid negative emotions and thus pain. The important word, missing in the previous sentence, is *unnecessary*.

Stoicism's goal is to help to remove *unnecessary* negative emotions and save you from *unnecessary* suffering and pain.

There is a difference between *suffering* and *struggling*. Even if you don't know the difference between the two, innately you know these two words, though almost interchangeable, have different meanings. A dictionary defines *struggle* as "to make strenuous or violent efforts in the face of difficulties or opposition." Dictionaries equate *suffering* to pain (experience of unpleasantness). I view *struggle* as *suffering* with a purpose. The purpose provides you with the *why*. *Why* is the fuel that makes you overcome the pain.

Things that are worthy, the ones that have the *why*, usually come with some amount of pain: Writing, kids, marathon running, dating, investing. You cannot have a good workout and not experience pain. This pain is not needless, but necessary. Once you figure out why you are doing something and that why is important to you, suffering turns into struggle and thus becomes more tolerable. Or as my son Jonah's favorite artist, J. Cole, said, "There is beauty in the struggle, ugliness in the success." Our favorite Roman emperor, Marcus, agrees with J. Cole and takes it a step further: "The impediment to action advances action. What stands in the way becomes the way."

185

Overcoming obstacles creates, as Mark Manson puts it, "a sense of meaning and importance" in our lives, and as a bonus it brings happiness. In the long run, the things we struggle for are the ones that have the most meaning in our lives.

If you avoid problems, then you are destined for an empty, sad existence. Happiness in life comes from having and solving good problems! Viktor Frankl goes beyond that to state: "Happiness cannot be pursued; it must ensue. One must have a reason to be happy." And thus, we should be on the search for good problems. Paradoxically, if we embed this attitude deep into our operating system and embrace the happiness that comes from solving good problems, then we won't look at life's many obstacles so much as problems but rather as sources of happiness. As Seneca said, "Difficulties strengthen the mind, as labor does the body."

I have a close friend. He is in his early 40s, single, smart, kind – a terrific human being. He moved to the West Coast a decade ago, so I see him in Denver only once a year, in December. Over the years he has struggled with his weight. Last year he hit his personal absolute worst – 360 pounds. As we went out to dinner, I asked him when he was going to start dating again. (Yes, we have that close a relationship.) He said once he lost weight.

Fast-forward a year, and I am having dinner with literally half of my last year's friend – he has lost half of his body weight and now tips the scales at 180 pounds (true story). I asked him the same question: When are you going to start dating? I was secretly hoping that he had already signed up with every dating website available. To my surprise, he started listing all the inconveniences and frustrations that come with dating – going on dates, texting before and after dates, rejection, keeping his house constantly clean, etc.

I responded by quoting Freud: "One day, in retrospect, the years of struggle will strike you as the most beautiful."

I'll let Epictetus have the last word here: "All human beings seek the happy life, but many confuse the means – for example, wealth and status – with that life itself. This misguided focus on the means to a good life makes people get further from the happy life. The really worthwhile things are the virtuous activities that make up the happy life, not the external means that may seem to produce it."

Share this chapter with a friend:
https://soulinthegame.net/xhs/

What Pain Are You Willing to Sustain?

LET's SAY I chose an "If this, then..." material goal of growing my firm's assets to $100 billion. Hopefully by this point you can see glaring problems with this goal. But let's say I choose to ignore my own advice and set that as my goal.

The question I should then ask myself is: "What pain do I want to suffer through to reach this goal?" All the obvious benefits of the upside would not come pain-free; they'd come with plenty of pain that I wouldn't see at first.

I'd be managing not just $100 billion but thousands of employees. We'd have a marketing department and all sorts of other departments, and of course interdepartmental meetings and a cumbersome bureaucracy. I'd have to travel all over the world visiting our offices, something I wouldn't mind at first – I love seeing the world – but after a while the travel would lose its luster and turn into a chore.

I'd have to work more hours running the firm and would spend less time on what I love the most: Researching stocks.

Most importantly, I would not have the relationships with my clients I have today. Our firm's clients would turn into digits – impossible not to at that size. Finally, I'd have less time to spend with my family. All these things are, for *me* (and this is the key), pains that I am not willing to suffer. In the end, these pains would make me less happy, and so even if $100 billion under management was an attainable goal, I wouldn't be willing to endure the pain required to achieve it.

These thoughts and stories were in the back of my mind when I decided not to set a goal for IMA to be in the top 20 largest investment firms in Colorado by asset size and thus grace the pages of the *Denver Business Journal.*

See, being number 20 in Colorado is not ambitious enough for me. I want to be number one in the world – based on my internal values and the goals I will describe next, which have nothing to do with the quantity of IMA's assets under management and other external yardsticks.

But what are good values? Let's look at some.

Good Values

GOOD VALUES AND goals are internal – we have a lot of control over them, though not perhaps complete control. They are process-based. There is an immediate feedback loop. A lot of times our values completely overlap with our goals and are often indistinguishable from them. IMA's long-term goals and values are one and the same.

As I discussed earlier, our internal goals for IMA are very simple: Have an awesome, disciplined investment research process; provide flawless, excellent service to clients; run operations with the efficiency of a Swiss watch; communicate a message to the outside world consistent with our value of leaving the world a better place than we found it; have soul in the game in everything we do; and have fun while doing it.

We are coming back to Epictetus's dichotomy of control framework. When our values system is linked to external metrics that we cannot control, we are strapping ourselves into the bus of life in a way that gives us little control over the journey or destination. We are letting external factors like someone else's success or failure determine our state of happiness.

When our values are internal and process-based, we are in the driver's seat of the bus. The road will likely still be rocky, with plenty of disappointments (that's life). But we are in much greater control of our destiny. Paradoxically, the pain we experience along the way may also bring us joy.

I've mentioned before that the ultimate personal value by which I live my life, something I keep asking myself all the time, is: "Did I leave the world a better place than I found it?"

It is an ideal. I strive, but don't always succeed in it. It is internal to me. It is under my control. There is a short feedback loop. I think about it throughout the day and before I go to sleep. There is no room for anger in it. A lot of room for kindness. As Marcus said, "Waste no more time arguing what a good man should be. Be one."

Tranquility
in Motion

EPICTETUS SAID, "NO person is free who is not master of himself."
My goal is self-mastery, and I aspire to achieve this through what I call
tranquility in motion.

Tranquility means I am at inner peace, what Stoics would call equanimity,
where I have control over the amplitude and frequency of necessary
negative emotions. I am calm and cool – the magnitude and frequency of
positive emotions exceed the magnitude and frequency of unnecessary
negative emotions.

All the frameworks we have discussed (dichotomy/trichotomy of control,
EJR, reframing, negative visualization) should bring us closer to the state
of tranquility and equanimity. Tranquility comes from exercising the Stoic
operating system.

In motion means I live according to my values. I am solving good, interesting
(to me) problems. I have meaningful, fulfilling relationships with people I love
and admire. As Zeno put it, "Happiness is a good flow of life." For me, *in motion*
is Zeno's flow.

Seneca wrote about this tranquility in motion like so: "Once we have driven
away all things that disturb or frighten us, there follows unbroken tranquility
and unending freedom... a joy that is unshaken and unchanging, followed by
peace and harmony of the soul, and true greatness, coupled with gentleness,
since ferocity is always born from weakness."

A Story of
Four Books

MY BOOK WRITING adventures are good examples of internal versus external goals.

Publishing my first book, *Active Value Investing*, was a very traditional process. I had a book idea and a publisher, John Wiley & Sons, who liked it. After 18 months of working on the manuscript, I sent the first draft to my editor at Wiley, Pamela Van Giessen. A month later, I got an email from Pam in which she said, "Vitaliy, this book is unpublishable!" Eighteen months of writing, 90,000 words later, and "This book is unpublishable!" This was the most depressing day of the first decade of the century for me.

Here is what happened. I was so intimidated by the fact that I had to produce 60,000 words that I sat down and wrote every single investing thought that came to mind. I had a 90,000-pound sumo wrestler of a book that was dripping with unpublishable fat. Pam's advice was simple: Start fresh, write out an outline, and start copying and pasting from the old book into the new book. In the process, cut mercilessly. After a few days, I manned up and followed Pam's advice; and after a few months, my sumo wrestler of a book turned into a rather muscular gymnast.

My second book, *The Little Book of Sideways Markets*, was just the first book rewritten for a different audience (from practicing money managers like myself to civilians – think your neighborhood dentist). Because it was part of Wiley's "Little Book" series, I cut it by one-third. I finished it in two months.

Interesting side effect: Though the first and second books had the same content and were based on the same research, I think my second book is a better read. Cutting a third made the book crisper, less wordy, and easier to absorb. But there is no way I could have written the second book without writing the first one.

And then came my third book, *The Intellectual Investor*. I wanted to write this book for myself. I decided not to get a publisher; I did not want to have deadlines or advances. It was my research; a thinking project. I worked on that book for two years, then I took a six-month break, and several other writing projects got in the way. When I came back six months later and started rereading what I thought was an almost finished manuscript of some 65,000 words, I realized that it was unpublishable. I liked many parts of it, but as a whole it was not a book that I'd want to see out in the world (at least not in that state).

What really surprised me was my own reaction. My blood pressure and my mood did not flicker, even a bit. I said to myself, "Okay, I'll have to keep working." That was it. I closed my laptop and went to the office like nothing had happened; like I hadn't just spent two years of my life on that manuscript.

This was the moment when I realized the power of Stoicism. See, with my first book, I had an advance and a deadline. There was an externally-based goal that I didn't have complete control over – the writing gods were in the driver's seat more than I was.

With my third book, my only goal was to write and to learn. That is all I did. I read, I wrote, I learned. It was an internal, process-based goal. I did not fail to complete that book, because that was not the goal. I did not waste two years; I learned a lot and enjoyed the process.

I hope by now you see the dichotomy of the control framework here. Just think about it: Two completely different states of mind could have arisen out of the same outcome – tranquil versus depressed. I was able to go with the former option because I had framed a goal differently. And I did this completely unintentionally, before I even knew how to spell *Epictetus*.

There is another interesting lesson here. Any creative endeavor has two modes – tinkering and focused. In the tinkering mode, you are letting the outside world in; you are openminded and mindful; you are letting ideas in and allowing them to play with each other; you are mixing and matching mental models. Your ideas may come from different places – from reading books, listening to podcasts, talking to friends, walking in the park, or even taking long showers. (The last two are the ones that my subconscious favors the most.)

And yes, from writing too. But it is an open-ended writing – you don't know where it will take you. Usually when you think about writing or another creative activity, you think focus. Well, in the tinkering phase, focus is counter-creative. It induces tunnel vision; you only look forward and thus probably don't notice the ideas that wait beyond the walls of that tunnel. Your goal is simply to finish whatever you are working on.

When I started working on this book, *Soul in the Game,* my editor, Craig Pearce at Harriman House, and I set a deadline. But the deadline was my idea. I was excited to get the book out. All I had to do was to organize and slightly edit what I had already written. Focus and tunnel vision were fine.

However, near the end of our editing process, while I was rewriting one of my articles, I realized that I really wanted to write about, and just as importantly, learn about Stoic philosophy. I told Craig that I just wanted to work on the Stoicism section; I wanted to keep exploring it for as long as it took. He agreed.

I switched from focused to tinkering mode. Craig and I agreed to suspend the publishing deadline. I needed to keep reading, thinking, and writing. If I don't like what I write, then I won't publish it; but I cannot fail here because the objective is to learn. If you are reading this, that means the tinkering was fruitful; I switched into focus mode; and the material made it into the book.

In the words of Marcus: "The happiness of those who want to be popular depends on others; the happiness of those who seek pleasure fluctuates with moods outside their control; but the happiness of the wise grows out of their own free acts."

One More Thing

STOIC PHILOSOPHY IS not an academic distraction; it is a practice. Though they were Stoic philosophers, neither Seneca nor Marcus was an academic. Marcus was running the Roman Empire and Seneca was busy being a Renaissance man. As I mentioned earlier, Stoic philosophy is an operating system for real life, and it's a way of life that requires practice.

What I write here is far from a complete overview of Stoicism. I have just scratched the surface of what this philosophy has to offer. If I have piqued your interest, I hope you don't stop with my scribbles.

I have found the following books to be very useful as introductory guides to Stoicism.

A Guide to the Good Life, by William Irvine. Just as its name implies, this is really a good, practical guide to Stoic philosophy and practice. You may want to skip the first three chapters if you are not interested in the history of ancient philosophies.

How to Think Like a Roman Emperor, by Donald Robertson. Robertson is a psychologist by training; thus he delivers unique insights by unearthing psychological elements of Stoic practice.

Stillness Is the Key and *The Obstacle Is the Way,* both by Ryan Holiday. Holiday has a gift for bringing key Stoic philosophy concepts to the reader through wonderful stories.

How to Be a Stoic: Using Ancient Philosophy to Live a Modern Life, by Massimo Pigliucci. Pigliucci is a recovering evolutional biologist and in his book he strives to modernize Stoicism.

Let me share a trick with you. When I get consumed by a subject and go deep into researching it, in addition to reading books (in some rare cases instead of reading their books), I spend a lot of time watching lectures on YouTube and listening to podcasts. Podcasts are a wonderful learning tool when I go on my daily walks in the park. I often get new, additional insights from these authors answering a question, or going on a new tangent that they did not have a chance to wonder about in their books.

Of course, there are also the original texts by Epictetus, Seneca, and Marcus Aurelius. I suggest you don't start with them but read them after or in parallel with the above books, as they'll provide needed context.

Soul in Creativity

What unleashes creativity and what stunts it? Takeaways from almost two decades of writing.

Don't Let Your Environment Control You

ONE OF THE biggest hazards of being a professional money manager is that you are expected to behave in a certain way (though I get the feeling this applies to other white-collar professions as well). You have to come to the office every day, work long hours, slog through countless emails, and be on top of your portfolio (that is, check performance of your securities minute by minute). You must watch business TV and consume news continuously, dress well and conservatively, all while wearing a rope (tie) around the only part of your body that lets blood get to your brain.

Our colleagues judge us on how early we arrive at work and how late we stay. We do these things because society expects us to, not because they make us better investors or do any good for our clients.

Somehow, we let the mindless, Henry Ford assembly line, 8 a.m. to 5 p.m., widgets-per-hour mentality dictate how we conduct our business thinking. Though car production benefits from rigid rules, uniforms, automation, and strict working hours, in investing – the business of thinking – the assembly-line culture is counterproductive. Our clients and employers would be better off if we designed our workdays to let us perform our best.

In the widget-per-hour industrial age profession, your output per day is a function of widgets produced per hour and number of hours worked. You want to increase your output, produce more widgets per hour, and work more hours. There is a direct *linear* relationship between amount of time worked and widgets produced.

Investing is a very non-linear endeavor and not an idea-per-hour profession; it more likely results in a few ideas per year. A traditional, structured working environment creates pressure to produce an output – an idea, even a forced idea. Warren Buffett once said at a Berkshire Hathaway annual meeting, "We don't get paid for activity; we get paid for being right. As to how long we'll wait, we'll wait indefinitely."

Dan Ariely, the well-known behavioral economist, was interviewed on Bloomberg Television. He was asked, "What can one do to lose weight?" He said, "Start with the environment around you. If you come to work and there is a box of donuts on your desk, losing weight is going to be difficult. Also, look in your fridge: All the stuff that is probably not good for your diet is staring you in the face, whereas the fruits and vegetables that are essential to healthy eating are buried in the hard-to-access bottom drawers."

Our daily well of creative energy is finite. The environment around us can either add, subtract, or be neutral to this well. Taking Dan Ariely's donut analogy further, not eating donuts that are sitting on your desk consumes willpower and thus a simple act of having donuts on your desk will result in reducing your well of energy. However, if instead of donuts you place a basket of fruits and vegetables on your desk, eating them will not consume willpower (unless you really hate fruits and vegetables) and at the same time will give you vitamins and energy.

Finally, if you have neither donuts nor fruits or vegetables on your desk then your well of energy is undisturbed. By making small but conscious decisions about the environment around us, we can influence our creative output and our ability to make good decisions. We have to be extraordinarily careful to choose the right environment – to work with, and even socialize with, the right people.

Numerous studies have found that humans are terrible at multitasking. We have a hard time ignoring irrelevant information and are too sensitive to new information. Focus is the antithesis of multitasking. I find that I'm most productive on an airplane. I put on my headphones and focus on reading or writing. There are no distractions – no emails, no social media, no instant messages, no phone calls. I get more done in the course of a four-hour flight than in two days at the office. But you don't need to rack up frequent-flier miles to focus; just go into "off mode" a few hours a day. Kill your internet, turn off your phone, and do what you need to do.

I bet if most of us really focused, we could cut down our work week from five days to two. Performance would improve, our personal lives would get better, and those eventual heart attacks would be pushed back a decade or two. For instance, there is absolutely no reason why we automatically have to spend the bulk of our creative time in the four walls of our office just because it matches the address on our business card, unless your office is the environment where you are most creative.

If we want to be completely mindful about our environment and maximize the energy in our creative well, we can identify major daily or weekly activities, then match them to the environment that is the most conducive to them. During the week, for instance, I do research (which is mostly reading), build and tweak financial models, manage the firm, talk to clients, read books, and write.

I find the office is not a great place for any kind of reading, whether research or books. I need to be able to focus and I get distracted there too easily. So I take my laptop or a book and go to a park (if it is not cold) or Starbucks. Also, I have a special designated reading chair in my bedroom for reading books and writing.

To build models, I need to be in the corporate or home office, where I have a computer with multiple screens. If I need to talk to my colleagues, then I'd prefer to be in the corporate office. Environment is not a factor when I meet clients or talk to them on the phone, as long as it is not noisy. Running the firm is an activity that can be broken down into its own sub-activities that are mindful and mindless. Mindful tasks most likely will require me to focus, which means Starbucks or a park. Mindless tasks can be done from anywhere. And finally writing. Environment is paramount because writing consumes an enormous amount of energy and requires significant concentration.

The environment in the investing profession is further poisoned by the stock market and the business news. Serious business news that lacked sensationalism, and thus ratings, has been replaced by a new genre: Business entertainment (of course, investors did not get the memo). These shows do a terrific job of filling our need to have explanations for everything, even random events that require no explanation (like daily stock movements). Yet many managers have business TV on while they work.

You may think you're able to filter the noise. You cannot, though; it overwhelms you. So don't fight the noise – block it. Leave the television off while the markets are open. At the end of the day, check the business channel websites to see if there were interviews or news events that are worth watching.

Don't check your stock quotes continuously; doing so shrinks your time horizon. As a long-term investor, you analyze a company and value the business over the next decade, but daily stock volatility will negate all that and turn you into a day trader. There is nothing wrong with trading, but value investors are rarely good day traders.

I have found that constantly looking at stock prices also impacts my mood and wastes my brain cells as I try to interpret data that contains very little information. I am getting better: I am down to checking prices only once, maybe twice, a day. My goal is to do it just once every few days.

Take the rope off your neck and wear comfortable clothes to work (I often opt for jeans and a "Life is good" T-shirt). Pause and ask yourself a question: If I was not bound by the obsolete routines of the dinosaur age of assembly-line manufacturing, how would I structure my work to be the best investor I could be?

How you get ideas is up to you. I am not a professional writer, but as a professional money manager I learn and think best through writing. I put on my headphones, listen to music, and stare at my computer screen for hours, pecking away at the keyboard. That is how I think best. You may do better by walking in the park or sitting with your legs up on the desk, staring at the ceiling. I do my best thinking in the morning. At 3:00 in the afternoon, my brain shuts off; that is when I read my emails. We are all different.

I wrote the bulk of this essay before the coronavirus pandemic. The pandemic, however, may have created an interesting, once-in-a-lifetime opportunity to escape from the Henry Ford's "widget per hour" work environment, with a lot less friction from the external environment (i.e., your bosses, co-workers, customers).

The pandemic has blurred the boundaries between traditional and home offices. Dogs barking in the background or kids strolling into a room while you are on a video conference call are the new casual Fridays of our work environment today. At some point, things may drift back to the old normal, but now we are given the unique opportunity to shape what the best, most productive version of *normal* is for us. And here is the best part: The new normal doesn't have to look like the old normal.

Take a first principles approach; assume you have a blank-slate day in front of you. How will you structure it? Assume you have no constraints. If it is easier, assume you have moved to a different city and started a new job where you are the emperor of your calendar. Don't assume that you have to do today what you did yesterday.

By the time you read this, I may have modified my daily regimen a few more times. And I'll keep tinkering with it. The key is that we are handed the opportunity to shape our days so that we can become the best versions of ourselves. Don't squander the chance.

Time Does
Not Scale

I GET ASKED A lot, "How do you work?" and "How do you find time to write?"

People wonder when I have time to do research. Do I do research at all? Or do I have someone else do it for me?

I'll share some thoughts about this here. I hope this will help other investment, and non-investment, professionals.

There are so many ways to answer this. I'll start by saying that I write about two hours every day.

This translates into 500–700 hours a year or about 40,000 to 60,000 words a year – roughly a small book. The more you write, the better you get, especially if you write daily. I've been writing since 2004. Thus I can spew out more words than a person who is not a regular writer. Though quantity doesn't mean quality, to quote the not-so-great Joseph Stalin: "Quantity has a quality of its own."

I normally get up very early, make coffee, put on my headphones, and write. My wife and kids are asleep, it's dark outside, and I enter my own world. I get two hours of uninterrupted, focused thinking. And that is what writing is – focused thinking. This is how I access the deep, dark corners of my subconscious mind. It's a necessity, because this is the only way I can string thoughts together. Writing probably overcompensates for my inability to sit still.

I love research! The only reason I can write about stocks I own or have analyzed is because I read their annual reports, listen to their earnings calls, build financial models, and debate them with others. The ease with which I write about stocks comes from understanding their businesses, which comes from doing primary research.

I am not the only one doing research at IMA – we have internal and external teams. I have a global network of investment friends (though the professional/personal boundaries were washed away years ago) with whom I share our research, with whom I can debate stocks I am analyzing, and who will share ideas with me. IMA does not have the large research department of a mutual fund company, but neither does it have the constraints of one.

I am driven by learning, creating, discovering.

When people ask me at social functions what I do for a living and I don't want to talk about the stock market, I tell them I'm a writer. But I don't really think of myself as a writer; just a person who thinks through writing.

I think of myself as a student of life – a moniker I borrowed from Rabbi Noah Weinberg. We are more than our professions. We are parents, spouses, children, friends; we are our hobbies and our interests. I love investing; I would do it 80 hours a week if my family did not remind me of their existence. But I'd like to be more than just that. Being a student of life is not just a moniker: It is a mentality; it is a slightly different – more open-minded – approach to life. This is why I write about topics outside of investing.

My explorations into classical music are an example of that. I cannot play an instrument, but I receive incredible enjoyment from listening to classical music. Without it my life would be far emptier. So I started writing about it, which in turn helped me to learn more about it.

And then I am also the CEO of IMA – an investment firm with employees and a lot of clients. My first and most important professional responsibility is to do research. Clients come to IMA, turn over the bulk of their net worth, and basically say, "Vitaliy, don't screw it up, please."

How do I make sure that being CEO of IMA doesn't interfere with research?

It took me plenty of trial and error to get to the place where I am today, but here is what I do to stay focused on analyzing and managing stock investments.

I outsource and delegate. I hired an assistant. I looked through all the tasks I had to do. The ones where I added little value and did not enjoy, I offloaded to my wonderful assistant Barbara. Try to schedule a call with me and you'll be interacting with her. Not because I am so important – I am not; but because even scheduling a call takes time – five minutes, three emails. If you do four of those a week, that's 20 minutes. I add very little value doing that task. These things add up.

Which brings me to this: I hire my weaknesses. Which is easy for me, because I have plenty.

I am horrible with emails; I forget to reply, or reply weeks later. Barbara has zero emails in her inbox; I have an embarrassing number.

When we hired an analyst, I looked for someone who would have the same passion for value investing and have the same values, and a complementary skill set, with strengths that offset my weaknesses.

I went to lunch with a guy who ran a Fortune 500 company, and I asked him what he looked for in the people he hired. He said, "Look for the two C's: Competency and character. Hire people that will own a task." This is what I do. Someone gave me another piece of advice that I also took to heart: Hire slowly, but fire fast.

I am protective of my time. Try to reach out to me through IMA's website and you'll get an autoresponder telling you that if you are a prospective client and would like to talk to me, first you need to read our brochure. I won't talk to a prospect who has not read the brochure. Most of the questions that prospective clients have for me over the phone have already been answered more eloquently in the brochure.

IMA doesn't do traditional marketing or selling. Clients refer their friends to us or people read my articles and my books, and they reach out to us. Then we figure out whether we are a good fit for each other. That's it. IMA is not a traditional investment firm; nobody here does seminars, cold calls, or country club social selling.

Therefore, I spend no time on direct selling. None! This frees up a lot of time.

I say no, a lot. Most of the conferences I attend, I am there to learn, not to speak. When I am asked to speak at a conference I usually decline, unless I have an ulterior motive – like a getaway with my wife. In a few cases, when I say yes, once or twice a year, I decline to do a traditional, monological presentation and only do a Q&A. Presentations require a lot of preparation and occupy a lot of mental real estate weeks before a conference. And to be honest, I don't enjoy doing them, so I stopped doing them.

I don't do "Let's meet for coffee." I used to feel bad about being selfish with my time, but then I realized that my most important responsibility is to my immediate family and close friends. The time I spend on a "Let's meet for coffee" meeting is time taken away from a game of chess with my kids or a walk in the park with a friend. Once I started to look at things from this perspective, any guilt I had from saying "no" dissipated.

I also say no to internal projects that are a time suck. Our director of marketing wanted me to do a podcast. I like being an occasional guest on someone else's podcast – this requires very little time and I enjoy it. But doing a weekly podcast requires a time commitment and doing something I don't enjoy. So I found an elegant solution. I have a professional narrator read my articles, and voila: We have a podcast. It requires absolutely zero time from me. It is produced by the IMA team.

I hope you see a pattern. My personal formula for happiness is: Take the things I enjoy and from which I receive creative satisfaction, and divide by the things that I don't enjoy (usually very detail-oriented, mundane things that have few creative calories). The goal is to maximize the numerator and minimize the denominator. Because I focus on doing things I love, I can be more focused and have greater stamina.

I avoid time-draining hobbies – I don't play golf or follow sports. There is nothing wrong with either, they are just not my thing. I watch probably two football games a year. This is not advice for others, but it frees up a lot of time for me to research, write, read, and spend time with family.

I time block. I am a morning person; I am more productive and creative in the first half of the day. I look at research as the most important thing I do. Research consumes energy and requires creativity; thus, I am very protective of my mornings. From 8 a.m. to 2 p.m. I focus on research and don't do non-research phone calls. Talking to clients or prospects takes less energy, and thus I can do it later in the day (from 2–3 p.m.).

I don't schedule any appointments or phone calls on Wednesday; that's an open day, when I have no obligations to anyone. I can be as productive or unproductive as I feel like. I can go to the park, go skiing, go see a movie, or go to Starbucks to read. It is *my* time.

I scale my time through writing.

I modeled IMA after Starbucks – a company I have tremendous respect for. Starbucks provides premium, consistent, high-quality products and great customer service. That's a good description of IMA's own North Star.

IMA is not just in the investment business; it is in the service business as well. There is an interesting paradox: Customer service means time – my time. Well, almost – operational issues are elegantly resolved by our very capable team in operations. But as IMA keeps growing and thus has more clients, those clients will naturally want me to address their concerns about the economy, their portfolios, and so on. Our website and brochure state that our portfolio managers are one phone call away. We promise that we'll answer clients' inquiries within one business day. This is not an empty promise. We always do.

I came up with a solution regarding portfolio questions. Every quarter I write an in-depth letter addressing client portfolios. These letters run to 20 pages. Through the magic of technology these letters are custom tailored for each client, because all clients' portfolios don't look the same.

In the letter there is a Q&A section where I answer questions sent to us by clients. The goal of these letters is to answer accessibly, honestly, and clearly any possible questions clients may have about their portfolios and the economic world around us. As a result, last year I probably spent 30 hours at the most talking to clients on the phone. Clients can always call me, but they don't often have the need – I have answered their questions in my letters. My writing is scalable; my time on the phone is not.

As Freddie Mercury said, time waits for no one. I am a bit paranoid about time. I try very hard to spend it only on the things that matter to me the most. I have structured my life to do more things I love and fewer things I don't like. I identified my edge: thinking through writing and focused research. Time does not scale; writing does. I delegate and outsource. I work with people I love. That's it!

Share this chapter with a friend:
https://soulinthegame.net/hzs/

Abracadabra

"**A**BRACADABRA." THINK ABOUT this word the next time you speak. It translates from Hebrew as, "I will create as I speak." We are creating our thoughts as we speak; we are writing to our hard disk (our brain) as the sound leaves our mouth. Furthermore, the way we speak with others has a significant impact on how much thinking we do (yes, how much) and on what we think.

But I am getting ahead of myself.

There are four modes of communicating: preacher, prosecutor, politician, and scientist.[30]

Let's start by talking about the first three modes – we'll discuss the scientist mode last.

If you are in preacher mode, you are fully convinced of your belief and are trying to get others to embrace your gospel. A politician is trying to win the approval of others with a message he may or may not believe in. A prosecutor is trying to build an argument to convince you to change your mind.

We all spend some time in each of these modes. As a CEO, I spend plenty of time in preacher mode when I communicate IMA's corporate values to employees. I go into prosecutor mode with my kids when I try to change their minds on the virtues of doing homework and cleaning their rooms.

---

30   I learned about this framework from Adam Grant's book *Think Again*. Adam borrowed it from his colleague Philip Tetlock.

In general, I am not a big fan of politicians and thus I was going to take the easy route and write something insulting about them – how they're liars, intellectually dishonest, and always changing their minds on issues with the prevailing winds of public opinion. But then I realized that we don't have to be politicians to be spending time in politician mode. We all go there, including yours truly. When I had job interviews a few decades ago, I am sure I was in politician mode as I told potential employers what they wanted to hear. Most of us have behaved as politicians on first dates – we want our date to like us, so we can get a second date. If I hadn't turned on my politician mode on my first date with my wife, I'd still be living with my parents.

Each one of these modes is important to our survival as a species, and they are important to our own daily lives. Steve Jobs, in addition to being a visionary, had the talent of being able to convince others to do what seemed impossible. Apple employees called it "Steve's reality distortion field." Jobs was in preacher mode. Our court system runs on the ability of lawyers to get judges and jurors to change their minds. But so do our common social and interpersonal interactions.

I don't want to be dismissive of the aforementioned modes, but it is important to note that we do very little learning in these modes. If you carefully think about the three modes we have discussed so far, each one is outer-focused – you already know what you think and are trying to change someone else's mind to your way of thinking.

And then there is scientist mode.

Before I learned about this framework, I had a different name for it: *Student of life* mode. However, *scientist mode* has its own appeal. A scientist treats ideas as hypotheses that need to be tested. Ideas are just malleable starting points (as opposed to hardened truths) for further investigation.

What stands between other modes and the scientist mode is our ego. I keep coming back to Epictetus when he says, "It is impossible for a man to learn what he thinks he already knows." Our ego tricks us into believing that we already know a lot more than we actually do. New information that potentially could have turned into new knowledge, a new way of thinking, bounces off the ego's impervious surface.

To let go of our ego, to quote Adam Grant, author of *Think Again*, we need to put curiosity above conviction and humility above pride. We don't need to believe (or defend) every thought that enters our mind. We don't want to let our thoughts and ideas automatically become our identity.

Identity tends to be unmalleable, which is both feature and bug. The feature can be used to our advantage – we can carefully craft our values and the positive traits we want to embody. We think of them as our identity and with time they will indeed become (harden into) our identity. We can tell ourselves, "I am a person who is..." – for instance, a person who is kind to others, who is honest, who is net positive to society, who is healthy, etc. If you think and behave according to values set by your identity, eventually you'll rise to them. I discuss identity in greater detail in "I Don't Eat Pork."

Only carefully crafted values should be part of our identity. Once our ideas become us, it is hard to change our mind on them. That could be a bug as well. If we let our identity become "I believe the world is flat," it will be difficult to change when we discover conflicting evidence. Ideas need to spend most of their time living in the state of hypothesis.

Adam Grant, in *Think Again*, tells a story about the first time he met Daniel Kahneman, the Nobel laureate and co-father of behavioral economics. He was giving a speech and noticed Kahneman in the first row. He was shocked and flattered. After the speech Kahneman came up to him, smiling, and said, "That was wonderful. I was wrong." Not a reaction Grant expected. Puzzled, Grant asked something along the lines of, "How can you be happy about being wrong?" Kahneman explained (I am paraphrasing), "No one enjoys being wrong. But I do enjoy having been wrong. This means I am now less wrong now than I was before. This means I've learned something."

Finding joy in having been wrong is a skill that we all need to cultivate.

Intellectually honest debate

I was in Israel with a group of friends. One of my friends offered to show us the biggest Yeshiva (orthodox Jewish college) in the center of Jerusalem, where he had studied years before. It's called Mir Yeshiva. We went there at 10 p.m. on a Thursday night. Our friend guided us into the "library." If you go to a library on any campus in the US, it will have two things: a lot of books and a lot of quiet. This library had a lot of books (which were packed against the walls), but it had all the quietness of a bar on Saturday night when ladies drink for free (minus the ladies and the music).

What we saw before us was an enormous room with several hundred students sitting in groups of two and three around modest wooden tables, debating. As my friend explained, the louder they argue, the better they learn. This was the time-honored process of learning through arguing. Students would pick a sentence or a verse in the Torah and argue about its meaning for hours (sometimes days).

I was mesmerized by what I saw. This was such incredible dedication to learning. Remember, we were there late on a Thursday evening. I cannot think of better gymnastics for the brain than this. It doesn't really matter what subject you want to learn – the Torah, investing, or physics. This sort of dynamic, confrontational process of getting at the truth will uncover every weak and unpolished angle of your understanding of any subject. These Torah students, though far removed from having a debate about science, spent the bulk of their days being in scientist mode.[31]

These students were involved not just in a debate but in an intellectually honest debate, which we'll discuss next. But before we do that, I'd like to note an interesting fact I learned at Mir Yeshiva: Students when they enter Yeshiva do not have a graduation date (there is no "class of 2025" type of thing). They graduate when they are done; and even after they graduate, they continue to study Torah for a few hours a day. This goes against the common and practical modern Western tradition of going to college, studying and passing tests, graduating, and then going off to a job. Somewhere between graduating and going to work, we tend to feel that we have exited the learning state and so we stop learning. I really like this Mir Yeshiva idea of not having a graduation from learning; it's the ultimate embodiment of being a student of life – you are a perennial student of life, for life.

Back to debating. When you are debating you can be in scientist mode or prosecutor mode.[32] If our goal is, by means of a carefully crafted argument, to

---

31   I've been wondering for a very long time why Jews – a population of less than 15 million people in a world of almost 7 billion (only 0.2% of the world's population) – have received almost 22% of Nobel Prize awards (41% of the prizes in economics, 26% in physics, 28% in medicine). There could be multiple reasons for that, and I describe one of them in "Parents of La Mancha." But what I saw in Mir Yeshiva that Thursday night is another reason. I don't know whether religion shaped the culture or culture shaped the religion, but debate is embedded at the core of Jewish religion and Jewish culture – Jews just spend more time in the scientist mode.

32   A prosecutor (at least in theory), in trying to convince the jury that a defendant is guilty, should be looking for the truth, but the defense attorney doesn't have this burden – he just needs to argue that his client is not guilty.

convince a car rental clerk to give a free upgrade, then we are in prosecutor mode. If our goal is to learn but not to change someone's mind, then we are in scientist mode. But again, our ego often takes over and the debate, instead of turning into a pursuit of the truth, only hardens our beliefs (what we already know).

If you are on a search for truth, debating in prosecutor mode can actually be dangerous, because by debating you may end up hardening ideas that you did not really have the chance to fully think through. In other words, what you end up believing is formed by this sequence: An idea randomly entered your mind; you did not think it through from different angles but debated it in prosecutor mode, and this idea became part of your core beliefs. This doesn't sound scary until you realize that if the opposite idea had entered your mind first, you might have ended up believing the opposite.[33]

If you are debating in scientist mode, you have strong ideas that are loosely held. For a scientist, the truth is out there, whether he or she believes in it or not. Just like gravity, truth doesn't care if you believe in it or not. Just climb the tree carelessly without believing in gravity. After a few broken extremities, gravity will have confirmed its existence. As Seneca puts it, "Time will discover truth." You may as well try to discover it before time does. Gravity existed long before Isaac Newton discovered it. Scientists are in some ways archeologists of truth.

To have an intellectually honest debate or conversation you have to enter it with a willingness to learn.[34] Here are the rules for an intellectually honest debate:

Be honest with ourselves. Make sure we are in scientist, not prosecutor mode. As Dostoevsky says in *The Brothers Karamazov*, "Above all, don't lie to yourself. The man who lies to himself and listens to his own lie comes to a point that he cannot distinguish the truth within him, or around him, and so loses all respect for himself and for others. And having no respect he ceases to love."

Acknowledge alternative viewpoints. Charlie Munger summed this up very well: "I'm not entitled to have an opinion unless I can state the

---

33 Now to make things even scarier, think about how others (not me or you, of course) are born into their religious beliefs. They did not really choose them.

34 I have to give credit to Mike Gene, who wrote an article entitled "Ten Signs of Intellectual Honesty." I used his signs as a foundation for this essay.

arguments against my position better than the people who are in opposition. I think that I am qualified to speak only when I've reached that state."

Acknowledge our assumptions. Once your assumptions are disclosed it is much easier to have an intellectually honest discussion, because now you can debate each assumption separately.

Acknowledge our own biases. If you disclose your bias, then your debating partner will be able to attach an appropriate weight to your opinion.

Admit where your arguments are weak. This goes to the core of intellectual honesty. This will only make the search for the truth more expeditious.

Address the argument; don't attack the person. This relates to my Dale Carnegie discussion in the chapter "Dale Carnegie – Better Late than Never." We are debating ideas, not character. Don't sink to the level of some of our politicians.

A great example of thinking and debating like a scientist was unsurprisingly generated by two giants in the world of science, Albert Einstein and Niels Bohr – both received the Nobel Prize in Physics in 1922. They were involved in one of the longest-running scientific debates ever – it lasted almost 30 years. The debate began in 1927 at the Fifth Solvay Conference on Electrons and Photons in Brussels, which was attended by a total of 17 Nobel laureates.

Niels Bohr was a Danish-born scientist who was one of the co-creators of quantum physics. Though Einstein also helped create quantum physics, for a long time he could not accept its probabilistic nature.

Quantum physics (also known as quantum mechanics or quantum theory) studies the behavior of atomic and subatomic particles. To understand Einstein's problem with quantum physics, we need to understand that classical physics – which Einstein helped to eclipse in the early 20th century – was a simple, elegant masterpiece. And most importantly, it was deterministic science, meaning you could determine with incredible precision, through the use of mathematics, what would happen to object A if certain forces were applied to it by object B.

Enter quantum physics. This new science did not have the certainty, simplicity, or elegance of classical physics. Where events in classical physics are solid and continuous, in quantum physics they are fuzzy, discontinuous, and uncertain. Even Einstein's post-classical physics could not account for the behavior of atomic and subatomic particles... but quantum physics could.

Quantum physics had busted out from the beautiful constructs of classical physics, but – and this is an incredibly important "but" – it worked! If it were not for quantum physics, I might not be writing this book, because the microprocessor would not have been invented. (I honestly don't know how anything could have been written before word processors, because I rewrite the same sentence a dozen times. But I digress.)

The Einstein–Bohr debate was not a private debate; no, it was a very public discourse with papers written, presentations given, and lectures held. Bohr and Einstein were intensely searching for the truth. Their disagreements were always about ideas, and their arguments were supported by experiments, formulas, and models.

Einstein, though he never arrived at full agreement with Bohr, changed his mind several times and agreed with a lot of Bohr's arguments. In the end, he still could not accept quantum physics' probabilistic nature and lack of elegance, and till the very end of his life Einstein was still looking for an alternative to quantum physics through his unfinished unified theory.

The debate forced Bohr to backtrack on several issues as well.

During this great debate and when it was over, Einstein and Bohr remained friends, and their admiration for each other had not withered.

Science and society as a whole were the beneficiaries of this intellectually honest debate that had the sole objective of uncovering the truth. The Einstein–Bohr debate should be the gold standard for intellectual honesty and honest debate.

Here is another example. Intellectual debate is deeply embedded in the Jewish legal system. By Jewish law, a court will not accept a capital punishment verdict if it was delivered by a unanimous decision of 23 judges who decide upon capital cases. Yes, you read that right. There has to be at least one dissenting opinion for the death penalty verdict to be accepted. The court wants to make sure there was at least one voice in the proceedings that forced judges to confront the opposing argument. In other words, the court wants to make sure the decision was not merely tribal, but was debated.

When I have a conversation with someone that turns into a debate, I ask myself, "What mode do I need to be in and what mode I am actually in? What mode is the person I am debating in?" Also, I have stopped debating or even discussing politics or religion with others. For most people (not you or me, of course), political and religious views are hardened into their identities.

The only thing that is worse than being in scientist mode and debating with someone who is in prosecutor mode is debating someone who is in politician mode. At least if they are in prosecutor mode you may learn something. If they are in politician mode, they'll just agree with you so you'll like them. You'll get a temporary ego boost, but you won't get closer to the truth.

There is a time and place for each mode, but we need to keep reminding ourselves that we only truly learn when we are in scientist mode. That is usually the most difficult mode to maintain. Our ego, our desire to be right, constantly shifts us from scientist mode into one of the other modes. If we want to keep learning, being students of life, then we need to program (or reprogram) ourselves to spend a large chunk of our life in scientist mode.

I discovered that I spend more time than I thought in prosecutor mode with my kids. I finished writing the bulk of this chapter on a plane ride from Denver to Chicago. Jonah (20 years old) and I went to pick up Hannah (15 years old) from summer camp. I shared the chapter with Jonah on the plane. In Chicago, Jonah, Hannah and I spent hours walking the Magnificent Mile, sightseeing and talking. A few times our conversation turned contentious. Jonah would remind me, "Dad, are you in scientist mode?" In that moment my initial reaction would be to say "Yes." But I'd pause, think about it, and realize that somewhere in the conversation my ego had taken over and what supposed to be a scientist-mode conversation turned into a prosecutor-mode one. I need to keep reminding myself that in scientist mode my goal should be not to prove but to improve myself.

This incident in Chicago gave me another idea for how to train myself to stay in scientist mode: I've shared this chapter with my family, my friends, and colleagues at IMA and asked them to let me know when I cross into prosecutor mode in our conversations. This may work for you, too, dear reader.

Share this chapter with a friend:
https://soulinthegame.net/qmd/

Opera. Pain. And Investing. (Or, What We Should Learn From Pain)

THE FOLLOWING ESSAY touches slightly more on investing than other essays in this book. If you are not interested in investing, your first reaction may be to dismiss it. I implore you to look at this as an essay about pain that I am communicating to you through the lens of my painful investing experience. I've been told that pain is not limited to the investing profession, and thus you may find nuggets here that can help you, if (God forbid) pain knocks on your professional door.

Let's discuss a subject that is rarely (if ever) discussed in the investing community: Pain.

Yes, pain. Pain is a very personal and, well, *painful* subject. Thus, it may be brought up by money managers in the comfort of the psychiatrist's office, but never in public. After all, we money guys are supposed to project a Teflon image of logic and rationality, while mere emotions and sensations – especially the pain response – are left to the "herd," the nonprofessional investors, the... civilians.

Yes, humility is not a commodity that is held in high regard in my industry. Because of this, it's likely that you will never have heard pain and investing discussed in the same sentence... until now.

Opera

My journey on thinking and writing about pain was actually not caused by pain, at least not initially. It came from an unlikely place – an opera. I love classical music and get immense enjoyment from sharing my love for it with the world. After my investment articles are published, I send them out by email. But life is too brief to think and write only about investing, so in my investment emails I throw in notes on classical music[35] and life in general.

My musical notes usually start with, "Today I want to share with you..." and then I highlight a classical music piece, give my thoughts on it, and include a few links to performances on YouTube.

When it came time to share one of my favorite operas, *Pagliacci* by Italian composer Ruggero Leoncavallo, here is what I wrote:

> For most people, *Pagliacci* is an opera about betrayal – an unhappy wife (Nedda) cheats on a rightfully jealous husband (Canio), who is a traveling comedy troupe owner. The husband discovers that his wife has been unfaithful. He is consumed by shame and jealousy and kills both his wife and her lover. The opera ends with these words: "*Finita la commedia.*"

The ending of the story had little emotional impact on me. However, I was touched by the scene in which Canio finds out that his long-held suspicions are true: Nedda is cheating on him. He discovers this as he is about to go on stage with Nedda to perform in a comedy in which Nedda will play a cheating wife and he'll be a husband at whom everybody is laughing. As he is putting

---

35   You can find my notes on classical music on myfavoriteclassical.com.

on his makeup, he sings the aria *"Vesti la giubba,"* which translates as "Put on the costume." Just imagine the emotions racing through him at that moment.

Here are the lyrics from the aria:

To act! While out of my mind, I no longer know what I say, or what I do! And yet it's necessary... make an effort! Bah! Are you not a man? You are Pagliaccio! **Put on your costume, powder your face. The people pay to be here, and they want to laugh.**

As I sat down to write about *Pagliacci*, I really did not know why I loved this opera. Staring at the blank screen and listening to *Pagliacci* in the background is like a free visit to a therapist. I fell in love with it when I was a college student. However, that day, as I sat down to write about it, I found a very new meaning in it. I realized I could relate to opera on a very new and different level, through pain – I could relate to Canio's pain.

Just to clarify: No, my wife did not have an affair with a circus performer. I refer to the pain involved in investing.

Pain and investing

Investing is a nonlinear endeavor that is full of ups and downs. Every investor will have periods when his or her strategy is completely out of sync with the market. When the market is roaring on its way up and your portfolio is down, you may be sure that pain will rear its ugly face.

Value investing is almost by definition a contrarian endeavor. Growth investors ride the train of love, harmony, peace, and consensus – they buy companies that Mr. Market is infatuated with and thus prices them for love. (But just so you know, love ain't cheap and is rarely forever, at least when it comes to growth stocks.)

Value investors, on the other hand, live in the domain of hate – they buy what others don't want. Ironically, value investors may end up owning the same companies that growth investors used to own. When the love is gone, hate goes on a rampage; and trust me, you won't find anyone who'll pay extra for hate. It is cheap.

Investment styles go through cycles. Sometimes your stocks are really out of favor. Nothing you do works. You keep telling yourself that in the short run there is little or no link between decisions and outcomes. That's a truism of investing. You believe it on an intellectual level. Every day you come to work and the market tells you that you are wrong, you are wrong, you are wrong.

These negative confirmations are like Chinese water torture, undermining your confidence one bad day at a time until you are riddled with self-doubt. You are bleeding inside.

The world around you doesn't know that. You still have to "put the costume on," come to work, meet clients, analyze stocks. The pain you carry inside of you is constantly on mute.

This has happened to me several times in the course of my career. In 2012, it lasted a bit more than a year. Every stock I bought declined. Every stock I contemplated to buy and did not went up (many doubled). I was training new interns, and I vividly remember teaching them about our investment process almost on autopilot. I had to wear a brave face and ignore the burning pain inside of me. That year passed. The next was much, much better. Stocks that had caused me pain ended up being star performers. But I still remember the disconnect between how I felt and the public face I had to wear.

However, the pain of 2012 was nothing to that I experienced in 2015. The year started out okay, but then almost like clockwork, every month a stock in my portfolio would get halved. A new month, a new stock got killed. The grand finale was in November, when a stock that I thought was experiencing temporary fundamental weakness collapsed in a matter of a few days.

I've been investing for a long time, and this was not the first time my portfolio had declined, but in 2015 we had a lot of new clients. Unlike clients that had been with us for a while, had seen us weather previous down cycles and then seen us make money for them, our brand-new clients only saw the value of their portfolios shrinking. Also, 2015 was a benign year for the market; the market was slightly up or slightly down throughout the year.

I knew that in the long term our portfolio should be fine, but long term always lies well past short term. I was concerned that the new investors would panic and liquidate their accounts, thus cementing these losses.

I was on a trip to Israel that had been scheduled a year in advance with a group of friends. We were on a guided tour of Tzfat – one of the gems of Israel, a birthplace of Jewish mysticism, and one of its oldest cities. It was my first time visiting my historical motherland, and it should have been a once-in-a-lifetime experience.

All my friends were mesmerized by everything around us. They were inhaling their Jewish heritage through a fire hose. I, on the other hand, was suffering through excruciating pain. Pain that I had never experienced before and hopefully never will again. I had never thought before that day that emotional pain could also be physical. Every muscle in my body seemed crushed by an enormous weight. I had huge pain burning through me. I was surrounded by friends, but yet I felt very alone.

Never in my life, even in that moment, had I ever contemplated suicide; but that moment helped me to understand the pain people feel when they commit suicide. That is how great the pain was. I desperately wanted the pain to stop. I feel a little embarrassed writing this, because in hindsight my problem seems so small compared to what many people go through.

After we arrived at our hotel, I sat down and wrote a letter to my clients – something I had never done before mid-quarter. I knew they were concerned, and I did what I'd expect my money manager to do for me: I told the truth. I explained what had happened to the stock that collapsed. I also explained that with this particular company, we found ourselves in a situation where we did not know what we did not know. I explained that because of events like this, we have a diversified portfolio of stocks, not just one stock. As I was writing, the pain slowly subsided, though it did not completely go away. Writing ended up being incredibly therapeutic.

Sending this letter to clients was anything but easy. But to my great surprise, the response was very positive – some clients even consoled me and gave encouragement.

There are actually two issues here: The first is the pain, and the second is the duality between how we feel and our public face.

Let's start with pain; I'll address duality at the end. Once we have reduced our suffering (Stoics are useful here), we need to focus on acting rationally and then we need to make sure that we *harvest* this pain, so that we don't let (even temporary) suffering go to waste.

I suggest you read this section only after you've read "Stoicism – Life's Operating System."

Reducing pain

Stoics have so much to offer in the pain department; after all, the Stoic philosophy was created by its founder, Zeno, after he lost all his wealth in a shipwreck.

All the Stoics I've mentioned endured plenty of suffering: Eight out of 13 of Marcus' children died at birth or as infants; his wife of 30 years died in an accident; and he lived and (most importantly) governed through the Antonine Plague (a 15-year pandemic), many wars, revolts, and betrayals. Seneca lost his only son. Seneca was also sentenced to death, and the sentence was exchanged at the last minute for an eight-year exile. Epictetus... well, we don't know much about him, but he was a slave for almost two decades, and we do know that his master deliberately broke his leg.

Oh yes, Stoics knew pain and knew it well.

After reviewing my 2015 predicament, Epictetus would have suggested I start with his dichotomy of control framework. If we apply this framework to investing, we find that the only things within our control are our research, investing process, and communication with clients. Neither I nor any other money manager has any control over how the stock market will price our companies, or when the market will take our stock prices higher or lower. Believe it or not, this is a feature, not a bug, of the stock market. (I don't want to go down the rabbit hole of this topic here, but if you're interested, I suggest you read my essay, "Six Commandments of Value Investing," at SixCommandments.com.)

Yes, since *when* is not under my control – it is external – I should have ignored it in 2015. Separating externals and internals is paramount here. I should have just focused on internals – stock analysis, portfolio construction, designing and following a disciplined investment process, and only paying attention to stock prices from an opportunistic perspective (that is, the market's irrationality giving you an opportunity to sell or to buy more stocks to your advantage – which I actually did).

Being an investor who also writes worked somewhat to my disadvantage in 2015. I made things worse by using a lot of colorful words to talk up the situation in my head, greatly elevating my pain. This is where Marcus would have told me, "Don't be a Sophist, be very careful with the choice of words you use to talk to yourself."

He'd add, "Break things down to their fundamental essence, remove the fancy outer layer. Instead of 'My stocks collapsed!' say 'One stock declined 80%; this decline may be permanent [it was]; and the impact on the portfolio is this much. A handful of other stocks declined between 30% and 50% and their decline is temporary [it was].' List these stocks. Write down how much each stock is worth. [These numbers were significantly higher than the prices the stock market was quoting at the time.] Then value the portfolio not on how the market prices these stocks today but on what *you* think each company is worth."

Going through this exercise would have reduced my pain significantly in 2015, because, despite the one stock declining 80%, the fair value of our portfolio was significantly higher than the market priced it at the time.

If Seneca had time traveled to 2015, though, it would have taken him a bit of time to overcome the shock of the Roman Empire having crumbled and Caesar's Palace being a Las Vegas attraction. But he'd have put those things in the externals bucket. Then he would have calmly sat me down and told me, "Did you really expect that stocks in your portfolio would never decline? Did you really think that once or twice in the decade you were not going to step on a stock mine? You are human; you'll miss something and the stock will get halved or more, and that decline will be permanent. You'll have bad luck. You really expected this never to happen to you? If you didn't, you shouldn't be investing in stocks."

Seneca would have inadvertently quoted himself and said, "We suffer more in imagination than in reality." And he'd be so right – all my suffering at the time was in my very rich imagination. In fact, if I had framed my problem properly in the context of combined 2014 and 2015 returns, I would have noted that our portfolios were still up.

I did not know this at the time, of course, but if I had gone into hibernation at the beginning of 2015 and woken up in 2017, I'd have experienced only the joy of returns and no pain. This is why Seneca would continue quoting himself and say, "A man who suffers before it is necessary, suffers more than is necessary." I should have reminded myself that the market price for any company is an opinion (which is fleeting) and anything but a final verdict; it is external (thus I should spend very little time thinking about it). My suffering was unnecessary.

Epictetus would have reminded me, "It's not events that upset us, but our judgments about events." If I simply reframed 2015 in a broader context, the pain would have been much reduced.

I could have pulled negative visualization from my Stoic toolbox. Let's start with premortem: Visualizing my portfolio being down 20–40%. By visualizing this possible future event in advance, at the point when it does occur it won't sting as much (I should have done this before 2015 and should be doing this now).

We are often more afraid of the uncertainty of a negative outcome than the actual negative outcome. If at the time I visualized that loss and accepted it as a *fait accompli* (something that already happened), this would have removed a tremendous amount of stress. I also would have realized that my losses were recoverable.

The Stoics would have told me, after I followed Marcus' advice and listed my issues as plainly as possible, to write a letter as if these events had not happened to me but to a friend, and give him advice. This third-party perspective, kind of like what I am doing now, giving advice to the 2015 version of myself, is incredibly therapeutic, because by giving advice to someone else you are separating yourself from the emotions that are engulfing you and causing you pain.

As I have mentioned, this was not the first or the last time my portfolio declined in value. I would have benefited from writing a journal, for several reasons. If I stuck to very plain, black-and-white language it would have helped me to reduce my pain. Also, during future portfolio declines, which are inevitable, I could go to this journal and read my thoughts, which would remind me that though such declines are unpleasant at the time they are happening, they are par for the course. There is a reason *fishing* is not called *catching*, because there will be days or weeks when sitting in the boat will bring you nothing but frustration.

I wish I had meditated more then. It would have helped to lessen the pain. Writing is my form of meditation. Let me give you this analogy about meditation. Imagine your brain is a bottle that has two types of thoughts, rational and emotional, bottled up in it. Your rational thoughts are clear water and the irrational thoughts are dust particles. When you are calm and pain-free, the bottle is not moving much and so your emotions are resting at the bottom of the bottle and the water is mostly clear. But pain stirs up the bottle, and now all you see is murky water; the clarity is gone. Meditation (or writing, for me) allows you to gradually stop shaking the bottle. The dust settles, clarity prevails, and pain subsides. (I cover meditation in much greater detail in "Attend a Party in Your Own Head.")

What helped tremendously in 2015 was having a circle of trust. If you invest for a living, it is important to have a support group – other investors you trust, people who understand what you're going through. That circle of trust gives you an important escape valve; it allows you to not keep your emotions on mute. Unburdening lessens the intensity of the pain and its duration.

Reading fiction also helped me because it temporarily replaced my painful world with one that was pain-free (or at least if there was pain it was not mine). Walking in the park and exercising worked for me, too. I am sure that there are scientific studies that use a lot of Latin terminology to tell us how trees and rocks are great for us. I am sure they are right. Personally, walking in the park de-stresses me. Working out in the gym helped, because I temporarily traded mental pain (the breakdown of my portfolio) for physical pain (the breakdown of my muscle tissue). And then there is this wonderful sensation after the workout when I feel my muscles are growing – it is harder to be depressed when you feel like the Incredible Hulk.

An acquaintance, a very successful and respected value investor, managing billions of dollars, went through a long stretch of underperformance and shut down his firm and mutual funds (his mutual funds showed positive returns, but they were lagging indices by a few percentage points over the span of a decade). A few days after, on a sunny Monday, he went to his Manhattan office, took an elevator to the tenth floor, and plunged to his death. He had hundreds of millions of dollars in the bank and not a worry about how he was going to pay his bills for the rest of his life. He had a wife and kids. He had mistakenly linked his self-worth to the performance of his portfolio – it became his sole identity. But he was so much more than an underperforming (at that moment in time) value investor. He was a father, husband, son, mentor, friend, book reader ... and the list goes on. We need to keep reminding ourselves about this.

If you are doing what you love (you should not be investing, for example, if you are not madly in love with it), remember that though you can do a lot to lessen and manage the pain that comes your way, it is a necessary part of the journey of solving good problems. No matter how intense the pain is at the time, it is temporary: It will pass.

I'll let Marcus Aurelius have the last word here: "Whenever you suffer pain, keep in mind that it's nothing to be ashamed of and that it can't degrade your guiding intelligence, nor keep it from acting rationally and for the common good. And in most cases you should be helped by the saying of Epicurus, that pain is never unbearable or unending, so you can remember these limits and not add to them in your imagination."

Acting rationally

If investing were an exact science – a formulaic process by which you could constantly test and retest your hypotheses and repeat your results – then the pain might not be necessary. But though we come armed with the backward-looking precision of income statements, balance sheets, and financial ratios, as investors we never have complete, perfect information, so we never quite know what the future has in store for us. The paradox of investing is that flawless analysis can lead to a bad outcome (let's call it bad luck) and flawed analysis can lead to a great outcome (let's call it good luck). You can thank randomness for that. In the long run, good and bad luck will cancel out, but in the short run (which can last years), bad luck may cause you gut-wrenching pain.

The first thing you'll want to determine is whether you are a casualty of bad luck or if your analysis was flawed. In 2015, a half-dozen stocks were at the epicenter of my pain. I re-analyzed them as slowly and as rationally as I could at the time. On one stock I had made an analytical mistake – it was not bad luck; my analysis was wrong. But the others had been temporarily marked down by the market. Their short-term fundamentals might have weakened, but their fair value had not changed much.

I added more capital to a few and did nothing with the rest. Fast-forward a year or two. The stock for which my analysis was wrong never recovered, but all the other stocks delivered either modest or very significant gains (more than offsetting the loss caused by their fallen comrade).

This is where a systematic, rational process becomes paramount. Documenting your research (including your assumptions) and your thinking when you are thinking clearly (when the dust particles are comfortably settled at the bottom of the bottle) is important.

Harvesting pain

Though creativity and imagination are not big parts of your local university's finance curriculum, they are at the core of investing. They help us to translate the certainty of the past into mental models that deal with the ambiguity and uncertainty of the future.

Our creativity and imagination are just like a musical instrument: They require tuning. Occasional stress from pain is a perfect tuner.

Here is one example: Sergei Rachmaninoff went into the history books as one of the most accomplished Russian composers of the 20th century. However, Rachmaninoff had to live through tremendous failure and pain before the pieces we love and treasure came to life.

The premiere of Rachmaninoff's first symphony in Saint Petersburg in 1897 was an utter disaster. How bad? One music critic compared it to the ten plagues of Egypt. It was under-rehearsed by the orchestra, and there is even a theory that the conductor was drunk. Rachmaninoff wrote, "If the public were familiar with the symphony, they would blame the conductor (I continue to 'assume'), but when a composition is both unknown and badly performed, the public is inclined to blame the composer."

This failure plunged the 24-year-old into a three-year depression. His self-confidence was shot, and he composed almost nothing during that time.

Pain is an incredible instigator; it slips deep into your soul and unearths emotions and creativity you did not know existed. For Sergei Rachmaninoff, the culmination of his three years of pain resulted in his 2nd and 3rd piano concertos and "Symphony No. 2," which he wrote ten years after the first one. I am not sure if Rachmaninoff would have willingly traded three years of depression for the creativity that it produced. But undoubtedly the failure of Rachmaninoff's first symphony and subsequent pain paved the road for his future masterpieces.

In investing, pain causes you to reexamine every facet of your investment process, shedding light on the deficiencies you did not know were there.

It also reignites creativity, and if you let it – if you accept it as an important part of your life as an investor – then it will make you better. After all, pain without purpose is just meaningless suffering. We seem to learn a lot more from our failures than from our successes.

It is important for all of us to realize that investment pain is not unique to us mere mortals. Even investment icons, the ones we put on a pedestal, went through years of pain and may yet go through more. We are just not aware of it, because they were wearing their public masks of normality. It is important not to tie our self-worth to the performance of our portfolio, so that we don't strap ourselves into an emotional rollercoaster ride over which we have little or no control.

Ben Graham, the father of value investing, was wiped out during the Great

Depression. I am fairly certain that was a very painful period of his life, but it led to his writing *Security Analysis,* which later became the bible of value investing, *The Intelligent Investor.*

I am a tremendous beneficiary of investing pain. Both the concept of sideways markets and my first book were born as a result of the pain I went through in 2002, when I observed how the valuation of our high-quality (but overvalued) portfolio was melted away by what I later described in my books as the price-to-earnings compression of a sideways market.

I have to admit I squandered the pain I experienced in 2012. In hindsight, if I hadn't done so, the pain of 2015 would have been a lot smaller or completely avoided.

The pain of 2015 will likely prove to be a blessing and save me from a more significant future pain. I dedicated 2016 to reexamining 2015. I was determined to improve our investment process so the mistakes of 2015 would not be repeated.

To my great surprise, while working on bulletproofing our investment process against a 2015 *déjà vu,* the searing memory of the pain of 2015 unleashed creativity I did not know I had, and I ended up elevating our investment process to an unexpected level. That probably wouldn't have been possible without the 2015 journey.

Here is the bottom line: Don't squander pain – it is an opportunity to unleash your creativity. As Marcus Aurelius put it: "The impediment to action advances action. What stands in the way becomes the way."

Work-free oasis

Now to the duality between our feelings and our public faces. Our culture doesn't deal well with failure, and demonstration of any emotions beyond a polite smile often goes unappreciated. But the reality is that all investors go through pain at some point and may even suffer depression when we feel we've failed.

When I am in the domain of pain, I do an okay job of hiding how I feel around strangers, but pain impacts the way I behave around my loved ones. I am impatient and easily irritated, which is very unfair to them. It took me a while to link investment pain to the impact it has on my family.

After 2015's painful experience, I realized that it is important to have a stock market-free oasis in your life. I made a deliberate decision not to accept clients from my circle of friends or even from my immediate community (people I see on a regular basis at the synagogue, for instance). To maintain a rational mind, you need to carve out an oasis from the outside world. I can follow a rigorous investment process, buying only high-quality companies that are significantly undervalued, but I still cannot control how the market will price them in the short run.

In 2015, if I went out after work to drink a few beers with friends whose money I managed, an inescapable feeling of guilt (or at least discomfort) would travel with me to the bar. It was not a logical feeling – after all, I am not the one who decides how my favorite undervalued companies are priced today. Current price is a fleeting opinion of what a company is worth, not a final verdict.

Over the years, I discovered that most of the time people can tolerate downside volatility on an intellectual, theoretical level, but they really don't know how they'll react when they see their portfolio down 10% or 20% – behavioral finance calls this the *empathy gap*. As a fiduciary it is also my job to stand between my clients' emotions and their money.

I found that there was a very beneficial side effect to taking this approach: There is no unspoken ambiguity in my relationships with friends, and there is never even a hint of a perception of a hidden agenda on my part. Thus I have told all my friends and acquaintances that I will never manage their money. I'll help them with free advice, but will never have a professional relationship with them. This is liberating.

On Writing

I NEVER THOUGHT I'D be writing articles and books, or even worse, giving writing advice. I was always the worst student in my literature class in Russia, and I never received a grade higher than a C on any Russian essay I ever wrote. I have a theory that my teachers got sick of reading and grading my horrible essays, so they stopped and automatically gave me a passing grade out of pity. Honestly, I don't blame them.

When I came to the US, my grades in English class in college were not spectacular either. In fact, English was the only class I failed in college and I actually had to retake it in my senior year. My writing has improved slightly since then – and you now get to be the judge of my scribbles. However, if the prequalification for giving writing advice was based solely on quantity – on how many words have blackened a perfectly fine white screen or besmirched innocent paper – then I am beyond qualified. I have been at it for more than a decade now. My writing "career" started in 2004, when I was hired as a writer by TheStreet. com. They didn't hire me because I was any good – believe me, I wasn't. But I had an investing background and TheStreet.com was not very picky; it needed warm bodies (ideally with CFA next to their names) to comment on the markets and stocks. TheStreet.com paid almost nothing, and it was overpaying me.

I had zero experience, but I was ambitious. I took writing very seriously, and therefore my articles were serious. They were filled with big words, and, quite frankly, they were enormously boring. In addition, I was extremely self-conscious about grammar. Sentence structure and punctuation drove me nuts, and I was afraid of confusing words that were spelled similarly but had unrelated meanings (like comma and coma).

This brings me to the first lesson that I want to impart about writing, and it's one that will drive English teachers insane: **Don't worry about grammar.**

Once I stopped worrying about grammar, I felt a huge weight lifted from my shoulders (as all those little punctuation marks emptied themselves from my brain). I completely gave up on *a, an* and *the* (my son does a great job at fixing those for me), I stopped obsessing about commas (and comas), and I stopped trying to ferret out all the other marvelous secrets of English grammar. I let copyeditors – who are very talented and oh so skilled at this – catch me out in all my little peccadilloes.

Writing is a very creative process, and more importantly, I love writing. But grammar is the least creative part of writing. I found that I spent one-third of my writing time fixing grammatical errors. And the sad part is that even after I put in my best effort, I still don't catch all the nitpicky stuff.

I broke the writing process into two parts: the creative part – downloading thoughts from my conscious and subconscious and crafting them into an article, client letter, or book. And then there is the less creative part, the nuts and bolts. I started to worry even less about grammar than before and began bringing talented copyeditors (they are editing this, so I have to say that – though they are!) into my writing process much sooner. This allowed me to write more and, in my humble opinion, the quality of my output has not suffered at all.

Instead, **I channel my energy into being a storyteller and making my writing interesting and funny (when appropriate).** As I mentioned, when I started writing, my articles were technical and boring. I still feel sorry for the people who read them and especially for my dear friends who felt an obligation to read them.

Then, my TiVo accident happened.

It was six months into writing for TheStreet.com that I wrote about the digital video recorder company. In that article, I dared to use a little bit of humor to describe the painful experience I had getting TiVo's phone auto-attendant to understand my Russian accent. I had to ask my then-three-year-old, Jonah (who by that time had already acquired a perfect "Disney" accent), to talk to the auto-attendant instead, and of course it understood him just fine.

That article was not brilliant – it contained as many or as few insights as my previous articles did – but it was not "proper," and it was not boring. Suddenly, though, the feedback from readers was much different. I received a ton of email. It was then that I understood the power of humor. But it was not *just* humor: I had been able to deliver my otherwise-boring message in an interesting way, and it connected with my readers.

This article singlehandedly changed how I write. I realized that knowing what you want to say is not enough; you also need to figure out *how* to say it. To this day, I spend hours staring at the computer, trying to come up with an interesting analogy or a compelling angle on how to say something I already know. I often use analogies to tell a story, especially if the topic is complex. They help me relate complex ideas through simple examples.

Let me illustrate. I have a very smart investor friend of German ancestry. True to his roots, he is very efficient in everything he does. (Yes, I am stereotyping here, but why not?) He has written a very smart investment book; if you read the whole thing, you'd learn a lot. But that is a big *if*. His book is as efficient and properly structured as you would expect from a well-engineered German car, or an instruction manual for that car. It doesn't have an extra word or a superfluous sentence. But unfortunately, in the process of making it efficient, he sterilized his book. I was excited to read it but could not get past Chapter 3. I got terminally bored... and I do investments for a living.

Our brain naturally looks for the most efficient way to communicate a point, the one that consumes the least amount of energy. A story that contains a metaphor is not always the most efficient instrument (judging simply by word count and the writing time needed), but it is usually highly effective, because it lets us connect with readers on a very different and often more personal level. In other words, the reader may actually finish reading what you wrote.

There is an unintended benefit to a writer when he communicates through a story. Storytelling taps into the right, creative side of our brain and thus stimulates the construction of mental models.

Identify your favorite writers, the ones whose voices you can really relate to, and learn (steal) from them. In his book, *Steal Like an Artist,* Austin Kleon writes: "Nobody is born with a style or a voice. We don't come out of the womb knowing who we are. In the beginning, we learn by pretending to be our heroes. We learn by copying." Kleon quotes Paul McCartney: "I emulated Buddy Holly, Little Richard, Jerry Lee Lewis, Elvis. We all did." We're not talking about copy and paste here, but trying to emulate the best qualities of others. Kleon adds, "Don't just steal the style, steal the thinking behind the style. You don't want to look like your heroes, you want to see like your heroes." In our effort to copy our betters, we'll mostly fail; but this very partial success, which makes us draw upon and improve upon our own qualities, will ultimately lead to shaping who we become – this is how we evolve.

Carefully choose the people who you are influenced by, but don't settle on just a few. Kleon puts it so well: "If you have one person you're influenced by, everyone will say you're the next whoever. But if you rip off a hundred people, everyone will say you're so original!"

Read to write. My father has been painting since he was seven years old. Being an artist is deeply embedded in his mind and heart. Whenever we traveled he took an easel with him and always looked for places to paint. We'd be on vacation, out walking. He'd stop, close one eye, squint with the other eye, stretch out his arms in front of his face and form a square with thumbs and index fingers – framing his vision for a painting. He was looking for beauty, for the next picture to paint. When I started writing articles, I noticed that I began to read differently. I started to pay much closer attention to sentence structure, to the voice and the stylistic tricks the author was using. I started reading not just as a reader but also as a writer. Writing also rewired how I observed life around me. I started to pay attention to little things, often turning them into metaphors.

Be respectful of your environment. This is not an ecological statement; I am talking about your writing environment. If you write long enough, you start to appreciate the importance of your external and internal environment. Stephen King, in his book, *On Writing: A Memoir on the Craft*, said that he listens to heavy metal band AC/DC when he writes. He feels it walls him off from the external world and helps him build his own worlds. I listen to classical music and, if I am really stuck, I start listening to opera.

And if that isn't weird enough, I write only in italics. This little trick makes my letters look a bit friendlier to me. If you find that you like your font to be pink, go for it. We writers (and thinkers) need any edge we can get, and you can always change back to a color and format that is acceptable to society when you are done.

Create your own quirks. Walter Isaacson, author of many of my favorite books, including biographies of Steve Jobs and Albert Einstein, writes at night. He writes on the computer and then prints out everything he has written. The next morning, he reads it on paper out loud to himself. He says, "That way it is easy and fun to read, because if you just read it on the screen you don't edit it properly." Whatever works.

Turn off the spell checker and just write, write, write. I don't always follow this, but I have found it to be very helpful when I'm stuck. I don't stop for anything. I don't correct misspelled or missing words. I just write; I keep moving forward and never turn back. I am doing a word dump. See, you cannot edit *nothing;* you can only edit *something.* This word dump fishes ideas out of your subconscious and gives you something to edit.

Be prepared for pain. Writing is a very personal process. Some of us are great thinkers, able to puzzle through very complex ideas in our heads and lay them out logically on paper. I have tremendous respect for those lucky ones. For most of us, writing is usually a painful endeavor that involves staring at a blank screen for hours on end and writing and rewriting multiple times.

In fact, let me take it a step further: I think through writing. A quote from George Bernard Shaw comes to mind: "Few people think more than two or three times a year; I have made an international reputation for myself by thinking once or twice a week." As I have mentioned previously, if you ask me a question about something I have not thought about before, even if you give me a minute to think about it, my answer will usually, well, suck. I have not written about that topic yet, and so I may not have thought it through, and the logical links may not have been made. That's just how my mind operates.

Quite frankly, I am embarrassed for my brain. It's like the dirty apartment of a confirmed bachelor, with unwashed clothes, empty pizza boxes, and beer bottles all over the floor. For an idea to be developed to the point at which it can leave the room, I have to clean it up, organize it, and put things in their rightful place. That is why I write. Sorry, dear reader – it's not about you, it's about me, me, and me again. That is how I think.

When you sit down to write, your thoughts may not be quite ready to come out – it's okay if they just haven't come to a boil yet. Don't blame it on writer's block. Author Tom Clancy once said, "Writer's block is just an official term for being lazy, and the way to get through it is work." Just take some time off, do something fun and then get back on the writing horse.

One last thing. When you read this (or any other) well-polished book and the words are smoothly flowing along in perfectly lyrical sentences, you need to realize that you are most likely reading a 47th revision. Writing is rewriting, with a lot of pain in between rewrites.

Share this chapter with a friend:
https://soulinthegame.net/nda/

The AC/DC Effect

DID YOU KNOW *that Mozart and AC/DC will help you activate the two sides of your brain?*

My son Jonah was born in 2001. Like most parents, my wife and I wanted to give him as many advantages as we could so that he could succeed in this world. We read about the *Mozart effect* in a study published in *Nature* magazine, which showed improved performance in kids who had listened to classical music. Actually, we went a step further: Jonah started listening to Mozart in his mother's womb. We bought a special speaker that was connected to a CD player, which my wife wore as a belt on her tummy for several hours a day.

After Jonah was born, he was surrounded by classical music, as we listened to it everywhere, all the time. But I have to tell you, because it was called the Mozart effect, we felt we were helping his development even more when he listened to Mozart's *Piano Concerto No. 21* than when we played Rachmaninoff's *Piano Concerto No. 2*.

At the time, the internet was in its infancy, at least from a usability perspective. So we did not read the actual, original study on the Mozart effect, we read an article about it. We were young parents desperate for any edge to give to our offspring. Our Mozart effect efforts may have increased Jonah's chances of falling in love with classical music when he grows up, but they probably contributed very little to increasing his IQ.

As we discovered later, it was called the *Mozart effect* because researchers used Mozart's *Sonata for Two Pianos in D Major* in their study. However, the choice of music turned out to not really matter. Nevertheless, I am thankful that the researchers had good taste in music. They could have used music by AC/DC (sorry, hard rock fans) in their research, and my poor Jonah would have been subjected to that instead when he was in his mom's tummy.

Listening to classical music from a negative age (if birth is the zero point, then time in the womb should have a negative sign) is not the worst abuse a child ever suffered.

Heidi Mitchell, in a *Wall Street Journal* article, interviewed Alexander Pantelyat, an assistant professor of neurology of the Johns Hopkins Center for Music and Medicine. Dr. Pantelyat said, "The Mozart effect hasn't been shown to have clear benefits beyond the 10 to 15 minutes during which subjects in studies were engaged in tasks." The type of music you listen to actually doesn't matter: "if you enjoy heavy metal, you might be more focused when you listen to it."

He added:

If you add lyrics, you're activating the Wernicke area, where language is processed, and other parts of the temporal lobe, and this may divert your attention or possibly overload the brain's attentional capacity. Imagine listening to two languages at the same time while working. Of course that's distracting.

"Around 80% of people process language on the left, or the analytical, side of the brain," Dr. Pantelyat said, "and everyone processes music on both sides of the brain." He added that "music activates as many, if not more, parts of the brain at the same time than any other activity."

To sum up: If you are listening to music while you think (work), music stimulates your brain; but the effect wears off after you stop listening. Even more importantly, though, because musical processing requires both sides of your brain, it helps build the bridge between the left and right sides. Thus, it connects the logical to the artistic sides of your brain, stimulating creative thinking. Some music will be helpful and some will be distracting – picking a playlist that is best for your brain is a highly personal experience.

Neuroscience is a very new science. A decade or two from now, we may find that all of the above findings were just the placebo effect... wishful thinking at work.

I look at anything I do in life and investing from the "What is the cost of being wrong?" perspective. There is no downside here. If you find that music distracts you, then stop listening to it while you actively think. If it helps you to merge the activities of your logical and artistic hemispheres, even if it is the placebo effect at work, do you really care?

I can only speak for my left and right brain, here. However, as I mentioned, anytime I have a writing or thinking block (which happens quite frequently), I listen to classical music (opera if I'm really stuck), and it helps me. In fact, it took me several symphonies, two operas, and a piano concerto to write this.

I am very thankful to the Mozart effect study because, at worst, it exposed my son to classical music from well before he was even born.

Creative
Rollercoaster

M Y PARENTS LOVED Tchaikovsky. Russia treasured him. I feel like Tchaikovsky's music accompanied my mother's milk. But my appreciation for him and his music increased exponentially when I learned how much fear and emotional pain he had to overcome to compose it.

I don't compose beautiful music, but I do write. Composing and writing, though they have quite different final products, do have one thing in common – the creative process. Be it musical notes or words, they somehow show up on paper from deep within our subconscious.

Tchaikovsky started working on *Souvenir de Florence* in 1886. It was first performed in 1890, and he kept revising it until 1892. Tchaikovsky experienced an emotional rollercoaster as he was composing this wonderful piece. This got me to thinking about the dichotomy between the beauty of the final product and the pain of creating it.

Learning of the difficulty Tchaikovsky had in composing *Souvenir de Florence* was liberating for me. I realized that if the greats like Tchaikovsky suffer through emotional tribulations, then it is okay for mortals like the rest of us to endure them as well.

Let's explore the emotional rollercoaster Tchaikovsky went through composing it.

Lack of motivation

"I jotted down sketches for a string sextet, but with little enthusiasm ... I haven't the slightest inclination to work..."
— Tchaikovsky's diary, June 18, 1887

The paradox of creative activity is that, unlike assembly-line widget production, time spent at the computer screen does not directly correlate to the quantity or even the quality of the words that appear thereon.

Writing appears to be a quite delicate activity that is dependent on the whims of an unpredictable and sometimes inconsiderate muse.

There are takeaways from this.

Create space and show up. Though the muse is not a words-per-hour kind of creature, you can't just wait idly for the muse to show up. Just like the assembly-line worker, I need to clock in daily.

If you don't like to "clock in," how about "Create space on a daily basis for inspiration to visit." I don't write for a living, and thus I can afford to dedicate only two hours to it. I go through a daily ritual. I get up early, around 5 a.m. (thankfully, I am a morning person). I make coffee. Sit down in my "writing" chair. Put on my headphones and start my "writing" soundtrack: Bach's *Concerto No. 1 for Harpsichord in D minor.*

If the words are flowing, I thank the writing god. If they are not, I stare at the blank screen and... I type. If I do not like what I wrote, which happens very often, I hit "ctrl" and "enter," which creates a brand-new blank page, and I try again.

I don't wait on inspiration; I create the space and time for inspiration to come. If the words are flowing, I milk that moment for all it's worth. Then life inevitably interrupts – kids wake up, we have to eat breakfast, I have to drive them to school, and so on. If the muse did not pay a visit, then I have put in two hours of typing. I close the laptop and come back the next day.

Write regularly. If you don't write on a regular basis, then it gets difficult (though not impossible) to restart the flow. Imagine you are in Minnesota in January; it is freezing cold outside. There is a fountain in the middle of St. Paul.

The fountain is covered in ice, but the stream of water keeps flowing. Here is the secret to this fountain: If the water is constantly running, no matter how cold it is outside, it will keep running. But if the water is stopped for even 20 minutes, it will take a lot of effort to restart the flow. Writing is just like that. That's why I write daily.

Go easy on self-criticism. There are times when two hours in front of the laptop results in complete nonsense (it happens often). I tell myself that my subconscious (the muse) was not ready today. But it's a continuous process, and I have kept the door open for something good to come out tomorrow. This reminds me of being a parent – when my kids succeed, I congratulate them; but when they fail, I tell them that there is always tomorrow.

Here is the secret: You don't stop writing when you close your computer screen; your thoughts are still being processed by your subconscious when you are taking a shower, walking in the park, or cooking. This is why coming back the next day is so important.

Self-doubt

"I'm beginning to fear that I am losing my powers of composition and becoming angry with myself."
– Tchaikovsky, a letter to a friend, July 2, 1887

Tchaikovsky's pain and self-doubt resulted in stunning pieces of music. One thought keeps coming back to me: Maybe (creative) pain is a necessary part of growth; maybe it's an indicator that we are pushing ourselves out of our comfort zone.

I experience a burning feeling of self-doubt every time I take a break from writing. Self-doubt is part of the price you pay for the water freezing on the writing fountain.

But even if I write daily, I still experience a trickle of fear and anxiety when I sit down to write a new piece. Someone compared writing to driving a car on a very dark night in a snowstorm. You can't see ten feet in front of you – that is, past the next sentence.

How do I overcome this fear? Curiosity. The fear is also accompanied by a trickle of curiosity. As you are reading this now, you are (hopefully) curious to know what I will say next. I want to know as much as you do, my dear reader, what this will look like when my subconscious is done with it, and what I will learn and discover for myself.

I've been writing for over a decade and a half, and still to this day the fear and curiosity are right here with me. As long as the curiosity keeps getting the upper hand, I'll keep writing.

Pushing your circle of competence

"I began it three days ago and am writing with difficulty, not for want of new ideas, but because of the novelty of the form. One requires six independent yet homogeneous voices. This is unimaginably difficult."
— Tchaikovsky, to his brother Modest, on June 27, 1890

Let me tell you a bit about Tchaikovsky's *Souvenir de Florence*. It is a sextet – a piece composed for six string instruments. In this case, two violins, two violas, and two cellos. Tchaikovsky was guilted into writing it. He had been awarded an honorary membership in the Saint Petersburg Chamber Music Society, and in thanks he promised to write a chamber music piece (music composed for a small group of performers).

Tchaikovsky had never written a sextet before. It was a new domain for him. I can relate to this so much. It is so comfortable to write about familiar subjects and remain on familiar turf. However, the real growth comes when you push the walls of your circle of competence further out.

I started out as an investor writing about stocks and the economy – that was it. It wasn't easy, but it was a familiar territory where I had spent most of my adult life. And then I pushed into writing about family and travel adventures, classical music (a huge step for a person who cannot even read music), diet, and exercise; and then I had the audacity to write about creativity and about writing. Every push into a new domain of writing was accompanied by fear. The fear undermined my confidence and made writing so much harder.

However, as I spent more time in new domains, I gradually grew more self-confident being there. I found unexpected benefits. Writing changed me,

241

rewired me as an individual. As I started writing about music, I found myself reading and learning more about it.

I developed a thirst to learn and found more meaning in life. I can thank my parents for this; but I know that the seeds they so diligently planted would have not seen the sunlight if they were not watered by my writing, constantly venturing into new domains and pushing my circle of competence. I started seeing myself as a student of life.

I can pat myself on the back and congratulate myself, but I won't. I just have to remind myself, the next time I venture into a new domain, that while the journey so far involved some fear, overcoming it made my life so much more fulfilling.

Share this chapter with a friend:
https://soulinthegame.net/qqc/

Melody of Life

The melancholic, quirky, and passionate world of classical composers and what we can learn from their lives and works.

Why I Write About Composers

MY FATHER BELIEVES that art does not need context; it should stand on its own. You look at the painting and its title. What the artist thought about it, his state of mind, is irrelevant. The art speaks for itself.

When asked what he was thinking when he created a particular painting, my father is often puzzled. He just painted. The outside world stops existing for him and it is just him and his paintbrush. He escapes into painting.

There are actually two issues here: The artist's conscious effort to communicate a message through this art and the artist's emotional state, spilling into the art.

My father does not paint program paintings. When he paints a forest, fishing port, or bouquet of sunflowers, he does not have a message that he is trying to communicate, other than to bring the beauty that he sees to the canvas. But this doesn't mean that his subconscious is not influenced by his emotional state.

This subconscious activity is what I am trying to glean when I read and write about composers.

Their emotions spill into their work. It is hard to be depressed or to be in pain and compose uplifting music. Or to be happy and compose a funeral march. The creation of art is not like writing computer code; it is not a highly logical "If this, then that" process. It is a nonlinear, highly emotional process. (I either just insulted or complimented computer programmers.)

Maybe my father can block out the world and leave his emotions behind him when he paints for hours at a time. But I'd argue that it is very difficult for artists to leave themselves, their emotions, out of what they are creating. I know from personal experience that my writing is highly influenced by my mood or even the music I listen to (and I am not even an artist).

Learning about composers' lives helps us to better understand their music; it enhances the music and gives it more meaning. Also, if you know about the person who wrote the music, then when you listen to the music you may get a glimpse into their soul. This is why I write about composers.

As you read the following short essays about composers, think about whether your understanding of their music and the impact it has on you has changed.

You will see the struggles and victories of these creative geniuses. Their lives were not always filled with fireworks and stardom. (Schubert died destitute and gained fame only after his death.) All of them overcame an enormous amount of suffering and self-doubt, and at times their success was overshadowed by the even greater success of their contemporaries.

As a creative person, these stories inspire me to get up and keep going forward when I hit a creative lull.

Tchaikovsky – Master of Emotions

I HAVE ALWAYS HAD a difficult relationship with Tchaikovsky's music. My parents loved his first piano concerto, and I've listened to it several hundred times over the years (I love it, too). At the same time, I was forced to listen to his music at school in Russia. Anytime I am forced into something, I naturally start resenting it. This applies to Russian literature as well: My teachers turned Russian literature into Mark Twain's definition of *classics*: Books that people praise and don't read. I am still trying to get back into Russian literature.

Tchaikovsky's music has been overpopularized in America. *The Nutcracker* has turned into a Christmas ballet, which is so popular that for some ballet companies it accounts for almost half of their annual revenues. *The 1812 Overture,* which was written as a celebration of a Russian victory against Napoleon, has been turned into a theme song for America's independence from... the British. *Swan Lake*, though it has not yet been fully Americanized, still has a good chance of becoming an American Thanksgiving ballet.

Luckily, as I have grown older, Tchaikovsky's incredible music has overcome my implanted childhood resentment, even if it took time.

Tchaikovsky's suicide note?

Tchaikovsky (1840–1893) was a master of emotions. He was a neurotic, highly sensitive person, full of phobias. For instance, he had a phobia that his head would fall off when he was conducting. (He eventually overcame this phobia, since at times he had to earn a living as a conductor.) His music is ridden with emotions; it is the manifestation of his emotions. It is his emotional confession.

There are several theories as to why Tchaikovsky died at age 53. The theory I heard when I was a child in Russia was that he died from cholera, probably as a result of drinking contaminated water. However, there is another theory about his death: That he committed suicide.

Tchaikovsky is a Russian national treasure, a symbol of Russian greatness, someone the propaganda machine could point at and say, "Materialistic Americans have their poisonous hamburgers (and a chicken in every pot, and toilet paper, and...), but we've got art." This is also why the propaganda machine would censor a little-known fact about its hero: Tchaikovsky was gay.

Russian homophobia goes back centuries, as it does in most places in the world. And in the late 19th century, Tchaikovsky's era, it was in full flight. Therefore, Tchaikovsky hid his sexuality his whole life.

Many think the cholera story was a cover-up. Tchaikovsky was caught having an affair with Duke Stenbock-Thurmor's nephew. The duke was going to write a letter of protest to the Czar. This would likely have brought disgrace to Tchaikovsky. A "court of honor" made up of his former classmates in Saint Petersburg ordered Tchaikovsky to swallow poison. He did. Or so the story goes.

We'll never know which theory is true, the cholera or the suicide, but we do know that Tchaikovsky's sexuality had an impact on his music.

Tchaikovsky's *Symphony No. 6,* called *Pathetique* (which translates from Russian as *passionate*), was Tchaikovsky's final symphony. He conducted its premiere just nine days before his death in 1893.

To understand this symphony, we have to understand the dark period in Tchaikovsky's life. Tchaikovsky wrote *Pathetique* when he was depressed and doubting his ability as a composer. (He had destroyed his previous symphony because he was unsatisfied with it.)

There is an argument that *Pathetique* is Tchaikovsky's suicide note. Historians and music critics are divided on this point. They don't know, and we will probably never know, the truth; but I would like to zoom in on the fourth movement of this symphony in order to let the music help you decide.

The first three movements are gloriously optimistic: there is a waltz; beautiful, lingering melodies; and ballet dances. You don't need much imagination to see a sunrise, vast Russian landscapes, troikas, and bright white snowfields (*Doctor Zhivago*-style).

The fourth movement is different. It starts with a cry for help (voiced with the violins). It builds on melancholic, depressive overtones. Tchaikovsky masterfully borrows melodic elements from the first three movements, but these melodies are barely recognizable, as they are painted over with deep sadness. And unlike Tchaikovsky's other pieces, which arrive at a natural finale (you can feel they are about to end), this symphony (like death) ends in nothingness, absolute nothingness – the music just fades out.

The story of two rejections

There is a great lesson that we all can learn from Tchaikovsky's *Piano Concerto No. 1*. It was common at the time to dedicate a piece of music to the musician whom you wanted to perform the music, usually a famous performer. Dedication ensured that a piece of music would see the light of day and also provided an endorsement of the piece.

Tchaikovsky dedicated his first piano concerto to Nikolai Rubenstein. Nikolai was considered to be one of the greatest pianists of his time, and he and his brother Anton Rubenstein were important figures in Russian musical culture. In fact, Anton was Tchaikovsky's composition teacher.

Excited, Tchaikovsky played the concerto for Nikolai, who listened in silence and then told Tchaikovsky what he thought of it. Here is what Tchaikovsky wrote about this scene to his pen pal Nadezhda Meck:

It turned out that my concerto was worthless and unplayable; passages were so fragmented, so clumsy, so badly written that they were beyond rescue; the work itself was bad, vulgar; in places I had stolen from other composers; only two or three pages were worth preserving; the rest must be thrown away or completely rewritten.

Just imagine that someone you respect and admire, who has incredible influence, just called two years of your work "pathetic."

Tchaikovsky was genuinely hurt, but he pledged that he would not change a single note. He reached out to a famous German pianist and conductor, Hans von Bülow, and asked if he could dedicate the concerto to him. At the time, Bülow was preparing to go on tour to the United States. He loved the concerto! And thus Tchaikovsky's *First* was first performed in Boston in 1875. It was a great success. Music critics still found a lot of faults in it. It did not fit the established framework: The introduction, the part that makes this concerto so grand, is almost a self-contained piece of music that is attached to the concerto.

Here is the punch line. Later that year, a few months after the Boston performance, the concerto premiered in Saint Petersburg and then in Moscow. Nikolai Rubenstein conducted the Moscow premiere. Rubenstein performed the piano solo many times and even asked to premiere Tchaikovsky's second piano concerto. Tchaikovsky would have consented if Rubenstein had not died.

Tchaikovsky's *Violin Concerto in D major* suffered a similar fate, except that it was rejected not just by one, but by two performers. Parts of it were difficult to play. Critics did not like this concerto, either. One called it "long and pretentious," and that critic continued, "The violin is not played but beaten black and blue." Just like Tchaikovsky's piano concerto, this violin concerto became a tremendous success and is now among the most beloved violin concertos.

Share this chapter with a friend:
https://soulinthegame.net/egt/

In the Shadow
of Others

Franz Schubert in Beethoven's shadow

"THINK OF A man whose health can never be restored, and who from sheer despair makes matters worse instead of better. Think, I say, of a man whose brightest hopes have come to nothing, to whom love and friendship are but torture, and whose enthusiasm for the beautiful is fast vanishing; and ask yourself if such a man is not truly unhappy."

Yes, think of that man. The man was Franz Schubert (1797–1828), and the quotation above is an excerpt from a letter he wrote to a friend. Schubert lived a very short life: When he was 25 he contracted syphilis, and at the time syphilis was a treacherous, painful death sentence (just like AIDS in the 1980s and early 1990s). Schubert died at the tender age of 32.

Just imagine a young man aged 25, his life supposedly lying ahead of him, but instead he is staring death in the face. Understandably, Schubert was depressed. You can hear this depression in his music; it is full of melancholy.

Schubert was an addict: He was addicted to composing. In the 16 years of his creative life, he wrote over 600 songs, nine symphonies, 22 piano sonatas, 17 operas, over 1,000 works for piano, and many other works. Most composers were not able to accomplish as much in a full natural lifetime.

"I hope to be able to make something of myself,
but who can do anything after Beethoven?"

– **Franz Schubert**

Beethoven's genius and fame were (unintentionally) very toxic for his contemporaries like Schubert and for composers who lived long after his death (Brahms and many others). Schubert grew up in Vienna, a few blocks away from Ludwig van Beethoven, and died less than a year after him. There are conflicting theories about whether Schubert ever met Beethoven. We know that he was a huge fan of Beethoven's music. He was Beethoven's pallbearer. He asked to be (and ultimately was) buried next to Beethoven.

Imagine living in Vienna in the early 1800s and trying to compose your own music when you have heard the ingenious *7th symphony* composed by a fellow who lives a few blocks down the road. Any sound that comes into your head will seem to pale in comparison, and anything you put on paper will somehow appear insignificant.

Schubert was able to, at least partially, overcome the toxicity of living in Beethoven's shadow, as he was one of the most prolific composers of all time, composing till his last breath. But living in Beethoven's shadow prevented Schubert from publishing a lot of his work, as he felt unworthy of publication.

Tragically, Schubert lived all his life in dire poverty and only became famous after his death. Schubert would have been utterly shocked that, 200 years later, his name would be mentioned in the same breath as Beethoven's. He would also be surprised that today he is known as one of the great symphonists. Schubert did not hear most of his symphonies performed, as they went unpublished.

Schubert's *9th Symphony* was rediscovered by Robert Schumann. Today Robert Schumann is known as a great composer (and as the husband of Clara Schumann – another great composer). However, in his time he was a very well-respected and popular music critic.

Schumann visited Schubert's brother in 1838, ten years after Schubert's death, and discovered the unpublished manuscript of a symphony. Schumann was shocked at how wonderful the symphony was and brought it to Felix Mendelssohn. Today, Mendelssohn too is known as a great composer, but at that time he was also a very famous conductor. Mendelssohn conducted the first performance of Schubert's symphony, which today we know as the *9th*.

Today we talk about Schubert's and Beethoven's symphonies in the same breath. We don't dare to compare their geniuses. The music of these Western European superstars elicits equal amounts of joy and tears from the music-listening public around the world.

Johannes Brahms in Beethoven's shadow

You cannot talk about life in Beethoven's shadow and not talk about Johannes Brahms (1833–1897). Brahms was born in Hamburg, Germany in 1833, six years after Beethoven's death. Unlike Schubert, as a composer he was never directly eclipsed by Beethoven's shadow. Still, the greatness of Beethoven's music haunted Brahms well into his 40s.

Brahms was a musical prodigy, a gifted pianist from a very early age. In his late teens he was already composing chamber music, for piano and voice. In 1853, when he was 20, he met Robert and Clara Schumann, the stars of the classical music scene at the time. The Schumanns were smitten by young Brahms, and Robert, in his excitement, wrote an article for one of the most important music periodicals of the time, proclaiming Brahms to be the next – wait for it – Beethoven.

The music historian Robert Greenberg called Schumann's well-meaning article an ultimate "curse" for Brahms. Suddenly, Brahms' future symphonic music would be held to a very different standard. Brahms exclaimed, "You have no idea how it is for the likes of us to feel the tread of a giant like him behind us!"

It took Brahms over 21 years to finish his first symphony.

Brahms' *Symphony No.1* premiered in 1876. It was a great success and critics accorded it the highest possible honor it could receive in the eyes of Brahms: They called it "Beethoven's *10th*." This success unfettered Brahms' creativity – he gained the confidence he had obviously lacked before. He composed a major orchestral piece almost every year after that, including three more symphonies, a violin concerto, and a piano concerto.

What is also amazing about Beethoven's shadow is that its true impact is unknown. Just as we'll never know how many more wonderful symphonies Brahms would have written if Robert Schumann had not written that fateful article announcing him as the next Beethoven, we'll never know how many composers stopped composing altogether or did not publish their works because they felt they could never measure up to Beethoven.

The greatness of others can be intimidating, and it can injure our own creativity if we let it. We should allow it to inspire us, and not allow it to put us down.

Whatever our field, there is always someone more talented and famous who came before us. Such people have big shadows. Don't step in them; create your own shadow.

Share this chapter with a friend:
https://soulinthegame.net/arb/

How Franz Liszt Revolutionized the Piano and Classical Music

ONE OF MY favorite childhood memories is walking home with my father on a sunny Sunday afternoon. I was maybe nine years old. There was the sound of classical music coming from the fourth-floor window of our apartment building. Our neighbor was listening to music very loud. My father said with admiration, "She is listening to Liszt." This was the first time I had heard of Franz Liszt.

I remember my father explaining to me the "z" in his name and that it was spelled differently from *list*, which in Russian means *leaf*. I don't remember the music, but I do remember a certain respect in my father's voice for the neighbor and her preference in music. This little moment, just a few minutes on a sunny Sunday afternoon, left a huge imprint on my life.

Franz Liszt[36] (1811–1886) was a Hungarian composer and pianist. I don't think you can talk about Liszt without talking first about the evolution of the piano. The piano you see today in concert hall or in private homes was not always like that. Though the earlier instrument had a similar shape and had a keyboard, its interior plumbing was completely different. In fact, it was called a harpsichord – think of it as a harp (wooden frame with stretched strings) with a keyboard.

Around 1700, the harpsichord started a gradual transition into fortepiano. This "gradual" journey took a long time, both instruments coexisted for a hundred years before the fortepiano permanently replaced harpsichord. Fortepiano had the same look as the harpsichord, but instead of the strings being plucked they were hit by little leather-wrapped hammers. The frame that held the strings was still wooden, and the strings were held at low tension. This is the instrument used by Mozart and the young Beethoven.

The sound of the fortepiano is different from the sound we are accustomed to hearing today: it is lighter, and the instrument did not have a double escape mechanism and thus could not repeat sounds rapidly – it speaks instead of singing. Each note is very clear and distinct, and the fortepiano has still not completely lost the sound of the harpsichord. If you listen to Mozart's piano concertos or sonatas, you can hear that they were written for the fortepiano.

Mozart died in 1791, just as the fortepiano (or simply, piano) – the instrument we are all familiar with – was starting to emerge. But from the late 1700s to the early 1800s, the piano underwent a significant transformation. This transformation had a major impact on the music that was composed; and, in a musical feedback loop, composers impacted the instrument.

Beethoven was one of the early adopters and beneficiaries of the piano's evolution and played an important role in the evolution of the instrument. At one point he had broken most of the strings in his piano. He complained to the piano manufacturer that pianos wore out very fast.

---

36 When I was in college, I took music appreciation class. Though (luckily) I continued to appreciate classical music after the class was over, I don't remember learning much about classical music in that class. I must thank Robert Greenberg for his lectures in "The Great Courses" for my understanding of classical music. A lot of the material here is based on what I learned in his lectures. Unfortunately, it is hard for me to specifically attribute what I learned from "The Great Courses" versus from other sources. I highly recommend that you watch or listen to his lectures in "The Great Courses."

The biggest differences between the fortepiano and pianoforte (the modern piano) are that the frame the harp strings are tied to is not wooden but metal; the low-tension strings have been replaced with high-tension ones; the instrument has a range of two additional octaves (14 extra white keys); and the hammers are covered with tightly compacted felt instead of leather. These changes transformed a delicate instrument into an incredibly powerful beast that can go toe-to-toe with an orchestra, but that at the same time retains the gentleness of its ancestors.

This brings us to Franz Liszt. Liszt was born 16 years before Beethoven's death. He was a child prodigy and a virtuoso pianist. He was the first rockstar of Europe – the Michael Jackson of his day.

As luck would have it, on a trip to Paris, Franz Liszt stayed in a hotel right across the street from Erard Piano – a trailblazing piano maker that invented the double escapement movement that sped up the piano and significantly reduced the limitations of previous generations of pianos. Erard was also the first piano maker to fit pedals under the piano.

As the story goes, young Franz wandered into the Erard store and started playing on one of the instruments. Mssr. Erard was smitten by the boy's genius and also recognized a unique marketing opportunity. He made an endorsement deal with young Franz, providing pianos for all of Liszt's performances. Liszt went on a three-year tour, giving several performances a day. No town was too small – he loved the attention and the applause. However, this tour was suddenly interrupted by his father's untimely death.

In 1832, Liszt attended a concert of the Italian violin virtuoso Niccolo Paganini. The violin had undergone its most dramatic improvements 200 years before the piano did, and it was a mature instrument by that time. After Liszt heard Paganini he remarked, "What wonderful things might be done with the piano if its technical possibilities were developed as those of the violin have been by Paganini." He decided to become the Paganini of piano. For some six years he limited his public performances while he practiced non-stop (putting in Malcom Gladwell's 10,000 hours).

Liszt invented solo recitals – before Liszt it was unheard of for an artist to give a solo performance (doing so was probably perceived as immodest). Liszt changed the way the piano is positioned on the stage, placing it, lengthwise, parallel to the edge of the stage and opening the lid toward the audience.

To me – and this is the extremely uneducated opinion of an amateur classical music aficionado – Liszt pushed the boundaries of what was possible on the now-evolved, much more powerful instrument, where the player's technique was the only limitation. To do this, he had to write his own music for the new instrument and vastly improve his performance technique.

Imagine that Intel had just created a new processor that was 100 times better than the old ones, and let's say Microsoft wrote a new operating system that vastly improved the capabilities of that new processor. But to truly shine, the new system would need new programs. The old ones might still run just fine, but to truly showcase the new box's abilities, it would need to be loaded with brand-new apps.

Liszt did not create the new hardware, but his technique (the new operating system) removed a lot of limitations and released the power of the new instrument.

To me, Liszt's *Sonata in B Minor* is the new software. Liszt made a solo piano sound, at times, like a full orchestra – something that I don't think had been done before him (though I'd be happy to be proven wrong). Liszt's contribution to classical music is incredible and immeasurable. It spans much further than his amazing music, because Liszt showed the likes of Tchaikovsky, Rachmaninoff, Grieg, and many others what the piano could do.

The Two Sides
of Chopin

THERE ARE TWO sides to Frédéric Chopin.

But before we get to that, by way of intro, we need to talk about two other composers: the two Franzs – Franz Liszt and Franz Schubert. We have a contrast of two Franzs.

Franz Schubert was introverted and a mediocre pianist. For Schubert, the piano was just a vessel to communicate his music and nothing more.

Schubert's *Fantasie in F Minor* is a great example of that. It is written for piano, four hands or what is called a "piano duet". This is speculation on my part, but if Liszt or Rachmaninoff had written this piece it would have been for two hands (or one virtuoso pianist). In this observation, I am not trying to detract anything from Schubert – quite the opposite – but I feel these small glimpses into composers' lives help me to understand and relate better to their music.

Franz Liszt was the complete opposite. He toured all over Europe, giving several performances a day. Women went crazy over him. For Liszt, the piano as instrument was as important as the music he composed.

This brings us to Chopin (1810–1849). Schubert's and Chopin's paths never crossed; Schubert died when Chopin was 18 years old. Chopin arrived in Vienna after Schubert's death.

Chopin left Poland at 20 and settled in Paris. He was a skinny, sickly-looking man. He was very shy – he only gave 30 public performances in his lifetime

(Liszt gave more performances in a month). Chopin was in poor health and he died young, just like Schubert, at 39. And where Schubert lived in the shadow of Beethoven in Vienna, Chopin was in Paris, a city completely smitten by Liszt.

It seems there are two Chopins. First, the one who reminds us of Schubert – the one in poor health; the depressed one; the one who wrote deeply emotional, melancholic music. Remember, this is the composer who wrote the *Funeral March* – happy people who look toward life don't do that.

And then there is another Chopin: The one who lived in the shadow of Franz Liszt; who was only a year younger than Liszt; who was in the same city and traveled in the same circles as Liszt. Yes, Chopin the virtuoso, trying to push the limits of the piano.

When we listen to Chopin's etudes you are listening to the Liszt side of Chopin. An *étude* is a short piece of music that is composed to improve a player's specific technique. Before Chopin, *études* were mainly composed for musicians, not for listeners. Chopin's *Études* changed that. Chopin's *Études* are very Lisztonian, as they pushed the then newly evolved piano to new, unheard-of levels.

And then when we listen to Chopin's *Nocturnes* (a short, romantic composition), we are hearing the Schubert side of Chopin.

Fantastic *Fantastique*

L OUIS-HECTOR BERLIOZ (1803–1869) was not a child prodigy; at age 12, he was a latecomer to music (by that age, Mozart had already completed his first performance tour). His father discouraged him from studying piano, so he did not. His parents wanted him to be a doctor (every Jewish mother wants her son to be a doctor), and Berlioz was sent to Paris to study medicine. At the age of 23, despite his parents' objections, he formally abandoned the study of medicine and focused solely on music.

It's hard to say whether Berlioz's musical adventure would have amounted to much if he hadn't fallen in love. When he was 27, he attended a performance of *Hamlet*. There he saw her: Harriet Smithson, Irish Shakespearean actress. He was fatally smitten. He wrote her love letters, but his love went unrequited. He rented an apartment across the street from her and then wrote her the ultimate love letter: *Symphonie Fantastique*.

Fantastique was written in the pain of unrequited love. Berlioz wrote:

Oh, if only I did not suffer so much! ... So many musical ideas are seething within me. ... **Now that I have broken the chains of routine, I see an immense territory stretching before me, which academic rules forbade me to enter**.

In another letter he wrote:

Sometimes I can scarcely endure this mental or physical pain (I can't separate the two) ... I see that wide horizon and the sun, and I suffer so much, so much, that if I did not take a grip of myself, I should shout and roll on the ground. I have found only one way of completely satisfying this immense appetite for emotion, and this is music.

I strongly believe most creativity in the world is unleashed by pain. If it were not for pain we would not have Rachmaninoff's *Piano Concerto No. 2,* which he wrote after suffering a three-year depression following the failure of his first symphony. Or think about this: Beethoven was deaf the last ten years of his life, and this is when he composed his best work.

Back to Berlioz. Either Berlioz could not take the pain, or he needed additional stimulants to access his newfound creativity; in any case, he consumed a lot of opium in the course of writing *Fantastique*. It premiered to incredible success in 1830 and turned Berlioz into a huge star. Harriet was unfortunately not at the premier and only heard the symphony two years later. By then Berlioz was famous, and she recognized his genius. They got married, but her acting career was in decline and she was jealous of his success. They then separated and Berlioz eventually remarried.

Nevertheless, we should all thank Harriet for this incredible masterpiece.

Here is how Leonard Bernstein summarized this symphony: "Berlioz tells it like it is. You take a trip, you wind up screaming at your own funeral."

Fantastique is a five-movement program symphony. (Program music means that the symphony follows written program notes; think of them as silent opera.) It's the love story of Berlioz's unrequited love for Harriet – on psychedelics.

Here is what Berlioz wrote in his program notes: "The Artist, knowing beyond all doubt that his love is not returned, poisons himself with opium. The narcotic plunges him into sleep, accompanied by the most horrible visions." The symphony continues with the murder of the artist's love interest, the execution of the artist after a stirring march to the gallows, the artist's funeral, and the artist's love interest's reappearance as a witch.

Berlioz was born only a few years after Franz Schubert, so he lived in the era when Beethoven ruled the classical music world. But he lived in Paris, which is 767 miles from Vienna – the epicenter of Beethoven's stardom – and in the days of horse and carriage it may as well have been 10,000 miles.

We know Beethoven's music traveled around Europe and Berlioz was highly influenced by his music; but maybe because Berlioz received little classical musical training, it was easy for him to break the rules of composition – since he didn't know them. Or maybe it was drugs and Berlioz's being madly in love; but Berlioz never fell under Beethoven's shadow, and thus his symphony *Fantastique* was a trail-blazing creation that set a new standard for orchestral music that has endured.

Bruckner – Humble, Odd, Sex-Deprived Religious Fanatic

I HAVE STOPPED TRYING to figure out why the music of one composer is popular and the works of scores of others are not performed but collect dust in the obscurity of music libraries.

At the beginning of the 20th century, the American public did not care for Edvard Grieg's *Piano Concerto in A minor,* but today it is one of the most-performed piano concertos. Mahler's music was not popular in the US until Leonard Bernstein popularized it in the 1960s. Neither Grieg's nor Mahler's music suddenly got better; public attitudes toward it changed.

Over the last few years, I've been actively trying to stretch the boundaries of my musical knowledge by going deeper into the music of the composers I am already familiar with and also by more widely exploring new (previously unfamiliar to *me*) composers.

When I listen to music that is unfamiliar to me, at first it's work. Yes, work. At first, I don't understand that music and it brings me little pleasure – it's just random, unconnected sounds. I may have to listen to a new piece half a dozen times before it clicks with me. I remember listening to Puccini's *La Boheme* a dozen times, and at first I was baffled at how this opera could possibly be one of the most-performed operas. Today, I don't see how it could not be.

Sometimes, even after a dozen tries the music won't click with me, and I put it into the "I don't understand" pile. I try very hard not to use "I don't like" when it comes to classical music, for two reasons. First, it implies that I am a judgment-worthy connoisseur (I am not!); and second, *don't like* has a finality to it, while *don't understand* leaves the door open for me to understand the music down the road.

I "understand" some composers quicker than others. Russian composers take the least number of tries – there must have been something in the water I drank as a child growing up in Russia. Mahler, Sibelius, and Bach, on the other hand, took a long time for me to understand. I still don't understand all of Mahler's work.

This brings me to the latest victim of my explorations: Austrian composer Anton Bruckner (1824–1896). Today Bruckner's music is not very popular. Critics say his symphonies are very long and somewhat slow and that they lack emotion and extended melodies. There is also a practical limitation: His symphonies require a much larger orchestra, and since they lack the recognition of Beethoven's or Mozart's, they are rarely performed.

As I've been listening to Bruckner's symphonies and reading about him, I have found that Bruckner the person is even more interesting than his music.

Bruckner's ancestors were farmers. His father was a music teacher. Bruckner was a diligent student and became a talented organist. Robert Greenberg writes:

> The Church was Bruckner's refuge and solace for the entirety of his life; he was as devout a man we will ever find outside a monastery or a foxhole. He believed completely that everything he did should honor God.
>
> Bruckner was a total country bumpkin: naïve, simple, overly trusting, deferential and pious to a fault. (Bruckner followed to a T the Church's proscription against sexual relations not sanctified by marriage.)

Bruckner searched for a bride all his life:

> He was 43 when he fell in love with a 17-year-old, whose parents put a stop to the relationship. He fell for another 17-year-old in his mid-fifties. Though the parents in this instance gave the relationship their blessing, the young girl tired of Bruckner, and his passionate letters

went unanswered. Later still he became infatuated with the 14-year-old daughter of his first love – that came to nothing and at 70 he proposed to a young chambermaid. Her refusal to convert to Catholicism ended that. Piety and pubescent girls are not an attractive combination. Bruckner died a virgin and was buried under the organ at St Florian.

What really fascinates me about Bruckner is that he started composing symphonies fairly late in his life. Per Robert Greenberg:

... the 'eureka!' moment he experienced in his 39th year, when in 1863 he heard a performance of Richard Wagner's Tannhauser in Linz. Bruckner was doubly blown away: not just by Tannhauser, but by the realization that what made Tannhauser great was that it broke so many of the rules of harmony and counterpoint he had so assiduously studied!

From that moment, Bruckner embraced Wagner's music with a mania that changed his life. Convinced that it was his mission in life to become the Wagner of the symphony hall, he composed a symphony in C minor in 1866.

Bruckner was writing his music for God. This is what he wrote to then-young Gustav Mahler:

Yes, my dear, now I have to work very hard so that at least [my] tenth Symphony will be finished. Otherwise, I will not pass before God, before whom I shall soon stand. He will say: "Why else have I given you talent, you son of a bitch, than you should sing My praise and glory? But you have accomplished much too little!"

Bruckner's drive to please God must have kept him going, as success came to him seven symphonies and 20 years later, when he was 60. Just imagine this: 20 years of constant writing and rewriting six symphonies, six symphony premieres, six flops. He kept going. I admire that.

I started listening to Bruckner with his *Symphony No. 4* – it is his most-listened-to recording on Spotify. It is one hour and nine minutes long. If you run out of patience, do what I did. Don't think of it as a novel, think of it as book with four independent stories (parts/movements). Listen to each movement separately many times, starting with the first one.

I am listening to the first movement as I am writing this, and I can hear bits from various symphonies in this one – there is the grandeur of Saint-Saens third ("Organ") symphony; I can hear parts of Berlioz's *Fantastique*; and Wagner's brass and violins are definitely in there. The beginning of part two has some of Mahler's "Funeral March"-like sadness. And then you listen to the last five minutes of the symphony and it sounds like nobody else but a humble, very odd, sex-deprived religious fanatic.

The Art of a
Meaningful Life

Art or craft

O N OUR TRIP to Europe, while in Venice, my brother Alex, my son Jonah, and I took a water taxi to Murano, an island 20 minutes away, where we visited a glass factory and watched a glassblowing demonstration.

The glass artist took a ball of molten glass, stuck large forceps into it, and magic happened – he pulled a horse's head, body, legs and tail out of it. A few strokes with a metal blade and we had seen the birth of a horse. This whole thing took less than three minutes. I felt that I was not at a glass factory, but watching a magic act.

After we left the factory, Alex, Jonah, and I walked the streets of Murano, bathed by gentle Italian sunlight, discussing whether this fellow was practicing an art or a craft. Our instinct was to call it a craft, because we kept seeing hundreds of horses, identical to the one we saw born in front of our eyes, in the windows of Murano glass stores.

I kept thinking about that Murano horse long after we left Venice. Then I had an insight: We need to separate the art and craft that reside in the final product – the Murano horse – from the art and craft that live in the process of creating that horse.

Is the Murano horse art? If it touches your heart, if it moves you, then it is art. But what touches *my* heart may not be the same thing that touches *yours*. Normally, I would not put a bookshelf turned toward the wall or an unadorned log into the art category. But these items are exhibited at the San Francisco Museum of Modern Art.

This is where we'll leave the discussion of art or craft in the final product and move to the subject that truly fascinates me – the art and craft in the creative process. As you'll see, it will provide a framework, a mental model, that we can apply to many parts of our lives.

Let's start with craft. Craft is a skill that accumulates with time and is formed by experience, practice, learning, and usually a lot of repetition. It is a fundamental layer of any creative endeavour.

And then there is art. Art needs tension. This tension is caused by the uncertainty, the fogginess, that lies between the present and a final outcome. It is filled with conflicting emotions. On one side they could be the allure of success, which may bring recognition; or a sense of accomplishment in the fulfillment we receive from learning. These positive emotions may be contrasted by a fear of failure, disappointment, embarrassment, and the pain that usually accompanies all of these emotions. I lump these emotions into a broad category that I gently call "creative discomfort."

When I write, I experience tension, which is caused by curiosity as to what my essay will look like when I finish it. I am excited to know what I'll have learned at the end. I constantly battle with the fear that all my efforts will amount to nothing. At times there is anxiety, discomfort, and frustration that can occupy my mental real estate for days when a thought or an analogy is almost ready to come forth but stuck in the birth canal. As we create, we each experience a different set of emotions, which varies by individual temperament and by activity.

Repetition gradually turns an art into a craft – as our skill improves, creative tension is reduced and art is replaced by craft. The tension is slowly drained out of the process. The creative process becomes a little less creative.

Here is how that happens: When we do something for the first time, most of the activity is processed by our conscious mind. However, after we have repeated that exact task a few dozen times, it goes into our subconscious and the process becomes a bit more mechanical. It becomes a routine – a craft.

Now, think about it. As great as the process of birthing that Murano horse looked, if you decided to change your occupation from part-time reader of this book to full-time Murano glassblower of only that horse, after a few years you would have learned the craft of making it, yet you would have to go on making the same horse day in and day out. You might as well join the assembly line at the Fiat factory.

Claude Monet rented an apartment by Rouen Cathedral in Normandy, and over several months he completed over 30 paintings of the cathedral at different times of day and in different seasons.

However, just because we paint the same subject many times doesn't mean that the final result is automatically a craft product.

Monet studied light.

He had mastered the craft involved in these paintings – the permanence of the cathedral's façade – after a few repetitions. But the light was fleeting and ever-changing and caused Monet a tremendous amount of frustration (this is a very good thing in the creative process). He wrote, "Things don't advance very steadily, primarily because each day I discover something I hadn't seen the day before.... In the end, I am trying to do the impossible." You can feel the tension in Monet's words.

There is a constant battle in turning what we do from art into craft – this is an inevitable process of improvement. The art is just like that constantly fleeting light on Rouen Cathedral. It's what motivates us to keep going forward, to learn, to get better.

Happiness in life comes from having and solving good problems. Monet's good problem was that fleeting light, and his need to create art kept him coming back to paint that cathedral for months. However, once our art turns into a craft, we need to move on. As did Monet – he still had 30 haystacks to paint.

Art + Soul in the Game = Meaningful Life

To have a meaningful life we need to find the right balance of art and craft in our lives. This balance, like an optimally concocted chemical reaction, will perfectly recharge our batteries.

But that is not enough.

We need to have soul in the game, which gives us direction and purpose.

I have a friend who sells investment products. We went for a walk in the park, and he shared with me that he was dissatisfied with his job. He loves the process of selling – he finds art in it (there is a lot of "fleeting light" in it for him).

However, despite enormous financial success, he felt he was selling overvalued products that, down the road, might bring a lot of losses to the buyers. He did the best job he can, steering clients (who would have bought these products with or without his help) to the best among the bad investments, often at the expense of a lower commission; but he still felt that he had no pride in what he was doing. He would not want himself, his kids, or his parents to own these investments.

He had no soul in the game!

To achieve fulfilment and find deep meaning in whatever activity we are involved in, art is not enough. This activity has to be indistinguishable from our identity; we need to be throwing every last ounce of ourselves – our soul – into it without reservation. It has to have all of us. It has to be something we believe in. And yes, it has to be a net positive to society. It is hard to mentally be all in when there is an asterisk (*) attached to what you do – i.e., "I love what I make, except anyone I care about should never consume it."

Just imagine if Jiro were creating his incredible sushi while also harboring the belief that sushi is bad for his customers. Having the right mixture of art and craft in an activity that you don't believe in and that is not aligned with your values will create an internal dissonance, as your fully charged battery will be taking you into the wrong lane of the highway of life.

The Mixture of Art and Craft

Two of the most accomplished American pianists of the 20th century were Russian-born Vladimir Horowitz and Polish-born Arthur Rubenstein. Both were very mindful of the mixture of art and craft in performing classical music.

Rubenstein said, early in his career, that when his children were born, he did not want them to think of their father as a second-rate pianist. "I buckled down back to work – six hours, eight hours, nine hours a day. And a strange thing happened... I began to discover new meanings, new qualities, new possibilities in music that I had been regularly playing for more than 30 years."

But then as he got older Rubenstein dispensed what may sound like contradictory advice: Practice no more than three hours a day. He explained: "I was born very, very lazy and I don't always practice very long... but I must say, in my defense, that it is not so good, in a musical way, to overpractice. When you do, the music seems to come out of your pocket. If you play with a feeling of 'Oh, I know this,' you play without that little drop of fresh blood that is necessary – and the audience feels it."

Horowitz was also concerned about overpracticing: "As far as practicing is concerned, I usually try to do one to two hours a day. It isn't good to practice too much, or your playing becomes too mechanical." He went even further: "Perfect itself is imperfection."

If you are a pianist, should you listen to young Rubenstein, older Rubenstein, or to Horowitz? You should listen to yourself and be mindful of the right balance, for you, of art and craft. This applies to any creative activity – we need to be mindful of the right mixture of art and craft, at different points of our journey.

Divide and conquer

Pianists don't have the luxury that other creative adventurers often do: To maintain the right mixture of art and craft in our life, we need to know which part of the creative process we want to be involved in. Take Jiro for instance. You can break sushi making into two stages: Inventing new sushi and making it every day for customers. The ratio between art and craft tilts heavily toward art in the inventing (dreaming) stage. However, once a new piece of sushi has been invented by Jiro, repetition quickly takes over and it becomes a craft. At the craft stage, Jiro heavily relies on apprentices.[37]

A mental model

This art and craft mental model applies to a lot more than just art in its conventional sense. You can look at almost any creative activity through that prism. You can see why I stopped teaching my investing class at CU. The

---

37 I understand that some readers want only craft in their lives. They want calm and predictability today and tomorrow; they don't want the tension – the art. Everything I said above still applies to you; just invert it. Extricate the tension that comes with art from all of your activities.

repetition of teaching the same class semester after semester squeezed all the art out; the tension was gone, and all that was left was craft.

In fairness to teaching, I could have restrung the tension by constantly tweaking the material I taught. Instead, I moved on. I found another activity that consumed me – writing. Writing brought a greater and more versatile challenge, involving a lot of art and little craft (at least in the beginning).

I need tension; without it I don't have the desire to write. For instance, when I started writing, I cranked out articles about individual stocks once or twice a week. I did not realize it then, but I was learning the craft of writing. Today these types of articles involve little creative tension. I write about individual stocks when I have to – in my letters to IMA clients. But even then, I try to bring art into my writing by introducing storytelling into the letters.

As investors, we need to constantly widen our circle of competence. When we are within our circle of competence – the area that we know well – the ratio of art to craft is very low. As we push the boundaries of our circle and thus try to convert newly entered domains of incompetence into competence, the amount of art increases. We learn about new industries, develop new mental and valuation models. This is why I love being a generalist (I don't specialize in a particular industry). There is always something new to learn.

In investing it is important to maintain a delicate balance between art and craft. All craft and no art leads to a miserable existence, at least for me. Imagine the horror of specializing in analyzing only utility stocks all your life, in an industry that moves at the speed of an archaic bureaucracy.

At the same time, if you venture too far outside of your circle of competence, then, to paraphrase Freddie Mercury, too much art will kill you. The unknown unknowns outside your circle of competence can destroy your portfolio. For this reason, when we enter into new industries where we are stretching our circle of competence, we make smaller investments at first. If we make a mistake, it will sting, but it won't kill us.

And then there is my most important occupation of all – being a parent. Imagine you are a tennis coach and all of your students are robots with identical programming. You can see how, after a while, once you have learned the craft of teaching tennis, the art will be gone – no tension; you'll know the exact response to every problem.

Now, instead of robots, your students are kids of different ages. Even if you've been teaching for a while and have a lot of craft, with every child you still need to find the right approach. There is an art to choosing which teaching technique (which craft) to use with each kid.

Every kid is different. Bribes worked well on Jonah. They never worked on Hannah. Mia Sarah – too soon to tell. Also, as kids grow, so do their challenges. My father likes to say, "Little kids don't let you sleep; big kids don't let you live" (I hope he is not referring to me).

I use the art and craft framework at IMA to run the firm as well as to manage myself. I have structured my job to retain the tasks with high art content – stock research, managing portfolios, communication, the firm's strategy (all areas where I still get plenty of help) – and have delegated high-craft-content tasks to very capable IMA staff.

When we hire new people or assign new tasks to employees, I keep this framework in the back of my mind. Some folks prefer high art content; others don't. I'll give you an example. When we created my podcast *The Intellectual Investor* (investor.fm), our marketing director was in charge of it. He chose the platform we were going to use to host podcasts, hired a narrator to read my articles, wrote a description for the podcast, worked with an artist to create art for the podcast cover, and wrote intros and outros. Then he produced the first five episodes of the podcast, and designed the weekly workflow process. After that, another employee at IMA, who prefers a higher craft mixture in her job, took over and has produced each podcast since.

Being mindful of this framework makes IMA more productive, and most importantly, it keeps everyone at IMA doing what they love and happy with their jobs.

Step Out of the Shadow

A creative process that has a high concentration of art is messy and nonlinear. It is a highly individualized endeavor. As I reflect on the "Melody of Life" section in this book, I see lessons we can learn from the lives of these composers.

Being in the shadow of others can be debilitating to our creativity and our confidence. The first step in stepping out of someone else's shadow is to actually realize that you are overshadowed and it's impacting you.

Schubert, Brahms, and dozens of other composers whose names we'll never know (as their music never got published) were impacted by Beethoven's enormous success. Each composer dealt with being in the shadow of others differently.

Schubert's Ninth Symphony could have disappeared if it had not been discovered by Robert Schuman after Schubert's death.

It took 21 years for Brahms to step out of Beethoven's shadow and complete his first symphony (that is one long writer's block).

Berlioz broke all the rules of classical music at the time with his *Symphony Fantastique,* possibly because he partially inverted Pablo Picasso's "Learn the rules like a pro, so you can break them like an artist." Berlioz broke the rules because he did not know them – he started studying music later than most composers. Or perhaps he was just madly in love.

Liszt took a very different route. He embraced the newly emerging technology of the piano. He became the best pianist of his generation through practicing nonstop and giving several performances a day. When he ran out of repertoire to match the power of the new instrument and his newly developed skill set as a pianist, he wrote his own music.

It was common thinking in the early 19th century that Beethoven's *9th Symphony* was the be all and end all of symphonies – it was the perfect symphony. I am glad Tchaikovsky and so many other composers never got that message, or we would have been deprived of a lot of wonderful music.

Bruckner showed that it is never too late to embark on realizing our dream. He started working on his first symphony when he was 39 and only saw success 20 years and six symphonies later.

Being in the shadow of others isn't just limited to classical composers. I can clearly see it in my own profession, investing. A lot of value investors have been living deep in the shadow of Warren Buffett. Their behavior has been shaped by Buffett's enormous success. For instance, Buffett avoided technology stocks for a long time. He said he did not understand them. I cannot tell you how many value investors I have met who were one-third of Buffett's age and who parroted Buffett's behavior and refused to own technology stocks.

The irony, of course, is that Buffett stepped out of his own shadow and poured tens of billions into the largest technology company in the world, Apple, which as of this writing has been the most successful Berkshire Hathaway investment (by dollar gains) ever.

The biggest lesson from all these musical geniuses is that creative discomfort accompanied all of them throughout their careers. It's par for the course for any serious creative activity. If it would make you feel any better, this small dose of negative visualization might be helpful: A Fiat assembly line worker is not facing any creative pain, at least not while at work.

Discovering that creative discomfort is an embedded feature of creative activity was liberating for me. A lesson I learned from meditating is that when you observe a thought that bothers you, it starts bothering you less. Observing pain and noting that it is sourced from creative activity lessens the pain.

Stoics and the fourth wall

In theatre, there is a term, *breaking the fourth wall*. This is when an actor steps out of the character and starts talking to the audience about the play. I'll do something similar here. At this point this book is almost done. As I am writing this (almost) last chapter, I am going to break the fourth wall, in part to answer a question I've been asking myself: How would the Stoics look at creativity?

Our old friend Epictetus might remind us of dichotomy of control (the "some things are up to us and some are not" framework). He'd tell us that in any creative activity you should always aim to satisfy an audience of one – you. What is the point of stressing over something you cannot control?

I shared a nearly completed version of this manuscript with a dozen friends. I wanted to get feedback from the perspective of readers. Most loved the book and gave me constructive suggestions, many of which I implemented. However, a few folks whom I respect advised me not to publish this book in this form. They thought I had violated cardinal rules of book structure.

They were right on the breaking the rules part.

I intentionally took creative risks with this book. It is not organized in chronological order. I am also quite aware that there is no traditional story arc – chapters are not always neatly connected to each other through a story line. And at the same time, the book has been put together to be read in sequence. I deliberately made these choices. Not for the sake of breaking rules – I just ignored them. I followed Picasso's dictum – learn the rules like a pro, so you can break them like an artist – to a tee.

I believe this structure has resulted in the best book *I* can write. Just as Jiro presents you with sushi in a particular sequence to create a certain theatrical experience of flavors and images, I have organized my themes and stories in the best way I could imagine. I had to assume that most readers would be able to overcome minor inconsistencies, such as my kids' fluctuating ages, and so I've organized the book thematically, not chronologically.

I am very aware that some of you will have been annoyed by the book's structure, and some will have liked it. Some will have found the book too personal, wondering who I think I am to write an autobiographical book on loosely interconnected subjects; and some of you will have relished the book's intimacy or even its dance on the edge of randomness.

All your responses are beyond my control. Ultimately, I wrote the book for an audience of one. I could only control the love, pain, and effort I put into writing. I received enormous creative satisfaction from it – I squeezed every last ounce of my soul into it. That's all I could do.

I keep thinking about Tchaikovsky's *Piano Concerto No. 1* and his *Violin Concerto in D major*. Both were rejected by musicians he deeply respected, the piano concerto once and the violin concerto twice. These pieces were too different from the norms of the time. Luckily for Tchaikovsky, they were beautiful, ingenious masterpieces and redefined the norms. These concertos are still performed today, more than 100 years after his death.

I am no Tchaikovsky, and breaking norms doesn't guarantee success – this book may be forgotten two weeks after it is released.

As I am writing this, my blood pressure is steady as a dolphin's. Stoics would call my attitude toward the book's success a positive preference (a kind of "I'd rather be rich than poor, but I'm fine with either" attitude).

Do I want the book to be successful? I'd be lying if I said I didn't care. There are three answers to the question of why anyone writes a book: A deeply personal one; one you share with friends; and one you share with the public.

All of these answers may be honest, but individually they are incomplete.

On the personal level my real goal with this book is to get my kids to read it. As I mentioned in the dedication, I wrote the book for them... because they don't read my emails. As a father, this is the most important bar this book has to clear – my kids. I am already two-thirds of the way toward clearing that imposing hurdle: Jonah and Hannah have already read it. Mia Sarah is only seven, so I may wait a few years before I spring it on her.

This answer is honest but incomplete. I did not have to publish the book for my kids to read it.

My friends who read the manuscript kept asking me, "Who is this book written for?" It is written for current and future fans, or my tribe, to be more precise. I really don't have any commercial aspirations for it. I have (negatively) visualized that it will fail to sell. Other than the book never making it to the bookstores at all, it cannot fail. If it succeeds or fails in the commercial sense, my life will not change a bit.[38]

Again, this answer is honest but incomplete. It was hard to visualize a *tribe* during those (thousands of) early morning hours I spent writing the book.

This brings me to my public answer, which is as honest, and ironically is even more complete, than the previous ones. You. Yes, *you*, my dear reader, are why I wrote this book. If you arrived at this paragraph by reading from the beginning and at times the book has brightened your day, made you think, or nudged you in a positive direction in any part of your life that needed nudging; if the book was a net positive for the time and effort you spent on it, then I have succeeded.

But the Stoics – those Stoics! – would remind me again that it's not up to me how you receive it.

---

38 It was not written as a marketing tool for my firm – IMA doesn't need it, and it is not that kind of a book. The publisher has different views on this – that is not up to me.

Intermission – Stop Eating Sugar

I HEARD A STORY about the French Impressionist painter Edgar Degas. He was a perfectionist and had an incredibly hard time completing his paintings. Often, when he would encounter one of his paintings hanging in someone else's house, he'd stare at it intensely for a while and then ask the owner of the painting whether he or she would mind lending it to him so he could finish it. Who could say no to this? As the story goes, sometimes the owner would never get the painting back, as Degas would ruin it in the process of trying to make it perfect.

As I was working on this book, I realized that I might have a Degas problem on my hands. I was not at risk of writing a literary masterpiece, but I enjoyed the process of creating the book so much that I knew I'd have a hard time abandoning it. I'd edit it down and then add twice as much as I'd taken out. I had a hard time saying goodbye.

Then I figured out a solution – inadvertently, with the help of my wonderful wife. When I first told her that I was writing a book about life, she gave me a puzzled look and said, "Don't you think you have to be much older before you write about life?" I was perplexed by her comment. But there is a nugget of truth in it. When you are writing about life you are summing up life experience, wrapping it in the wisdom that arrives later in life.

But then it hit me: Warren Buffett had realized that philanthropy should not be done after he was no longer with us, by his estate. If he started to distribute his wealth to charitable causes while he was alive, then he would help people sooner and actually get to see how his philanthropy transformed the lives of others. (He came to this realization in his 70s. Who are we to judge him.)

I realized that sharing my life experiences, no matter how unpolished and imperfect they are, should not be reserved for my old age. I decided that this book would be called *Soul in the Game: Volume 1*. This open-ended title allows me to correct my youthful mistakes in future volumes.

Let me tell you one last story.

A mother brings her son to the Dalai Lama and says, "My son eats too much sugar. Can you please talk to him?"

The Dalai Lama looks at the mother and then at the son. He contemplates deeply and then says, "Come back in a month."

In a month, mother and son are back. The Dalai Lama looks at the son and says, "Stop eating sugar."

The mother is surprised. "Why did you have us come back in a month? You could have told him to stop a month ago."

The Dalai Lama smiled and said, "I had to stop eating sugar first."

This book – *Soul in the Game: Volume 1* – is my way of not eating sugar. It is my exploration of life, striving to be a student of life, making mistakes, correcting them, learning from them – all while I strive to have soul in the game in all of my adventures. I hope a story or two in this book inspire you to stop eating sugar in the parts of your life where you consume too much of it.

In the meantime, I will keep exploring, learning, and writing.

My dear reader, this is not goodbye, but an intermission between now and the next volume.

In the meantime, you can continue reading my essays on **SoulintheGame.net**.

Enjoy life and prosper.

Postscript

I really had a hard time letting go of this book. I kept doing the Degas thing: I was in full writing and rewriting mode eight months after I wrote the "Intermission" chapter just above. What started out as just a collection of articles morphed into so much more than that. Maybe not a traditional book, but a book, nevertheless. Even as I am typing this, I keep thinking about so many ideas I want to learn and write about. But it is time to let this book go into the world.